THE
THRILL
of the
DEAL

How This Logger
MADE A MILLION
in the Bush

ED REIERSON

Canadian Cataloguing in Publication Data
Reierson, Ed
The Thrill Of The Deal

ISBN 0-9685977-0-X

  1. Reierson, Ed   2. Loggers — British Columbia — Biography.
3. Cariboo Region (B.C.) — Biography.   I. Title.
SD537.52.R44A3 1999   338.1'7498'092   C99-911026-8

Published by
ED REIERSON
250-833-0941

Designed, printed and bound in Canada by
HUCUL PRINTING
Salmon Arm, British Columbia

I DEDICATE THIS BOOK TO

*My wife Vicki, my son Blaine
and my daughter Joann,
to my stepsons Steve and Brian
and my grandchildren
Kyle, Nikki, Candi, Mandy
and Morgan*

April 2016

To Colin

all the best

Ed Revision
H

Acknowledgements

I would like to recognize several people who helped me greatly as I worked on this book. My sister, Shirley, suggested I write it and then encouraged me as I went along. My wife Vicki untangled my handwriting and moved the book from ballpoint pen to the typed page. Keijo Isomaa of Morriss Printing advised me of the necessary steps between manuscript and printing, and Ann West, my editor, was patient, understanding and firm in the final stages. Designer Jim Bennett gathered the pictures and text and made it work as a book and Morriss Printing produced the finished product. I would also like to acknowledge all my friends and associates, some of whom I have referred to in this book. I trust and hope this effort reflects the appreciation I have for you all.

CONTENTS

CHAPTER ONE

The Early Years

*M*y heart was pounding as I waited for something to happen. My half-sister, Edith, had taken me into the playhouse. The urgency and secrecy of her actions as she dragged me along were baffling and scary. She sat down and started to play with herself, then started fondling me at the same time. She was puffing hard, she gasped a couple of times and then she was calm. She tidied her clothes and mine, then she grabbed me, shook me and said, "If you ever tell Mom about this, I'll kill you." I didn't know what we'd done, but whatever it was, I knew it must be wrong and I was scared. I was seven years old. This scenario happened many more times in the following year and the threat and secrecy of it was tearing me up. I was so afraid of being found out, of Edith's anger, of my Mom's anger, that whenever my Mom called my name, for any reason, my bladder would let go and I'd think, "Oh, oh, she's found me out." It's funny how a mind works . . . without even understanding what was happening, I thought of my seven-year-old self as the bad guy.

One night or early morning, somewhere around my eighth birthday, I was awakened to the sound of crying and talking. I peeked out of my bedroom door and saw Edith crying and hugging my Mom and Dad. Her long black hair was combed, she had her good clothes on, and her suitcase was nearby. She was leaving. In the morning, my siblings and I were told Edith had gone away. We were not told why. I dreamed up all kinds of reasons, mostly of course that we had been found out. It was a very, very scary time for me, but as the weeks went by, nothing happened. When nothing happened, I closed the whole experience away, tight in my head. That year shaped my whole attitude toward my sexuality my relationships and myself . . . and has caused me no end of problems in my life.

To this day, I don't know why Edith left. Parents, back in the days when I was a child, made the mistake of not sharing information or communicating with their kids. They assumed we either didn't care or didn't need to know. So many problems could have been avoided if we had been told things and included. I often felt very alienated and alone, and I suspect my brother and sisters did too. In defence of my parents, they were doing the best they knew at the time. As for Edith, she had come to live with us out of the blue. One day she just showed up. There was no explanation when she arrived or when she left. She was nine years older than I was, which would make her sixteen years old that year. I remember her as being very pretty with long dark hair and white skin. She would talk grown-up talk with Mom and Dad, in which we kids were not included, and she would also talk and play with us just like a kid herself.

Early memories are odd things. I remember bits and pieces from my childhood, some good, some bad, some scary. All of those memories, whether remembered or mis-remembered, understood or misunderstood, shaped the boy I was and the man I became.

I was born in 1936 near Lesser Slave Lake, Alberta. My Dad was a Jack-of-all-trades, taking work where he could find it, mostly carpentry. My Mom worked at home. I had, at that time, one brother and two sisters: Roy, the oldest, me, Ines and June.

My father moved us around a lot. He was a wanderer, never content to stay put and stick to one thing. Early on, my parents, Roy, Ines, June and I, were living in a log house in Canyon Creek, a small town on the shores of Lesser Slave Lake. My Dad was working as part of a crew hired to build a drainage canal. The house we were living in was pretty basic. It consisted of two cabins, 12 feet × 16 feet, pushed together under one roof, with a porch in front. The first cabin was used as a kitchen and dining room and there was a walkway to the other cabin. The second cabin was used for sleeping.

Roy and I had our bed next to the log wall and we took turns sleeping against the logs. We didn't like sleeping on the wall side because in winter, it was very cold there. I remember many times at night, when it was my turn to sleep against the log wall, that I heard a tap-tap-tapping sound from outside the logs. A steady rhythmic tapping. The first time I heard it, I got frightened and woke my brother. When he woke, however, the tapping stopped and (of course) as soon as he went back to sleep, it started up again. This went on for many months. I told my Mom about these night-time tappings and she said "Oh Edward, that's just some loose bark on the outside and the wind flaps it against the house," and she would dismiss it with a wave of her hand. After one particular night of tapping, I went outside to fix this loose bark but the logs were clean and bare. Nothing loose. I was mystified. I quit talking about it as everyone figured I was imagining it or just making it up or behaving like a baby. But, the tapping didn't stop and I began to think it had to be a ghost. My Dad told stories of strange happenings with ghosts, and I imagined that this was my ghost. One night I woke up to the tapping, my bladder was bursting, and I was too scared to get up to go to the slop pail (kid's chamber pot), so I peed against the logs in the corner. I thought to myself at the time, "Take that! You tapper you!" I had tried everything on this tapper. I had tried anger, praying and I'd said, "I'll be good," but nothing worked. None of my promises, threats, or "treatments" worked and I never did find out the source of the noise.

At this time in my life I also had a recurring dream. It would start with me running away from something I couldn't see. Then I would be able to see it. It was a shadowy, dark figure coming to get me. I would run but never fast enough. As "it" was about to get me, I would wake up in a cold sweat. Sometimes I was so frightened, I would wake up my brother but he would just mumble, "Go back to sleep, it's just a dream." He didn't take my problems in the night too seriously. This dream followed me along for years, resurfacing to threaten me every once in awhile, until I was about eleven years old. One night I went to bed thinking, "I have to see what's chasing me!" I had decided to try and see my dream demon before but the nightmare would not cooperate and repeat itself on a night I was ready to deal with it. But, this one night, my dream started. In my dream, I turned around as I was being chased (this was very hard for me to do) and I confronted the shadowy figure. It was huge at first but as I tried to see its face it got smaller and smaller until it turned out to be a small black puppy who wanted to play with me. I was so relieved, and I was upset with myself because I had been running from this cute puppy for so many years. I never had the dream again. The dream that had tormented me for so long just stopped.

Today when I hear a kid talk about a bad dream, I listen. Those dreams are real. Parents in my day didn't seem to take any time to talk to their kids, especially about serious stuff, saying, "that is for grownups." It seemed to me as a child that my mother was always too busy to take time with us kids for talk or comfort. And she was busy: four kids in a small place, no bathroom, no water, not much to cook with, sewing and repairing most of our clothes by hand, wood heat and a cook stove, and no electricity. I guess a crowded place with no amenities and little money and having to do everything the hard way kept her very busy.

Anyway, this was the time that Edith showed up out of the blue, and after about a year, left us in the same way. Nothing was ever said about why she had come or why she left. Us kids didn't find out until much later that she was our sister. Dad told me when I was in my teens. There seemed to be a lot of family secrets in that era. I'm finding out now, many years later, after reading books like Suzanne Sommers Family Secrets and watching Oprah Winfrey's TV segment on family secrets, the damage that these hidden things do to families and the long-term hurt they cause. Edith was my father's daughter. My mother also had a daughter from an earlier relationship, a person I never got to know. Apparently, she lived with her paternal grandparents, as their daughter. I learned about this half-sister when, as with Edith, I was in my teens. It seems a tragedy that these two girls were denied a traditional family life to protect a family secret. Children born out of wedlock, back then, were shameful, people to be hidden just to keep a secret. When I talked to my mother about these girls in later years, she got a sad look on her face and changed the subject. She did the same thing when I tried again. I feel for my Mom, the heartache she must have felt. People seemed to be ruled by a cruel society back then. Actually, I guess society is still cruel, but just in different areas. When will we learn?

In 1946 my parents moved to Salmon Arm, B.C. (I was ten years old) from Lesser Slave Lake, Alberta. My Dad bought an 80-acre homestead just off the Salmon Valley bottom. It had a 10-acre field, about 70 acres of trees and a barn and a cabin. The cabin was 12 feet × 16 feet, with one room for our family of two boys, two girls, Mom and Dad. How did we fit, I wonder? I remember at bedtime the table was where the girls slept. The first morning going to school was bad. We had to walk half a mile to the main road, then one mile on the main road. No bus back then. The walk wasn't bad but the anticipation of school was awful. We were shy and back-woodsy, and I was withdrawn, repressing memories of Edith. In any case, we were on the main road heading for school when we saw two figures coming toward us fast. They were running. They caught up to us and passed us without a word. They were identical twins. They were wearing green britches, green army jackets and pilot skull hats. Their round faces were red and their large eyes never left us as they went by. They were Allen and Albert Fowler, boys I was to come to know well over the course of my youth.

As we arrived at the school and went in, everyone starred at us, because we were these funny dressed newcomers. We wore homemade clothes, and when you are from a different area, you seem to have a different look. I was very uncomfortable. Finally we were introduced, seated and work started. We could be lost in anonymity for a while. My teacher was Miss Semple and she lived in the valley at what they then called a "teacherage." A house where she had board and room. She was very strict and she had grades 4, 5, 6, 7 and 8, about 40 kids in all. Five grades in the same room. Grades 1, 2 and 3 were downstairs with another teacher. Sometimes it was quite hectic. Two months went by. In order to feel important I took to sticking my tongue out at her whenever her back was turned. The class was impressed at my bravery. One time I made a face at her as she read at her desk. Her glasses were reflecting the light and I didn't see her looking at me. As she dismissed the class for recess she said, "Oh, by the way Edward, you can stay." When the class had left the room, she got up and said "Edward, I am very surprised and disappointed in you. I never would have thought you would do something like that." She opened her desk drawer and took out her strap. This was a piece of belting half an inch thick, 2 inches wide and 2 feet long. She came to stand at my desk. I was dying a thousand deaths by this time, my heart was pounding and my bladder was feeling weak. She said, "Stand up and give my your hand." She held my wrist, and said, "For this behaviour, you get six on each hand." I can't describe the pain as the strap descended on my palm, the second was worse, tears squirted from my eyes, and by the third my fingers were numb. I felt a low animal sob start deep within. By the time the sixth landed I was a sobbing mess. She then took my other hand and it started again. When she was done, I was completely devastated, a quivering, beaten, horrified small boy. I had completely lost control of my bladder and wet my pants. She pushed me down in my desk and went back to hers. I never left my desk until noon when she said "Edward, you can go for lunch now." This was far too severe a punishment for such a sensitive boy. I was never able to meet her eyes again. After that day, I developed a chin quiver, which I imagined she would take as another face. I was afraid to go to school and it affected me until she left the school, one year later. It was a lesson learned to be sure, one I would never forget. Albeit overkill! When I think about it now, I realize I wasn't doing anything to her personally, just trying to please the class, and with that, in my own mind, my crime wasn't that serious.

One time a small girl got hurt when a play fort made out of the school's cordwood sticks collapsed. One of the Grade 8 girls got blamed. Miss Semple carried on about this, and then said to this girl, "Come to the front of the class and take the strap." This girl said "No, I didn't do it and I won't take the strap." Miss Semple said, "Take the strap or leave the school forever." This girl gathered up her books and left. Her name was Frieda Mashborn, and I was secretly so proud of the way she stood up to this teacher. I think of her as an Icon. Even to this day, when I think of that event, I am proud of Frieda. I still see her off and on. She raised a family and went on to drive a bus delivering seniors to appointments and errands.

In 1947 my sister Shirley was born. She was a long-awaited addition to our family by our Dad. She was not planned but once they knew she was coming Dad, especially, was excited. I was indifferent. I had two sisters already, Ines the oldest born in 1939 and June one and a half years later, and so far they'd not been much fun. Roy and I did not like our sisters very much back then. Dad was always saying things like, "Quiet down, you'll wake the girls" or if we ever made them cry, intentionally or otherwise, we were sure to get heck. So we kind of ignored them. I remember when June was born I was five years old and Dad took my brother and me into Mom's bedroom and said, "Look, this is your new sister!" June was born at home. Anyway, Dad was so sure Shirley was going to be a boy that he had "his" name picked out already. He had read a book that obviously impressed him, by Lowell Thomas, and that's what the name was going to be, Lowell Thomas Reierson. It was not to be. Lowell Thomas was a girl. Dad wanted to name her that anyway but Mom said, "Don't be silly!" So the new baby was called just that — Baby (for a long time until they decided on Shirley

Anne. I wonder if Shirley had a bit of a problem with her identity later because of that.

One thing that stands out from that time was when Shirley started to crawl. She must have picked up a tack in her leg. Dad used them to fix loose soles on shoes. Tacks are very sharp and one had obviously fallen on the floor. Shirley was crying for a couple of days until Mom finally found it. She said, "Hey come and look at this." The tack was buried in Shirley's leg between her knee and ankle, and you could only see the head. It was all red and swollen. Mom popped it out and that ended Shirley's crying.

Shirley was a novelty that soon wore thin when I realized I couldn't hold her or tease her. We had already learned about babysitting. Mom and Dad had left Roy and me to babysit Ines and June while they went some place one afternoon. Well, wouldn't you know, an airplane went roaring over our house. We ran to see what it was and we saw this neat floatplane going to land on the lake. We couldn't resist. We ran down to the lake to look at this awesome creation, the first real plane we'd ever seen. I don't know how much time passed before we ran back but Mom and Dad had made it home before us, and were waiting. Dad had a wood stick and he sure used it on us. He hollered, "I told you to watch the girls" as he laid it on. Well, he was right, but it didn't make the girls popular with us even though they were innocent of any of the dynamics. My parents kept us separate although I don't think it was intentional. The boys worked outside and the girls inside. Ines and June played together and Roy and I played together. In the end it didn't work out very well as it kept the "boys versus girls" syndrome alive.

At that time I was always trying to please my parents. One time, a lady came by to buy some eggs (we had chickens). She commented to Mom, "Agnes, I like buying eggs from you because your chickens are penned up and can't get bugs and things." They went to the hen house to get eggs when I came running around the corner with a mouse. I excitedly called out, "Mom, I've caught a mouse and I'm going to throw it to the —," her hand clamped over my mouth to stop me from saying "chickens." This lady didn't catch on that we fed mice to the chickens. Thinking about it now I wouldn't eat eggs if I knew they had eaten mice. It goes to show you that what you don't know won't hurt you.

15

In 1948 we got a new teacher named Fred Davis. A young man from Vancouver, he was 21 years old. He was an excellent teacher. He was friendly and not so serious as Miss Semple. I thrived under him. One afternoon as class was ending, he asked the class if anyone had any special plans for the weekend. No one spoke so he asked if anyone liked fishing? My hand shot up on its own. I loved fishing. He then said, "Would you like to go fishing with me on Saturday?" I said, "Yes, Sir," and felt so proud. Saturday morning at 9 a.m. saw me at the teacherage knocking on the door and asking for Mr. Davis. He came out, said, "Good Morning," then frowned as he looked at me. He wanted to know where my shoes and fishing rod were? "My shoes are for school," I said, "and anyway, when I go fishing I wade in the water and that would ruin my shoes. And my fishing rod well, I have an army pack sack on my back and in it I have fishing line and hooks. I'll cut a willow with my knife down at the river." This seemed to satisfy him and off we went. We had to go through a field, a small slough and an alder grove. About half way to the river he stopped and said, "Hey, we forgot worms!" I said, "Oh, we can find worms in the alders." He looked skeptical but we kept going in toward the alder patch. I moved some old logs aside and sure enough there was a bunch of worms. He was impressed. When we got to the river, he snagged a worm with his hook and threw his line in. I cut a small willow with my jackknife, about 10 feet long, cut the limbs off, then topped the pole leaving a small fork at the end. Next, I took about 20 feet of line, tied it to the fork and wound 5 feet or so on the end in case I needed some more length later on. Finally, I tied a piece of clear line about one foot long to the end and put a hook on, followed by a small lead sinker, 10 inches from the hook. A worm finished the process and I was in business. I don't remember who caught the first fish but I sure enjoyed that day. There were many more fishing days to follow. I was crazy about fishing. I would fish any chance I had. The farm I lived on required lots of work, but on weekends Dad said, "You boys have to work one day and one day you can play." I always went fishing on my day off.

I made friends with Allen and Albert Fowler, who were my age and lived next door (the same twins that had run past us on the first day of school). These boys were to become my best friends, and we did everything together. Allen liked to hike and Albert liked to fish. On my play day, I either went fishing or hiking or both. Those four years, from age 10 to 14, were the happiest days of my life. Summer holidays I worked at the farms in the area, picking beans or weeding spinach, for spending money. The days were long and hot. One summer, after we got paid, Allen and I celebrated at the local store. We bought a "lime-ricky" pop and an Eatmore chocolate bar. They were sure good. Some weekends we peddled our bikes to town to see the show. I distinctly remember one show, "The Red Stallion in the Rockies." What a show. Two thumbs up for that one.

Doug Haines was another fishing buddy of mine at that time. He was an ardent fisherman, seeming to find fish where there were no fish! One memorable time Doug, Albert Fowler and I were spear fishing when we found a big spring salmon. This salmon had wriggled in behind a logjam. Albert and I were trying to flush him out while Doug waited downstream. Finally, we flushed the salmon and he took off downstream. We hollered, "Here he comes, Doug." Doug had been sitting on a log, definitely daydreaming, when we yelled. He was up on a bank, ten or so feet from the river, not in a prime position. But, he just grabbed his spear and threw it at the salmon. His aim and his luck was good, because he got the fish. I remember the spear hitting the salmon and it continuing downstream for a ways, with the spear sticking straight up. When we finally landed the spring, we were sure happy. It was a 20 pounder.

About that time, around 1947 or '48, hydro power came to the Salmon Valley. Most of the residents hooked up to it, including us. One neighbour, Neil Campbell, got one of the first televisions in the area. Neil had a sawmill and provided work for a lot of the local people. There wasn't much work around in those days. Most people in the valley worked for Neil at one time or another. But, the neighbour kids had to go and see this TV, and the Reierson brood was no exception. The Campbells were very hospitable and would invite us in to watch this new phenomenon. They had a large family and I was friendly with the kids my age: Murray, twins Chris and Carol, and Maynard. We would sit around and Naomi, their mother, would bring a big bowl of Ritz crackers for us to munch on. I can't remember any particular program, but I do remember the reception was very poor and the picture snowy.

One evening I was going to look for the cows by the river at the back of our barn and I heard a splash in the water. I couldn't think why on earth the cows would be in the river but, when I looked, they weren't there at all. It was a large salmon splashing in the river. My heart started pounding with excitement and I thought, "I can catch this salmon." My Dad had made me a small spear to catch whitefish with and I had it cached in a hollow log not far from the barn. It was small but it was my only hope. Dad had made it from cut-off bicycle spokes, which he drilled into a wooden frame. He then attached them to an 8-foot handle. These spokes were about 2 inches apart, making the spear about 8 inches wide. I crept up on the salmon, holding my spear, and scooted out onto a log to wait until the salmon came down the river to where I was. When the salmon drifted under my log, I struck with my spear. I didn't think my spear would hold this fish so I slid down the handle to sit on it. What an experience that was holding down the spear and sitting on the thrashing fish. I got it out on the bank and sat there admiring my prize. I hurried home with the salmon, my clothes squishing all the way. My Dad loved fish and was happy to see me. An 18-pound salmon. The cows were forgotten for the time being.

In 1950 my Mom and Dad decided to move back to Alberta. My Dad was a mover, not a mover and a shaker, just a mover. He was full of unrest, never happy, always thinking things would be better somewhere else. By this time we had a large family, two boys and three girls, and none of us wanted to move, especially me. I loved Salmon Arm. In our valley, in the mountains near the river, I felt safe. It was home and I had my friends. But what can you do? No amount of whining from any of us did any good. Dad just dug in harder until finally we moved.

He traded our lovely farm for a General Store in Garden View, Alberta. It also had a post office. A horse and buggy went with the post office, as the mail had to be picked up at another small place four miles away. My brother and I used to have that job. I was in Grade 8 and, since B.C. was a year ahead of Alberta, the teacher said there was no use coming until test time, since we had already done the work. I went working for a grain farmer until June and until school exams. This was a very hard job for a 14 year old, four cows to milk, morning and night, in the field by 7 a.m. and done at 7 p.m. I was so tired at night I had no trouble going to sleep.

After school was out at the end of June (by the way I passed my Grade 8 exams), my brother and I decided to go back to B.C. We were going to go on our bicycles. We got carriers for the front and back, then packed for our trip. It's hard to describe how lonely I was for my friends back in B.C. I missed them and my old home terribly. We had sleeping bags, groceries, a frying pan, hatchet and various other odds and ends. So, bright and early one morning off we went. It was a different experience. We travelled for about a week, cooking out and sleeping in the bush alongside the road. One day it started to rain, we had no rain gear and were soon sopping wet. It was not fun. We stopped that night and built a big fire but everything was wet and very uncomfortable. The next day found us cold and wet again. By that night we were miserable and completely soggy. We hit a small town and rented an Auto Cabin. I made a fire in the wood stove and we were soon warm. I cooked bacon and hot cakes. When they were done, I said, "it's ready Roy." Hearing no reply I looked over at the bed and saw he was fast asleep. That looked so inviting I went over and lay down beside him, and went right to sleep too. We sure had a good sleep but needless to say our supper got cold. The next morning we talked it over and decided to head back home. Our B.C. adventure was put on hold. When we arrived home some four days later, my Dad said to my Mom, "I told you they would be back!" Now there's support and encouragement for you!

Well, we'd been back in Alberta for less than one year when another change came along. This store business wasn't working out very well. My Dad was not a people person and most of the farmers needed credit. This was frustrating for him, so he traded for a 12-acre farm five miles from Vernon, B.C. We arrived in October: Mom and the girls on the train with all our packed up belongings and Roy and I with Dad, in his 1949 Austin car. Vernon was a midsize town with a large high school. The girls started elementary school as soon as we arrived and Dad took Roy and me to see the high school. It was a military-looking building, cold and dreary. We thought, "No way, we aren't going to school!" We had poor clothes and shoes, and we were too intimidated to go. Dad said, "Well, you will have to go to work then."

Original schoolhouse in Silver Creek, 1911

My Dad, Grandma and Mom with Roy and myself, 1938

Roy and myself in Canyon Creek, Alberta, 1945

Roy, Ines, June and myself in Canyon Creek, Alberta, 1945

Silver Creek School, 1947. *Back Row: left to right;*
Allen Fowler, Bill Hansen, myself, Thelma Howell, Gordon Wilby and
Albert Fowler.

Silver Creek School, 1998

Second house my Dad built in Silver Creek in 1947.

My sister Shirley taken at Silver Creek on a hot day in July – she was three years old.

Salmon Valley General Store, 1945

CHAPTER 2

Working for a Living

So, it was 1951 and Roy and I had abandoned formal schooling. Dad put us to work on the plum farm, but how much work is there on a 12-acre farm in the winter? This farm bordered Swan Lake and he had a plan in mind for the coming season — so we helped him build six rowboats for rental in the spring. We also did some ice fishing — there are some nice Kamloops trout in Swan Lake — and odd jobs that Dad gave us. Finally, in the spring we grew restless. Dad said, "Okay boys, I'll help you find a job and then you will be on your own." Why did it have to be either one way or the other in those days? We were too young to be on our own but too old to want to stay at home all the time. There should have been some way to have a few transitional years: go out working for a while, then back home for a while. But it had to be one way or the other. We chose to leave. We wanted to do things, have some money for a change, buy a car and some clothes. I was 15 years old and Roy was 17.

Along with Ines and June and Shirley, we left behind two new sisters: twins Jean and Joan. They were born in early summer of 1951 and, boy! were they something. I remember Dad building them a side-by-side potty chair, with two holes and two pots underneath. My Mom would sit them there after meals. She'd tie them to the back with a cloth diaper snugged around their middles. They'd sit on their seats, playing and cooing and looking cute. I didn't see these sisters a whole lot as they were growing up but I remember they were always dressed alike and I remember them learning to walk and, later, riding tricycles. They were happy, smiling, little blondies. It wasn't until much later that I got to know them and appreciate them as adults. I thought that, like my Dad, they would think that once I was gone, that was it, I was gone. Not so, a happy discovery I made years later.

Roy and I started working in a tie-mill at Ewings Landing, 30 miles from Vernon, on Okanagan Lake. A tie-mill is a sawmill dedicated to making railway ties. The outfit was Monkhaus & Worth. Tom Monkhaus and his wife Bertha had a large old house where the crew boarded. Bertha did the cooking. They were good people. Tom was a small, wiry man who spoke with an English accent and Bertha was a tall, full-figured woman with a sunny disposition. The job paid $100.00 per month and if we panned out they would hire us steady at $1.10 per hour. We worked nine hours a day, six hours on Saturday. Thinking back now, this was too much for young boys. We needed to get used to this hard a pace slowly and work up to it, not start with nine hours a day. We knew how to work but this was a bit much.

Tom put me skidding in the bush with a horse, working with his nephew, Willie Pollock. Willie was easy to work with and he showed me the ropes — and he taught me how to smoke. He had a package of tobacco and papers, when he stopped for a smoke he would show me how to "roll your own." Willie was 19 years old. At night when we went to camp I would see my brother, tired from his day in the mill. One day I noticed his jacket sleeve was in tatters from packing slabs and I felt really sad for him. Roy was easily taken advantage of and I felt he was being worked too hard.

One Saturday, at the lunch break, Tom said that a friend of his had agreed to help him butcher his two pigs but that the friend, unexpectedly, couldn't make it. I opened my mouth and said, "My brother and I can butcher pigs, no problem!" Tom said, "Really?" and, "Would we?" We said, "Sure." Tom said, "Okay, how about Sunday morning?" On Sunday we got ready.

That's one thing Dad had taught us was how to butcher pigs. We got a fire going under a 45-gallon barrel filled three-quarters full of water. We put the barrel on two timbers (built up boards will do) and then built a fire underneath it. Then we put a tripod over the barrel; the tripod was made of 15-foot poles tied together on top, with the legs apart at the bottom. You can then hoist the pigs up over the barrel. With the fire going nicely and the other preparations ready, including an old table pulled up beside the barrel, we were ready for the pigs. We got the 22 rifle and sharpened the knives. I could not butcher an animal in this fashion now but at the time it was an accepted practice.

When the pigs were bled, we cut an opening above the back feet and looped a piece of sinew over a wooden tree we had made. Using a piece of wood two feet long and with tapered ends to slide under the sinew, you then tie a rope on the center of the tree, loop the other end over the tripod, and hoist the pig up and over the barrel. Proper water temperature is important for a good scald. If you can plunge your hand in the hot water three times and no more, the water is okay. Next, you lower the carcass in the hot water and gently lift it in and out. The idea is to have it in long enough so the hair falls out or scrapes off easily, usually about 5 minutes. You test occasionally until the hair is coming off nicely, then you place the carcass on the table and start scraping. There is a tool for that but we used a knife — careful not to cut any tough area. As needed, you can pour more hot water over a tough spot using a tin can. We repeated the same process with the other carcass, then hung them up by the wooden trees. Using two-foot trees to open the back legs makes dressing them out easier. Cleanliness is very important and this is the time for careful work. In another hour and a half we had these two pigs hanging up, cleaned and ready to go. Tom was very impressed. He later told Bertha, "You know those boys made that job look easy." We were very proud. Recognition was something we weren't very used to.

A friend of my brother, Willie Howell, had come to visit and talked of a dam being built on the Nechako River, just outside of Vanderhoof. He was going to see if he could get a job there and wanted Roy to go with him. Roy seemed to think that sounded okay and they both left. Roy had worked for one month. Now I was alone.

Tom moved me into the mill and I started at the back end packing slabs and stacking ties. This tie-mill cut squares 6 × 8 × 8 feet long and 7 × 9 × 8 feet long, and then shipped to the railroad. These ties were very heavy and the work was hard. When the truck came to the yard to haul Tom's load to Vernon, I helped him load. Tom had a 3-ton Ford flatdeck. Bill Geare was Tom's driver and I soon made friends with him. He was a clean-cut 25-year-old with a trim muscular build. He was married to a gal named Sheila and they lived close by our camp. I soon got to be friends with both of them. Sheila's Mom and Dad lived at Ewings Landing, a few miles away on Okanagan Lake. After work, we were to spend many happy hours swimming in this big, clear lake. It was a beautiful piece of water, blue green, clear and inviting.

My first introduction to the lake came in early April. Working in the mill, in the sun, was very hot and we could see the lake as we worked. It looked so cool and inviting. One particular hot day we decided to go for a swim after work, the "we" being Bill Geare, Willie Pollock and me. Off we went in the company's Model A pickup. Ewings Landing had a large wharf and not much else. The wharf had been used in the past as a freight dock. Supplies were delivered up and down the lake between about 1900 and 1945, and offloaded at a large dock. The dock had been idle for many years now but was still in good shape. It was high above the water, about 15 feet, and had a surface of roughly a 1000 square feet. We parked the Model A on the land edge and stripped off. Bill and Willie suggested we hold hands and run off the end. I said okay and off we ran. When we reached the timber that bordered the drop off, they let go of me and I went tumbling in alone. Was the water ever cold! Gasping and shuddering I came to the surface, struggling for air. The water was at least 20 feet deep at the end of the wharf. I swam to one of the pilings to climb out but it was too slippery, so I had to swim to shore about 100 feet away. I was frozen. The weather was warm but the lake hadn't warmed up yet. Bill and Willie were up on the wharf laughing their heads off. They knew how cold it was likely to be and had no intention of going swimming. They did wash off in the lake. All in good fun.

Later on that summer Sheila's sister, Vi Ewing, came to spend the summer with her folks. The four of us had many a memorable time together. I think I was in love with Vi, but I kept it hid as I was still afraid of girls or of their hidden secrets. All too soon summer ended and Vi had to go back to Banff where she worked in Gohrleys Drug Store. I still have a tender spot in my heart for her to this day.

I had the chance to try something new that summer but I goofed it up. Our main town was Vernon. We spent our weekends there. One Friday, Bill said, "There's a celebration happening this weekend in Vernon. It's called their Diamond Jubilee. It's like a circus and fair put together. Would you like to go with us?" He meant with Sheila, Vi and him. I said yes of course. Saturday after work, off we went. We had a nice supper and they wanted to go to the dance, so off we went. Vi said, "Do you dance?" I said, "Sure, but I don't want to." I'm sure she knew I was lying, I was so afraid of the truth in those days. I felt bad as she danced off with somebody else.

Dancing was something I had no experience with. The only time I had anything to do with dancing was at school, in Grade 7 gym class. Most of the class took to it fairly well, but I didn't. I stumbled around with my partner that first time. After that I sat on the sidelines. I was so self-conscious and had such low self-esteem that I couldn't bring myself to be a part of something that was new and might open the door to off-the-cuff comments or looks. I regretted not having learned to dance but not enough to risk learning how. My inability was to haunt me many times in the next few years. Sports and dancing seemed to go hand in hand, and I couldn't do either without being self-conscious. I was tall and uncoordinated and poor at sports, especially volleyball. That was the "in" sport at that time. I lived with low self-esteem for many years, perhaps lots of young people do. I did, eventually, tackle the problem but it was not until many years later.

◆ ◆ ◆

The sun was glistening on the silver conches lining the saddlebags on this gleaming black and silver motor bike. I was staring at it and daydreaming of what it would be like to be cruising down the road on this beauty. It was mid-August and I had worked in the sawmill for six months, had saved my money, and now I was going to spend it. I had hitchhiked to Kelowna and was in a bike shop downtown. The bike I was looking at was a Harley Davidson. It was a beauty, but it was more bike than I wanted or could afford. I ended up buying a Francis Barnett 250 cc, a very nice English bike. I paid $235.00 for it. It was solid black. Later on I installed a silver-trimmed windshield. Oh boy, was I proud of this bike. My first machine with an engine. I knew how to ride a bicycle and thought, "Well, a motorcycle can't be that hard." The shop owner showed me the gears, clutch and brakes. I had the Owner's Manual, a toolkit and off I went. I was very careful as I went through the gears and tested the brake. I drove around and around his shop yard until I figured it was familiar and I was brave enough to tackle the main highway. I didn't have a licence but in those days, that didn't seem to be that important. When I turned 16 in September I planned on getting a driver's licence. Before I took the test and got my licence, I used to stop driving the motorbike on the outside of Vernon and push it through town. That probably attracted more attention than if I had just driven through, I was 15 years old.

In October Tom and Bertha decided to go to England for a visit. They needed a new man to take over the mill while they were gone. Tom hired Bunzie Bunzinmire, and his wife. A friend, Fred Rathgaber, came along with them. We didn't need another labourer but Tom said he'd find something for Fred to do. Things were not the same after that.

By this time I had graduated to the front of the mill, working with Tom as a cantor. A cantor is someone who turns the log with a cant hook. When Fred started sawing I also canted for him. A log is rolled on the carriage and secured there with two metal spikes called "dogs." The sawyer then moves the carriage with a lever and the log is carried to the head saw; when it goes through the head saw a slab is cut off. As the log comes back, the sawyer would give a signal to lift the dogs, turn the log and reset the dogs all on the fly. The sawyer and the cantor would get good at hand signals, as the noise was too loud to talk. The logs were skidded to the skidway with horses and rolled down to the cantor as they were needed. The cantor would have one ready as the last one was cut up.

Bunzie and Fred changed the pattern of the crew and there was some unrest. One of the results was, logs were not getting rolled down to the cantor properly. I reached as far as I could for logs, came up short, then just cut the last one. Fred looked back to signal for another log but there weren't any. He shut the mill engine down and said, "What's going on? Why aren't there any logs down there?" I explained that the crew hadn't rolled them close enough to me. He said, "Look it's your job to roll these logs down!" and I said, "I can't do my job properly if I have to roll logs." He started for me, hollering. Bill, who was loading his truck, jumped on the mill deck and said, "What's the problem here?" Bill stuck up for me and Fred told him to mind his own business. Bill said, "This is my business. Ever since you and Bunzie started here things have not gone well." Fred said, "Look, I'm the boss here and what I say goes!" Bill said, "Yes, you're the boss and I'm not working here anymore!" and off he went. I said, "Hey Fred — me too, I quit!" I was proud of Bill for sticking up for me. Sometimes when a change in crew happens, things just don't work out. There was resentment on our part, and Fred and Bunzie needed to let one man go to make room for them. This all happened without words to that effect. Tom had thought he was doing the right thing putting Fred in charge. Willie and I had thought Bill should have been put in charge. The problem with that was, Bill was not a sawyer, and the sawyer was usually in charge. Looking back now, I was ready for a change.

I was standing waist deep in Christmas trees, trying to keep a straight face as Sheila Geare moved around to get a proper focus on her camera. She was taking a picture of Bill and me and our Christmas trees. After Bill and I left Monkhaus and Worth, we started cutting trees on Bill's mother-in-law's place. Christmas trees were a big item in the 1950s, in the Okanagan Valley. Bill had talked to an agent from the Emerald Tree Company, Bob Kershaw, in Kamloops and secured a contract with them for as many trees as we could cut. Bob showed us what kind of trees to cut, the desired length, and how to trim the base. Trees could be from 2 feet to 12 feet. The property we were cutting on was 160 acres of rolling sidehill above Okanagan Lake and was thick with trees. We cut from the 1st of November until the 15th of December. I really liked this job. It was fun working with Bill and Sheila. They moved into a cabin on the lake and I stayed with them. Cutting trees was a welcome change from the sawmill. The smell of needles and the pitch in the clean mountain air was euphoric. The only sound was the chop, chop of our axes and a sliding sound as we dragged the trees to the road. At the end, we split the money for the trees four ways, and there wasn't much left!

After finishing my Christmas tree job, including cleaning up the leftovers and burning the branches and ends, I said goodbye to Bill and Sheila. I headed to Vernon to join up with my brother who had come back from his job in Vanderhoof. Bill and Sheila were moving back to Banff, Alberta, where they were from. Bill went working in the oil patch and was killed in an accident. After that, Sheila went to work on a horse ranch in Montana. I saw her last in about 1974.

I found Roy in Vernon without any trouble. He was eager to buy a car and there was a car auction in town. He bought a Hillman panel at the sale. It was an ugly panel, the back higher than the front, but it was in good shape. He paid $250.00 for it. He didn't like it, so he promptly traded it for a nice 1937 Ford sedan. I parked my motorbike in a friend's shed and Roy and I headed up north to find work. Williams Lake was our destination and the plan was to try and find work all the way along until we got there. We left Vernon around Christmas time. We were a little sad, as most of our friends were spending their holidays with their families and our family wasn't that close. Roy and I were close, but we didn't feel we were wanted around home, so we chose to stay away. We weren't being paranoid about feeling unwelcome at the folks' place, or at least with my Dad. One day we stopped at home and my Dad said, "What do you boys want?" That didn't make us feel too great, I'll tell you.

We stayed overnight in Kamloops that first night. We had sleeping bags and extra clothes, but we stayed in Auto Cabins as we had some money saved. Between us we had, maybe, $200.00; and little did we know how fast this would to run out. It was a bad time to be looking for work. We didn't even go into some of the business offices we stopped at, we just parked in front. We didn't talk about it but, the truth was, we were too shy and insecure go in. Sometimes we said to each other, "Okay, why bother, they probably aren't hiring," and then we'd drive off. No wonder by the time we hit Quesnel we were broke and discouraged. Nobody seemed to have a job for us so we turned around on Main Street and headed back to Vernon. At least Vernon was a familiar place.

The trip back was uneventful and upon arriving in Vernon we heard of a woodcutting job at Okanagan Landing, about 15 miles on the east side of Okanagan Lake. We drove out to this place. It was a summer lodge and cabins, and they burned wood in the lodge. The owner, Major Hodson, had been in the war and had a plate in his head. He seemed a fair man and said he would like 25 cords of wood cut. He would pay $6.00 per cord. He took us up to the top end of his property and showed us a nice patch of fir trees, around two feet on the stump. He said to cut this wood four feet long and split it into about 8-inch pieces, then pile it up in cord piles. A cord of wood is four feet wide, four feet high and 8 feet long. That's a lot of split wood but we knew how to cut wood. He then said, "Okay boys, you have the job, but we have people all summer and in winter we want our privacy so you'll have to find your own place to stay." That was okay with us and we were happy to get the job. A place to stay was the least of our worries.

Off to town we went. We borrowed an eight-foot Royal Chinook cross-cut saw from a friend, a real beauty. A crosscut saw has a long thin blade, 8 inches wide with long teeth and a handle on each end. If it is sharp, it will cut real well. With a saw to use, the next stop was the secondhand store, where we bought an axe, a sledge hammer, some splitting wedges, pots, pans, dishes and utensils. Then on to the General Store for some groceries and back to the Hodson property and our job.

After talking it over, we decided to build our own cabin right on the job site. In those days you could just do that, when you were out in the country. I suppose we should have asked somebody's permission to put up a cabin but it didn't even occur to us. Our spirits were high as we started out. We didn't get too much done that first day as we got a late start. We slept in the car and were back the next morning, early. We had porridge cooked on an open fire. We picked a spot for our cabin up against a 50-foot rock wall, in a patch of very large fir trees too big to cut down for wood. We cleared off an area 20-feet square, moving brush and pine needles to bare ground. We figured we would make our cabin 8 feet by 10 feet. That seemed big enough on the ground.

We cut a bunch of logs 8 feet and 10 feet long and then dragged them to our site. These logs were about 6 to 8 inches in diameter. We put the first two logs down and notched the next ones into those bottom logs, then it was just a matter of notching each log as we went round for round. We realized as we got started that by notching the logs and having a small overhang, that our cabin was closer to 6 feet by 8 feet than our planned 8 × 10! We worked hard and it was a small cabin so, by the end of that day, we had the walls up. We built bunk beds in one end out of dry poles, cutting poles to length and wedging them in between the logs until a row of poles about three feet wide was made. The first bed was about a foot from the floor and the second row of poles was about three feet above that. We put a larger pole on the outside to serve as a border for the mattress. Our mattresses were about six inches of small fir boughs. With our extra clothes piled onto the bows and our sleeping bags on top of that, we each had a better bed than some we'd had as kids! That night we slept in our roofless cabin looking up at the stars.

The next morning we cut out a door in our cabin and started on the roof. We put an extra log on one side to allow for a slope on the roof and then we put up poles for rafters. At an old mill site not far away, we scrounged some old lumber to sheet the roof. When the roof was on we chinked the logs with moss and built our door. There were no windows. Back at the mill site we found an old heater made from a 10-gallon drum. It didn't have a door so we fashioned one from a flattened piece of tin. We carried this and an old table we found back to the cabin. That used up that day. Over porridge the next morning, we took stock. We needed roofing for the roof and a stovepipe for the heater. Off to town again for a roll of rubberoid roofing and a length of 6-inch stovepipe with a damper, as well as a handful of roofing nails and a can of tar for the seams. Back to the bush in Roy's '37 Ford (that little V8 purred like a kitten) with just enough daylight left to put the roofing on and hook up the stovepipe. The heater had no legs so we just sat it up on about six inches of dirt. We cut a square hole in the roof, through the boards, and then cut a round hole in a piece of 2-foot-square tin. When it was tarred down, the stovepipe got poked through it. We built our first fire in it that night and cooked hot cakes on top in a frying pan. We had to flatten the top a bit for cooking. We soon learned that you didn't build too big a fire in it or you were roasted out in a short while. We slept inside again that night, snug, warm and dry. The next day we finished up the cabin, chinking the cracks with moss. The roof was only 5 feet high so we dug down a foot inside the cabin, allowing us to stand up somewhat straight. This cabin was to serve us well for the next two and a half months and we'd built it in five days and mostly with scrounged material.

The next day we started cutting our wood. We would fall a 2-foot tree (on the stump), limb it up, measure the tree into 4-foot lengths and then start sawing with the crosscut saw. When we had finished sawing, or were tired of it, we would start splitting. To split logs, you placed a wedge in the centre of the log, toward one end, then banged it in with a hammer. Once that wedge was nicely started you would start a second wedge. We would take turns hitting each wedge until the log split apart. Once it was halved it was easy to split into quarters. The object was to end up with long pieces about 8 inches thick.

This was a memorable time in my life and I remember it as though it was yesterday. We supplemented our store-bought food with rabbits and blue grouse, which were plentiful around there at that time. Our favourite dish was stew. We would take a rabbit or blue grouse, cut it up, throw it in our large pot and cook it overnight or as long as we were up. The next morning we would put whatever veggies we had in the pot, usually onions, carrots, and potatoes, and leave the whole thing on the hot stove while we went to work. It was a surprise when we came back later, because we never knew if it would boil over, run out of water or if the fire would go out. But, sometimes, more often than not, it turned out perfect. Beside the rock wall was a waterhole, a spring I guess you could call it. It ran about six feet across and about one foot deep. It did not freeze all winter. In the mornings after a snowfall it was neat to see how many different animals had come to drink — and while we admired, we figured those animals probably wondered what the heck we were doing there! We shared the spring with our animal neighbours; they came down at night and we used it by day as our drinking and cooking water supply. Roy and I liked where we were living and the work was just fine. Each week we would cut and split the wood, measure our output, and drive down to Major Hodson's and he would pay us. We would usually cut about two to three cords a week.

We got to know a neighbour about one month into our work for the Major. His name was Howard Russell. He lived on the next place up the lake, on a beautiful piece of property. The Russell family had a granite quarry on their property. The Vernon Courthouse had been built with rock from this quarry. Howard was a bachelor and he lived with his mother. His mother was 82 years old and had an exceptionally good memory. She was interesting to talk to. She knew the history of the Okanagan Lake, right back to the 1890s. Sometimes Howard would ride his horse to the Sutherland Arms Hotel, about eight miles away, have one too many drinks, and his horse would bring him home. As our place was on his way home, sometimes he would stop in and wake us up. At these times, boy was he talkative. One time, we had come home and it was very wet. We parked our car and the next week when we went to go, the car wouldn't move. It started but would not move. So, we figured there was something seriously wrong. The next time Howard came by after a visit to the Arms we told him what had happened. He laughed and said, "Boys, when it's wet and then it freezes, your brakes are frozen to the drums of the wheels. To fix this problem, you pour hot water on the inside of your wheels and it will thaw out." We did this and what do you know . . . that's all it took. We had a new appreciation for Howard after that. Howard wasn't the only critter to visit us at night. One time, we heard scratching and sniffing around our cabin. We were too scared to get up and investigate. We figured we were safe inside our cabin although it was a bit unnerving. The next morning we discovered fresh cougar tracks around our cabin. We didn't go out at night for a while after that.

There was a large fir tree beside our cabin; about three and a half feet at the stump and it had a hollow base. We started a fire in this base, just for fun. It burned good as there was lots of pitch in there. This fire burned for about a week. One morning before we got up, we heard a creaking sound and then a tremendous crash, right beside the cabin. We got up and ran to the door to discover that our big fir tree had fallen down, barely missing the cabin. Most of the wood at the base of the tree had burned away, leaving just a small ring of wood. A slight breeze was it all it took to topple it. That day we cut it into cordwood. Hard to get work closer to home than that. When we rested in between logs or dreamed over our supper, we compared wishes. We both wished for the same thing, a pickup truck and a chainsaw!

Soon the winter gave way to spring and we grew restless. Major Hodson came by and said, "Okay boys, you have reached my request for 25 cords. Nice work, thank you very much, and maybe we'll see you next year. Clean up around here before you go." He paid us up to date and back to Vernon we went. It didn't take long for our money to run out even though we were careful. We slept in the car at night and hung around town during the day. We were hopeful, enthusiastic and ready for any opportunity that came along. We would take any kind of work we could get. But work of any kind was scarce, so we bided our time.

◆ ◆ ◆

A bright blinding light shining somewhere around or in my head woke me up, and for a moment I was lost, unable to focus. Reality came back and I awakened to the sound of rain splattering down on the roof and the light of a policeman's flashlight shining through the window of the car. I had been asleep in my brother's 1937 Ford Sedan. It was March 1952 and my brother and I were without work and money. We used the car for our hotel. We had parked it behind some bushes at the back end of Polson Park in Vernon. We had sleeping bags and were quite comfortable although it was cold and hard to stretch out. We had been there for a month and knew we would probably be there awhile yet as work in Vernon in winter was particularly hard to find, especially for two boys with little experience and limited education. Vernon was the fruit and vegetable capital of the Okanagan in the 1950s. There were packing houses and canneries. Also a sawmill and box mills. The sawmills slowed down in winter and of course gardens and fruit stopped until spring. There was no welfare and we knew nothing of U.I.C. so we learned to live by our wits. Around 7 a.m. a bakery we got to know opened its back doors and the baker sorted out his bread and buns. Sometimes bread and buns hit the dumpster. If he saw us he used to say, "Here boys take this" and would hand us a bag of day-old bread. If we were lucky there'd be some butterhorns. Back to our car and, Oh what a feast! Coldstream Creek ran through the park where we were parked, so we had fresh drinking water. I was 16 years old.

The sound of axes rang in the cold morning air. There were six axes chopping in various rhythms and fairly close together. We were hacking out a powerline right-of-way. Finally, after a lot of time scrounging, somewhere around June, Roy and I had managed to land a job with Joe Findleson and his foreman, Pete Dimion (we called him Pete Diamond). They had a contract with B.C. Hydro to slash a 100-foot-wide right-of-way for a powerline from Chase to Salmon Arm. This job paid $1.40 per hour and we were very happy to get it. There were six of us on this job and we stayed in a bunkhouse trailer, supplied by the company. Louis Adams, the oldest man on the crew at 27, did the cooking and the rest of us shared the cost of groceries. One month into the job, Roy and his friend, Willie Howell, went off to work somewhere else. You'd wonder where Willie was when we were in need of work. Roy left but I stayed. I had gotten my bike serviced and running and was using it to get around.

One fellow I worked with and I got to be friends over the summer. I was 16 and he was 18. His name was Roy Undershoults. I had a pair of boxing gloves, which were popular in those days, and we used to spar a lot after work. I never could beat him — he was tough. He was 6'3" and 185 lbs. At that time I was 6'2" but only 160 lbs. We had fun though, banging away at each other.

One of the memorable events to happened that summer involved our breakfast. The crew trailer moved every two weeks or so, to keep us closer to our work. One particular time, we moved it to a small clearing near a cheery creek. A farmer's two cows used to spend the night in the clearing. Early in the morning, while we shared the clearing with these cows, Roy Undershoults would get up early and milk one. She was easy to milk, he just walked up to her and she would move her leg and he'd sit down and get to work. He would only milk two quarts or so, enough for our porridge, and boy was it good. Another activity I remember well from that summer was my official role as bee exterminator. Whenever we would run into a bee's nest, I was called. I thought it was because I was the bravest. I think now it was because I was the youngest. We had some powder and I had to get close enough to shake it onto the nest. You had to get real close to do that. Needless to say, I was stung fairly often.

Partway into the job, Pete Dimion got a chainsaw to tackle the larger trees that we had to clear. I was the only one with some experience and so I was chosen to run this saw. I had helped Willy Pollock saw some trees down and buck them up with a two-man McCulloch when I was working at Monkhaus and Worth. I had held the "dumb" end. A two-man saw puts one man at the control handle and one man holding the end of the blade by a handhold. This saw was a one-manner and Pete showed me how to start it and I was away. This was the start of my falling career. I had turned 17 in September and was to keep this job right to the end of the contract, falling danger trees with Pete until the end, even after the main job was completed.

The powerline job ended November 20th and it was back to Vernon for me. I met up with a friend, Jack Wilson, who I had known when I was out at Okanagan Landing sawing wood. Jack was a good guy and loyal to his friends. His Dad, Willie, had a fencepost contract and he needed help so we went to work. We cut and split cedar posts, and piled them in the bush for pickup in the spring. We also trapped for fur and shot some deer. Willie had some orders for deer meat in Vernon and as the orders came in we would pick up a deer we had hanging and deliver it. Jack's Dad had a nice clean 1951 Ford pickup and we got to use it for deliveries. One time we were delivering a deer in Vernon and Jack made a U-turn in front of the train station. He gave it a little gas to spin it around and this deer slid to the back with a bump and the tailgate popped open and the deer slid out on the street. We had covered it up with a tarp, as it was not hunting season. Jack was very cool and he backed up to it, we loaded it and carried on. We sold these deer for $25.00 a piece. We split the groceries three ways and Jack's Mom, Lily, did the cooking. She was a very good cook. She made the best breaded deer steaks I have ever tasted.

I was hunting that winter with Jack Wilson, in the Fly Hills area of Salmon Arm. We had driven to the end of a logging road, and then made a plan of where we would go. There was a sidehill going gradually up and we decided to split up, heading away from each other. Around noon we would veer over to each other, meet, and have lunch. I wandered up the hill, enjoying the clean, crisp air and the freshly fallen snow. I saw tracks of squirrels, rabbits, a coyote, and some old deer tracks. It's amazing what you see in the fresh snow when you are paying attention. Around mid-morning I started heading over toward where I assumed my friend Jack would be. I kept moving over that way, figuring I would either run into him or his tracks. Once I came upon his tracks I would be okay. Finally, I came upon upon fresh tracks and thought, "Yes, they look like Jack's. I'll stay on the other side of them and then I'll be okay." As I continued to go up and down hills, I began to wonder where the heck he was. I hollered a couple of times around noon, but no response, so I built a small fire and had my lunch.

When Jack still did not show up, I assumed he had run into a deer or a moose and that he would meet me back at the truck later on. I started meandering back down in the general direction of the truck. Around mid-afternoon something did not seem right. I felt I was in the wrong area. It's funny, sometimes you're okay and then you kind of wake up and you're not okay. Well, that's how I felt. I decided I'd better backtrack and figure things out. I returned to my lunch spot and hurried on, following my tracks, until I came to what I had thought were Jack's tracks. I realized they were my own! I had circled around and crossed my own trail. No wonder I was turned around.

It was starting to get dark and I was about four hours from the truck. I knew I would not be able to travel in the dark, so I looked around for a spot to spend the night. I was not very happy with myself. I found an old broken-off fir stump about 10 feet tall and 3 feet at the base. I was able to push it over (some old fir stumps are sometimes rotten and easy to push over). These stumps make excellent fires. The ground end usually has pitch pieces that are easy to light. I got a good fire started and dragged in as many dry poles as I could find and move. I stacked the wood close and then cut as many green branches as I could carry, and made myself a dry place to sit by the fire. I wondered what on earth I was going to do with the all the time until daylight. It wasn't that cold but as night settled in it seemed cold. Just sitting there didn't make it feel warmer. I tried chopping with my hatchet but got tired of that pretty quickly. I had my branches piled up against the old fir stump, that was now laying down, and was quite comfortable. I dozed off intermittently and would wake up and put more wood on the fire. I felt pretty safe as I had my rifle and my axe but it's funny how the smallest sounds are magnified when you are alone in the forest in the night.

I was getting pretty impatient, my wood supply was getting pretty low, and I was wishing I'd brought more food. About 4 o'clock in the morning, I thought I heard a dog bark. I wondered what on earth a dog would be doing way up here when I suddenly thought, "That's got to be Jack's Dad's dog." The barking got louder and finally I heard voices talking and saw a light coming up the trail. It was Jack and his Dad. Jack had gone home, had supper, changed his clothes, and collected his Dad to come back and help look for me. They followed my tracks with a gas lantern until they came on my camp. They had some coffee and sandwiches with them and boy did that taste good, especially the coffee.

I had to put up with a lot of good-natured ribbing about getting lost but I sure didn't mind. I was also glad I'd stayed on my trail. I explained to Jack what I had done and he laughed and said, "Oh, I can see that happening. No wonder I couldn't find you for lunch. You were over in the next county."

I had spent a lot of my childhood in the bush and always carried a hatchet and matches just in case I got lost. If you do get lost, the first thing is not to panic. The instinct is to hurry someplace, but if you do that you end up with no camp and completely in the dark. After not panicking, the second thing is to prepare a camp, gathering as much wood as possible and collecting branches to keep you off the snow and ground. Then stay put until daylight. The third thing is to get a good fire going and get as dry and warm as possible. Even though you can't do much more against the cold and dark, you will survive. I have spent many nights in the bush, but this was the most memorable.

As spring approached, the Wilsons decided to be by themselves so they said to me, "Ed, when have you last visited your folks?" I answered, "Oh a while back I guess." Lily suggested I should go and say Hello at least. I agreed, and they drove me to Armstrong to where my folks then lived. They dropped me off and drove away. I visited my folks for a while. It was a strained visit. I felt like I wasn't welcome. I stayed overnight and the next day started off for Wilsons, about 15 miles away. I planned to hitchhike a ride, shouldn't be too hard, I figured. Well, wouldn't you know, there were few cars that day and the ones that came by wouldn't pick me up. I ended up walking the whole way and arrived at Wilsons around suppertime. I walked to the door and knocked, Lily answered. She said, "Oh Ed, what are you doing here?" I told her I'd come back to work but she had to set me straight. "I'm sorry, Ed," she said "We won't be doing anything for a while. We had to send Jackie to Creas Clinic outside of Vancouver for some tests. His head was hurting something awful. We took him to the doctor and he referred him to a specialist at the clinic. And, we don't know when he'll be back." I'm pretty sure Jack was there the whole time and not in Vancouver. I must have seemed very naïve but I really would have understood better if they had just told me it was time for the family to be alone. I believe Jack was there because of an incident that happened when I was with them that should have clued me in. A lady friend of Jack's had come calling one evening. The Wilsons had a dog that gave them lots of warning if someone was coming. When she knocked on the door, Lily answered and when this lady friend asked for Jack, Lily said, "Gosh Jackie is not home. Would you care to come in for some tea?" She said, "No thanks, but would you tell Jack when he gets home to contact me?" Lily said, "Sure I will" and shut the door. Jack had been home all the while and when the dog started barking, Lily looked out and said, "Oh, oh, it's Ruth," and Jack made a dive under his Dad's bed. It was just a two-room cabin. His Dad had a quart milk bottle under the bed that he used as a chamber pot and, when Jack dove under the bed, he knocked it over. It was about half full. Well, he came out from under that bed a bit of a mess after Ruth left. We all had a good laugh over that one. But, what I'm getting at is that they most likely did the same thing to me and I was too slow to catch on. Maybe it was for the best.

Back to Vernon I went. My brother was working at Bolean Lake out of Falkland, for Vernon Box and Pine, a sawmill outfit. It would be a while before I would meet up with him again. My next job was for Maynard Munson doing farm and logging work. Maynard had a McCulloch 325 chainsaw and I honed my skill as a chainsaw operator on that machine. I ran it every chance I got. I worked for Munson for two months at $100.00 a month plus room and board. About the 24th of May, two school friends from Silver Creek, John and Sam Moore, came by and asked me if I wanted to go to Williams Lake with them to look for work. I said yes and then said goodbye to the Munsons. We were in Williams Lake in about a week.

Sam found work in 150 Mile House, in a sawmill owned by Khonke Bros. John and I found a falling job in Williams Lake for Vic Imhoff. He had a sawmill about seven miles north of Williams Lake. This was the job we were looking for. John had a 430A McCulloch chainsaw and I was his swamper. A swamper limbs and measures the trees, and the faller falls and bucks them. After about a month I bought my own saw, a real nice, used 430A McCulloch, from a saw shop in Williams Lake, owned by a nice man, Gordon Cole. I put $100.00 down and owed $200.00 on this saw. In those days a saw was very expensive and you financed them with some money down and the rest in payments. You also had to have insurance on them. We had a real enjoyable summer falling and bucking for Imhoff Sawmills. Later on we each had to have a swamper to keep up. John hired his younger brother, Melvin, and I hired my good friend Allen Fowler, from home, to help me. Allen was chopping out an undercut one day and he chopped his foot real bad. He sliced his second toe right up to the arch. What a mess. We took him to the hospital in Williams Lake, where they stitched him up and put his foot in a cast. He was in the hospital about a week, then was able to go home to Silver Creek. His falling days were over for that year.

Around about November 1st, when the rains came, we were shut down. We were feeling stakey and decided to head back to Vernon for the winter. I ran into my brother and we decided to go to work for a fellow in Lumby, a man that Roy had worked for in the fall. His name was Ernie Elgers. He had a trapline on Silver Star Mountain and a logging contract for Lumby Timber, cutting white pine logs. He had a nice base camp in Trinity Valley, 10 miles out of Lumby, with two other cabins along his trap line. We agreed to run his trap line three days a week and log three days a week. He would supply us with a horse and rigging. I had bought a car — a 1950 Desoto — so we loaded it up with our gear and headed out.

Working on this trapline was quite an experience. It was about 10 miles long with one cabin half way up and one cabin at the end. The idea was to make the first cabin, stay overnight, reach the second cabin for the next night and then hoof it all the way home on the third day. Sometimes this worked and sometimes it took longer. There were heavy snowfalls in those mountains and after a heavy snow it was quite a job digging traps out and breaking trail. These cabins on the line boasted only the bare necessities: a heater, beds and a rough table, but after a long day, they were a very welcome refuge. We usually carried some pancake flour and salt with us, and there were usually a few things left in the cabin. It was slim pickins on the line but we could feed up back at the main cabin.

This trapline had squirrels, weasels, mink and lynx as the main furs. Any animals caught would be taken out on the way up and the trap reset. They would be carried up to the next cabin, skinned out that evening and left there to be picked up on the way back. I won't go into any detail about how all these animals were caught, as trapping has become a difficult subject, and it even bothers me to write about it now. At the time it seemed okay to trap, but now I would not be able to do it as my love for the trees, nature and animals is too great and would not allow it (and, to be truthful, not only are there fewer animals about but I am less "hungry" and that makes a difference, too).

One day, not on the trapline, we butchered a domestic black rabbit from home to eat. We skinned it out and stretched its hide on a stretcher to dry cure. A stretcher is a piece of thin wood about as wide as the animal and a bit longer with a rounded end, usually made from cedar. You roll the skin over it, inside out, like pulling on sock, stretching it tight and holding it in place with thumb tacks. The skins are then stacked up and left to dry cure, usually a week or so, then taken off the stretcher, turned right side out, and stored in a mouseproof dry box. Ernie would pick the furs up every two weeks. When this tame rabbit was cured, we took it off the stretcher (we wanted to play a trick on Ernie), cut off the ears, rounding them close to the head, cut off the tail, then sewed a squirrel tail back on. It looked pretty good. We then told Ernie we had caught an animal in a trap that we didn't know what it was. Could he help us identify it? He said, "Sure, let me see it." We brought out our creation. I have to say he was fooled for a while, but, after adjusting his glasses, looking down his nose and stroking it, he eventually solved the puzzle.

Ernie was a very talented trapper; experience had been a good teacher. He loved trapping but his hips had started to bother him in the cold weather and he could not make the long hikes any more. He was in his late 60s at the time I met him. He taught us his tricks of the trade. He was showing us how to make mink sets one day, by making a hole in an over-hanging bank, placing a trap in there, and putting some artificial scent on a cotton ball beside it. I said, "Oh, I know how to do it another way." He got agitated and said, "Show me." I had learned an Indian method from my friend, Jack Wilson, the winter before. You dig a hole in an overhang-ing bank by the creek, small about 8 to10 inches in diameter and 2 feet deep. You then place some old meat entrails or whatever you have at the back end of the hole, place your trap and then shut the hole off completely with willow sticks, stuck in the dirt around the mouth of the opening. The mink smells this meat and discovering the closed opening, goes into a frenzy, tearing the sticks out, throwing caution to the wind, and of course gets caught. Ernie said, "Okay, you put yours on one side and I'll put mine on the other, and we'll see who catches a mink first." We did this. Ernie was a bit put out when my trap caught the first mink. Of course I was not very diplomatic about it, not even knowing that word, or anything about it. I certainly never intended to be a smart-alec but a lot of times that's how I came across. I just wanted to show people I knew things too, and be liked. This is not a good way to come across as a good guy, by showing somebody up. This was one lesson it would take me a long time to learn.

When we were not on the trapline, we were logging — falling, bucking and skidding white pine logs and cedar poles. The white pine went to Lumby Timber. They sawed cants out of them and sent them back east where they resawed them and made knotty pine boards, a popular look in the '50s. A cant is a squared timber, 4 inches × 6 inches; 6 inches × 8 inches; etc. The poles went to Bell Pole, who had a pole yard in Lumby. We skidded these logs and poles with a horse. Ernie supplied the horse, Jim, and what a horse he was. He was gentle and very seldom got rattled. One time when our car wouldn't start, we went for Jim and hooked him on. He wouldn't even tighten the traces. No amount of coaxing would work. He just would not pull. Finally we put him away and went back to work. Ernie told us after work that Jim had pulled a car once and it had run into his heels, and that scared him off that job. When he was skidding the cedar poles, however, you could let him go by himself. Poles were hard to skid because they were so long. When a pole got stuck, Jim would back up a bit, pull a bit sideways until it came loose, and when it slid a bit down hill he would just jump sideways and let it go, so as not to catch his heels. He was a pleasure to work around. We had a barn for him and good feed.

This trapping job lasted until spring and furs lost their prime. The logging was finished by the end of August, although we should have left those poles till spring as they were sure hard to peel in winter before the sap was up. We took a couple of weeks off and Ernie got a contract for some cottonwood bolts. These were 3' 6" long, peeled, and had to be split into 4" slabs. You then piled them into cordwood piles to let them dry. This wood was used in a mill in Vernon called Pad and Drum. They made a product called "excelsior," for apple box padding. Excelsior padding was, essentially, really fine, long, wood shavings. The Pad and Drum also made lathes. They were 1/4" thick, 2" wide and 3'6" long, used for lattice work and tacking on building paper. Getting the cottonwood cut to the right specs for the excelsior and lathes was a very hard job. We had to get out the sledgehammer and wedges to split these blocks. Cottonwood is hard to split in the summertime but easy to peel. In winter it's hard to peel but easy to split. You can't win. For this we got $6.00 a cord. We made about 40 cords in two months, and that finished Ernie's patch of cottonwood.

We had an old Clinton chainsaw at this time. You couldn't fall with it but you could buck with it. We would cut the trees down with the crosscut saw and then buck them up with the chainsaw. This saw was very temperamental. Once you had it running you didn't shut it off until it quit. When it quit we would start peeling and splitting, and when it cooled off sufficiently, we could start it up again. It would have helped if we had known anything about it. Chainsaws were just coming into their own and we knew little about them.

With no more cottonwood, the job was finished so Roy and I packed up camp and said goodbye to Ernie and went to the mill to settle up. They told us they had a patch of cottonwood at Cherryville, and would we like to cut wood for them. We said, "Sure" and, following their directions, we went out and found this patch of trees. There was no end to it! 160 acres of cottonwood. We thought, "Hey, let's make wood." We planned to stay in the car until we made enough money to buy or build a cabin. Why we did that I don't know. We definitely should have made living arrangements first. Anyhow we stayed in the car. We had groceries and sleeping bags, and we cooked on a campfire. The second or third day it started raining. The fall rains, I guess, and we got wet. It was hard to get dry, everything got damp even in the car. We put up with it a few more days, and then got discouraged. We had actually worked too long before we did something about a place to stay. We packed up and headed to Vernon, thinking surely we can find something better than this. How soon we forget! We went back to the mill and settled up, telling them that we had decided against this job.

On our way out, we ran into the pole buyer for Bell Pole, a man we'd come to know quite well while working for Ernie. He told us about a piece of land toward Mable Lake that was for sale. He said if we could make a deal on it, he would buy the poles. He said there were some nice cedar poles on it. Well, we knew about poles. We went and looked at the place. It was 320 acres with a farmhouse, barn and outbuildings, and 20 acres in pasture. The elderly man who owned it was friendly and said, "Yes, it is for sale." We asked if we could look at the timber. He said sure, and showed us where the lines were. Off we went looking at the timber. 300 acres is a big piece of land. I doubt we saw it all, but what we saw sure got us excited. Nice poles and white pine timber with some larch and hemlock mixed in. The hemlock was worth nothing at that time, but there wasn't much of it. Now the thing was to make a deal. We got back to the house and talked to the owner again. He told us he wanted $9,000.00 for this place and no, he wouldn't let us pay for it with the timber. He wanted to move to town and buy a house, so he wanted cash. We didn't have that kind of money. We had maybe $500.00. What could we do? We were certain there was enough poles on the place to pay for it and we just had to find the money. We drove to Bell Pole in Lumby and talked to them. Would they advance us the money on the poles? They said no, we couldn't do that although they would certainly buy the poles once we owned them. We tried Lumby Timber and Ernie Elgers. They both said no. It was hard as we were young and didn't have much credibility. I had turned 17 in September and my brother was 18-½. As a last resort we decided to try our Dad. We went to see him and laid out our deal. Our proposition was if he put up the money, we would pay him back from the timber and he could have the place when we were finished logging. We thought, what a deal for him! He'd end up with his money back and a farm to sell. But no way, he didn't even think about it. What he said was, "Do you boys think I'm crazy, that I would jeopardize my family (there was Mom and the five girls at home) for some hair-brained scheme that you boys come up with? I wouldn't even think about it! Now get out of here and leave me alone!" He didn't have that kind of money but he could have borrowed it. My Dad was not a dealer or a gambler. The trouble was, he didn't know anything about timber. When I think back on it now, I can see his point but for us at that time it was a bitter pill. No one would take us seriously. We sulked for days. I think the bitterest pill was that even our Dad had little faith in us. I think he could have talked it over and even if he didn't want to do anything, he could have merely made a suggestion or two, and helped us try to figure something out. I do believe a person should do things on their own, but a little help now and then, even just moral support, can mean a great deal. Back to Vernon we went. We thought about the banks but the only time we had been in there was to cash a cheque. The banks were very intimidating at that time, especially to people with little education or worldly experience. We had to give up on this project, and a bit of that still rankles, even after all these years.

Roy had a friend working for Vernon Box & Pine Sawmill, up at Bolean Lake, out of Falkland, and he went to work there for the winter. I found a job cutting stud logs for Buff Lumber at Monte Lake. I partnered up with a young fellow from Falkland named George Brown, a short, stocky guy who was always friendly and laughing. We worked for Joe LaFontain. Joe was a hard worker. He had a big team of Percherons and he skidded, George and I bucked. These stud logs were 8 feet long and cut from 12-inch jackpine. Joe's wife, Matha, cooked for us and we stayed with them during the week. Joe was a hard taskmaster and we never missed a day. One day we left the cookhouse to go to work and it seemed very cold. We said to Joe, "Boy it's cold!" He said, "Yes boys, it is that alright" and off we went. Later on that day we had a visitor to our landing. He was our closest neighbour, from about a mile away. His name was Mart Scott. He said, "Howdy," and we stopped to talk and have a coffee. Joe asked if he'd been given the day off. Mart said, "No, the mill closed today, it's too cold. I'm surprised you guys are working. It's 38 below." I suppose if we'd had a thermometer we mightn't have worked either. Goes to show you what you don't know. . . . !

On the weekends we stayed nearby with George's family. They were wonderfully friendly folk. There was George's Mom and Dad, Chief and Gladys, and his three sisters. We had lots of fun on those weekends. I never did find out how Chief got his name, and I never heard him called anything else.

This same winter I also got to know a girl, Thelma Lyness. Thelma was my first love or, perhaps, infatuation. I got to know her from the show they had every Thursday night in Falkland. After a while we, instead of going to the show, would drive around and sometimes park. We would hold hands and sometimes gently kiss a couple of times. It got to be a regular thing. I could hardly wait for Thursday to come around. We had to sneak around as Thelma was only 15. Her best friend would cover for her and I would have her back when the show got out, and then they would go home together. This continued all winter. One Thursday night, another young fellow, was driving past our parking place. He stopped and talked for a bit, then drove to town and told Thelma's Mom. That ended our Thursday night rendezvous. That was too bad because even though we were young, we had a good feeling for each other and I felt we should have been encouraged a little. At least Thelma's Mom could have said, come over to the house and visit, and maybe let us go out once in a while. I was on my own and had my own car, so I guess I seemed older than I was. And I guess I can't blame Thelma's parents. They were just looking out for her. Even though we had never done more than hold hands, talk and kiss goodnight. They didn't trust us or maybe they didn't trust me. It was tough but Thelma and I went our separate ways.

The next spring the mill stopped buying stud logs and that ended that job. Later on that fall I met a man named Art Smith. Art and I were to become good friends over the years. Art had a team of horses and was working for Vernon Box, skidding logs. He needed some help, so I hired on. Roy and I were reunited with Art and we all worked through the winter. Roy and I shared the falling and bucking, and Art skidded. Art was an excellent teamster and took good care of his horses and rigging. We would travel to work in a horse-drawn cutter we had borrowed from a neighbour. One day we cut a wood log to haul home that day after work. Art skidded it out of the bush and left it by the cutter. After work he hooked up to the cutter and hooked this wood log behind, and away we went. This was a 2 foot through and 24 foot long wood log. Well, halfway home we came to Jack Pine Hill, quite a steep hill. Partway down this hill I noticed this wood log catching up to us. I hollered at Art and he sprang into action. He stood up in the cutter and shouted to his team. "Patty! Goof! Ged-up, ged-up," slapped the lines at them and they took off. It was very close. If that wood log had of hit the cutter, it would have smashed it. Those cutters are built pretty flimsy. But we made it. Art was good in a pinch. The job finished when spring break hit in March.

I moved back to Brown's and later that spring I heard that Pondosa Pine was looking for fallers. I looked up Bill McEwan, who was their bush boss, and he hired me on. This was my first major job. Pondosa Pine was a good outfit, owned by the Hanburys from Kamloops. They had four cats in the bush, three D4s and one D7. The D7 built roads and landings and the D4s skidded. Each D4 had two fallers, falling and bucking in the bush, and two chokerman choking for the cat, one in the bush and one on the landing. These logs were scaled as they were skidded into the landing. My crew members were Bill Mehalchin on the cat, Tommy Mouser and Val Pringle choking, and Jim Johnston scaling. I liked this job and soon found a sense of camaraderie. I felt secure there. I was 19 years old. I had a 1950 Ford pickup and a 430A McCulloch chainsaw. My wish for a chainsaw and a pickup had happened although I didn't realize it at the time. I was to work here for the next four years.

George Davidson, Bill Hansen, Jack Turnbull
and Albert Fowler, 1950 camping trip

Brother Roy and myself with my Francis Barnett

Author trying out a rowboat my Dad built at Swan Lake, Vernon, 1950

1929 Model A Ford

1937 Ford

1950 Ford pickup

Author and Grandpa, Big Bill Enns,
1955 Silver Creek

1955 Pontiac

Allen and Albert Fowler 1955, note 1948 Dodge in back

Tie-Mill   BC ARCHIVES PHOTO: F-06050

Horse Logging   BC ARCHIVES PHOTO: F-04426

CHAPTER 3

Love and Marriage

*I*n the spring of 1956 I met a great girl. Her name was Barbara Bradley. She was 16 years old, pretty as a picture, with a lovely shape and a great smile. She had come down from Smithers to spend some time with her friends, the Schlosser family, who lived next to the Browns. We started seeing each other and soon were going steady. Later that fall on September 28 we got married. It was a church wedding in Barb's hometown of Smithers. All her family and friends attended but none of my family was there. My best man was Albert Fowler, from my Silver Creek days. Barb's bridesmaid was Betty Schlosser from Falkland. I had turned 20 on September 20th and Barbara was 17.

After the wedding in Smithers, we drove down to Monte Lake to live. We rented an Auto Cabin by the lake and set up housekeeping. I was working at Pondosa Pine and making pretty good money. We had friends in Falkland and would drive up there to visit some weekends. We spent the winter in the Auto Cabin and the next spring I bought a lot in Westwold, five miles away, and built my first house (second if you count the Hodson cabin). It was 16 feet × 24 feet. I used the laminated 2 × 4 method, which was popular for some small houses. These 2 × 4 are just piled one on top the other, on the flat and you just keep going around and around until the walls are up to 8 feet, then you cut out the windows and doors. Once the roof was on, we moved in. We had an outside biffy and I dug a well, 32 feet deep, so we had water. Barb helped me build, though we never got more than about half finished inside. We furnished the house with stuff bought at the secondhand store. That spring, Blaine, a son, was born. I took Barb to the hospital in Vernon, about 35 miles away from Westwold. Blaine was a bright, happy, beautiful baby and I was certainly a proud father. I was also a bit frightened about this fatherhood business and worried about no longer being able to be alone on my home ground, the place in the world where I was most comfortable. Barb and I spent the summer and fall finishing the house as we lived in it and discovering how to take care of Blaine. This was a mixed up time in my life. I was still working for Pondosa Pine and was seesawing between being happy in my new life and being overwhelmed by it.

The following spring another son, Douglas, was born. He was a blue baby and needed a blood transfusion three days after he was born. He and Barb were still in the hospital and the doctors said he would be fine so we weren't overly worried then or when we took him home. But he was a very weak baby, always crying, wanting to be held. We would take turns staying up with him. I remember always being tired during this time. When Dougie was six months old, Barb could not take it any longer and she moved back to Smithers. We hadn't been getting along for some time. You'd have thought that the two boys would have brought us closer together. The opposite happened. In January I received a telegram saying that Dougie had died from viral pneumonia. I flew to Smithers for the funeral and to be with Barb. I stayed for a week. My boss, Bill McEwan was very good, giving me this time off. Barb asked me to take Blaine back with me to Westwold. It was unusual in those days for fathers to raise kids alone but Barb needed to get her life back on track and she was struggling. I guess we married young, had a family really quick and then lost a child. It wasn't an easy time.

So, back home I went with my 18-month-old son. During the next two years I would get back together with Barb a few times but it never lasted. She was full of unrest and so was I. I loved my son Blaine very much and tried to keep him with me as much as possible. It was really hard being a single parent. A lot of jobs were camp jobs, one week in at a time. I would try to find a place for Blaine to stay while I worked but sometimes I took him to the camp with me. When I wasn't working, he was always with me. During this period I had given up my good job at Pondosa Pine and had various jobs around the province. I quit Pondosa thinking I'd get more time with Blaine. I know now that I should have just asked for a leave of absence. In hindsight, I think I can recognize two things: one, I probably quit Pondosa because I felt uncomfortable as a single parent around my co-workers and, two, that I should have had the nerve to go and ask for my job back when I realized I'd made a mistake. In any case, I took various short-term jobs, farming Blaine out when I took camp jobs and keeping him with me when I could. He always recognized me when I came to pick him up, even as a little tyke, and we would have a very happy reunion.

Barb and I were together for a short time when Blaine was four. It didn't last and in a few months she left again, this time for good. I had rented a house in Silver Creek and was working steady as a faller for Hickman and Howell Logging. I liked the rented house and wanted to stay in it awhile. It was a decent size and I figured I could get a housekeeper to look after Blaine when I worked. I advertised and tried out two different women. Something didn't work with both of them, either for them or for me. One day a new girl showed up. Her name was Sadie Carrol. She was 21 and in between jobs, and had met me in Smithers when Barb and I were married. I didn't remember meeting her. She moved in and took over housekeeping. She had liked me from before and I liked her so soon we were living together. Later on that fall Sadie got pregnant and I felt trapped. I started drinking and working in camps. I was running away.

One of the camps I escaped to was up on the North Thompson River. I was working for Arnold Hobbs. Every two weeks the crew would come in from camp for the weekend. One particular weekend was very cold, it was -38 when I got up in the morning. I wanted to start my car, a 1951 Dodge, which had a reputation for being hard to start in cold weather. It had been sitting for awhile and I knew it would not start without some help. I got a gallon of chainsaw gas, put a rag in it, lit the rag and pushed it carefully under the car on a 1 × 6 board. When it was directly under the oil pan I left it there. I then took out the battery thinking that I may as well warm it up. I took a 5 gallon (empty) metal can from my trunk, turned it upside down and placed the battery on top of it. I then poured some chainsaw gas and some chain oil around the base of this can and lit it also. I warmed my hands on the fire, then looked under the car to see the fire there burning nicely. I turned to go into the house to have some coffee when I heard this tremendous bang behind me. I turned back in time to see my battery going end over end up in the air, landing on the frozen road some 50 feet away from me. It shattered as it hit the ground. I then saw smoke coming from under the hood of the car. The fire in the can underneath had started to burn the flex hose joining the gas line to the fuel pump. The hose was a rubbery material that burned through before I could get it out and now gas was coming out of the line and burning. I pulled the can from under the engine, grabbed a pair of pliers and bent the gas line a ways back from the end, which put out the fire. Oh boy! Now I had no battery and a broken fuel line. I had to get another gas line from an old car I had, buy a new battery and enlist the help of my friend, Sam Moore, to get me going. That was one morning I should have stayed in bed. I did learn, however, never again to pour gas on a gas can that has had gas in it, light it, and expect to walk away without consequences. I was lucky that time, all I got was singed eyebrows and lashes, burned mitts and some burns on my hands and arms. It could have been much worse.

◆ ◆ ◆

I was having a nightmare. I didn't know where I was. I heard loud noises. My body was sore and stiff. I was very cold. My head ached and I could hardly open my eyes. I slowly became aware of my surroundings. I was not having a nightmare. This was real. I was in the drunk tank in the Vernon Jail. There was nothing in this 10 foot × 10 foot cell, just a pot and a hard floor. I can't describe the terror and anxiety I felt. I was very sick and very confused. I knew I had been out drinking the night before but beyond that I had no memory. Bad feelings were going through me in waves. I tried calling out! No one was around, it was too early. There were noises coming from other cells. Snores and muted talking. The cell doors started clanging as somebody else was brought in and locked up. I said to the officer, "What is happening here? Why am I in here?" He said, "You don't know?" I said, "No." He said, "Yeah, well you'll find out at eight in the morning. That's when they open up in here," and out he went, clanging the door behind him. I imagined all sorts of things, horrible things. Did I kill someone? I desperately tried to remember. No luck! Just blank. Eight o'clock came and they let me out of my cell into a holding room with a table and chairs, a sink and toilet. There were about six men in there with me. They had brought us breakfast on trays. I opened mine up and saw two hard-fried eggs and dry toast. I couldn't have eaten even if it had been a good breakfast. I asked what was going to happen, would somebody tell me why I was in here? They said an official would be in at 9 o'clock.

The time dragged on and finally an RCMP officer from Falkland, Howard Turner, whom I knew, came and asked for me. I wondered what he was doing here. When we got to an office and he closed the door, I said, "Howard what am I doing here?" He said, "Boy, are you in tough shape." I guess the desperate look on my face prompted him to say, "Hey, it wasn't that bad." He explained that I had smashed up my car because I was driving drunk (it was a U-drive I had rented) and when he came to help I was like a wildman. I wouldn't listen and he had to get help to get me into his car. Because I was ranting and raving and out of control, he took me to Vernon where they had better detox and detainment facilities. He said by the time we got to Vernon, I had passed out and was semi-comatose when they locked me up. He said, "It was for your own good, Ed! You didn't know what you were doing. We'll have court this morning and you'll be charged with impaired driving, and I advise you to plead guilty. You'll get a $250.00 fine and you'll be able to go. Nobody got hurt, you just ran off the road."

I went to court and what Howard said happened. The judge's name was Billy Smith, and he lectured me about driving and drinking. I asked for time to pay my fine and he allowed me three days. Back then, there was no backlog of the court. You went to court Monday after the weekend. I was very happy and relieved when this ordeal was over. I felt ashamed. I had to face the rental agency. They were good, telling me that the car was insured but I would have to pay the deductible. It was $300.00. I also lost my licence for 30 days. In order to get it back, you had to go on what was called "assigned risk." This was expensive: $300.00 the first year, $200.00 the second year and if you were accident-free the third year, you were back to regular insurance. This was only the liability insurance. Collision was extra. To put the cost of messing up into perspective, regular liability in-surance cost around $45.00 in those days. What a costly weekend that was. I was a poor drinker. Sometimes I could drink, be happy and every-thing was okay. Other times, I would get angry, belligerent and eventually black-out. If only I could have recognized which time was which, I could have saved myself some very bad, anxious mornings. In 1972 I had to give up drinking altogether. Drinking was common among my peers, everyone drank and it was the thing to do. Bad drinking caused a lot of problems among my friends (me too, I guess). Some were killed in car accidents or wrecked their home life or destroyed their cars and lost their jobs. We are supposed to be intelligent human beings; sometimes I wonder if we are all that smart.

I will give Sadie credit, she stayed by me through some bad times. It wasn't all bad; we had some good times. The big problem was me, I didn't love Sadie. In August of 1963, Joann was born. Sadie was very proud. I was too. When Jo was six months old Sadie said, "I'm leaving," and she moved back to Smithers. I missed Joann terribly. I was not to see her again until she was 15 years old. So, it was Blaine and me again. He was six years old by then. I thought he might miss Jo and Sadie but he didn't seem to, he just wanted me near by. If he was aware of or worried about my drinking (which I did try to keep hidden from him), he never let on . . . or not in a way I recognized.

With Sadie gone, it was back to working in camps and farming Blaine out. Farming out is a term used for finding a place like daycare, only there wasn't daycare around then. Some family would take in an extra child and that's the place I would put Blaine. It was very hard on us both when I had to leave him at a strange place with the promise to be back in a week. One summer I got hurt and was on WCB. I moved a trailer onto a friend's property on the Salmon River and we spent an enjoyable summer there, fishing, sunning ourselves and swimming.

I worked one winter at Lillooet with my brother Roy, falling and skidding for a sawmill owned by Paul Fisher. Paul had two boys, Gary and Lloyd. Lillooet was quite different to log in winter from what I was used to, as it was warm in the daytime and cold at night. It made for tough skidding on those steep slopes. Lillooet has some very steep terrain and the trails would melt in the daytime and freeze at night, creating really icy and slippery conditions. We were using a HD11 Allis Chalmers cat with a track arch and we slid down many a hill, despite our best attempts not to: cat, arch and a load of trees both! Like most logging jobs, our work ended with the coming of spring.

Fisher Sawmill was contract sawing for Moha Planer Mills in Lillooet. They hauled their rough lumber to their mill in town, where it was planed and packaged. I became friends with the Moha Planer Mill timber manager. He was a young, likeable fellow and we had many a good visit together. You know, sometimes you just click with a guy. Roy and I left Lillooet and went back home to Falkland. Roy lived in Falkland with his wife, Deanna. They had two kids at the time, Debbie and Wesley. I sometimes stayed at their place and Deanna would look after Blaine. I sorta hoped to see my timber manager friend again, even though Lillooet was a fair way from Falkland.

In midsummer I received a call from this friend in Lillooet about a job. B.C. Hydro was building a dam on the Bridge River out of Lillooet and they needed the timber cut within the dam site. They needed someone to log the timber and my friend thought maybe the contract would work for me. I said yes I was certainly interested, and he said, "Okay, I'll send you down the tender package." He sent me a contract about a half inch thick. What an opportunity! It would be a whole new aspect of logging if I could get it. All I had to do was get some equipment.

Another friend, Sam Moore, and I went to look at this timber and came back excited and full of ideas. We were sure we could work together on this and do it up right. We went to Vernon and met a guy, Jason Brown, who was Sam's mother-in-law's new boyfriend. He claimed he was a sales rep for Finning Tractor. Just the man I wanted to see if I was going to tackle this job. I told him I needed a D7 tractor to do the roadwork required and, probably later on, a smaller cat. Sam had two John Deeres at the time and they would be for skidding. Jason Brown said, "Yes I have a D7 in Vancouver and I could rental purchase it to you." That would work for me, so we shook hands on the deal and he said he would get the tractor shipped to Lillooet on the train and we could do the paper work when it got there. I agreed. He then gave me his business card. It said Jason Brown, Sales Rep — Finning Tractor, Vancouver. I felt 10 feet tall. We all went to the Kalamalka bar to celebrate. Jason said he was going to drive to Ontario, leaving tomorrow to buy a new car. Finning Tractor was paying the shot. He said he would like to take the train but in order to do that he would have to sell his car. He said to Sam, "You wouldn't be interested in a car, would you?" Sam said he wasn't sure and Jason threw the keys on the table and said, "Take it for a drive around the block. You can have it for the same money the dealers were going to give me on a trade, which is

$500.00." Sam said, "Wow, that seems cheap." Jason said, "Well they don't pay much in Ontario for a well-used car." Sam took it for a drive and thought it was a pretty nice car, one he wouldn't mind owning. He asked Jason if he could give him a cheque. Jason said, "Well you could but I'm leaving early in the morning so could you get me cash?" Sam went off to try and managed to get the cash at the bank before closing. He came back and Jason had a set of transfer papers right there. So, a deal was made. Jason said, "Goodbye boys" and away he went. Sam went back to work and I went back to my river to wait on developments. Sam left his car at home as he had a jeep truck which he used in the bush.

One evening a week later, when Sam came home from work, the Sheriff and a Laurentide Finance guy was waiting for him. They had put a sticker on his car and seized it. Apparently, Jason had not been making payments and was avoiding the finance company. Once they located the car they were quick to grab it. Sam said, "Hey! I bought that car, look here's my bill of sale." They informed him that you couldn't sell something you don't own. So, there went Sam's car, just like that. Now this started me thinking and getting mighty uneasy. What about my cat deal with Jason? I called Sam's mother-in-law, Bernice, and asked her if she had heard from Jason? When is he coming back! She said she didn't know. He had just said he was going to Ontario. The next morning I went to Vernon to see Finning Tractor. I asked for the sales manager, he took me into his office and said, "What can I do for you?" I told him about my deal and asked him about Jason Brown. He had never heard of Jason Brown. He said he'd phone Vancouver. I handed him Jason's card. He spoke to Vancouver for a while and when he hung up, his face was dark. "Nope, he doesn't work for us. I didn't think so," he said, "I was pretty sure I knew everybody on our staff." I talked to this sales manager about the job and about renting a cat from him. He said they were not renting cats at that time. They might arrange a rental purchase for one but it would depend on my credit, and he would need the first and last rental payments up front. I would have to rent it for six months. He took down all the information from me that was necessary and said he would get back to me. One week went by and he finally called. Bad news! Finning Tractor was not prepared to deal with me at this time. Their reason was simple. I was not established and had a poor credit rating. I was pretty discouraged. I talked it over with Sam and we spent another week trying to round up another cat or find some financing. No luck, so I reluctantly phoned Moha Planer, talked to my friend and explained the situation. He was very understanding but said he wouldn't be able to help in that respect, and would have no choice but to give the job to someone else. We had already passed our startup deadline. I was upset for days. I was 25 years old.

Well, some time passed, I spent a bit of time on WCB with a work injury, and continued my life with Blaine. Then I went to work falling for Walt Bradford in 70 Mile House. Walt was logging for Wayne Nyman who ran a sawmill in town. Walt was a good logger. He was in the bush before anybody else and he was still there when everybody went home. He was all business. It paid off too. You have to be on top of everything to be successful at logging. Well, anything for that matter. I used to think Walt was hard on his crew but you are under a lot of stress when you run a business. I learned that later.

One time that winter, on a Friday after a full week, we all ended up in town. I can't remember why and after a few beers, we were away. At closing time Walt said, "Hey guys, come to my place. I'll get Shirl (Shirley was his wife) to cook us up some bacon and eggs." We all said okay and away we went. Henry Harrison, Shirley's brother, who was working for Walt, was driving and upon arriving he said, "I better go in and check with Shirl, see if it's okay for us to come in." Away he went and in a while he came back laughing and said, "I don't think so boys. I went in, the house is dark and I saw a red glow coming from the front room — Shirley's cigarette and she wasn't talking." Needless to say we all went home except Walt, who had to face this warm reception. Walt and Shirl had two girls and were a very nice family.

We logged the rest of the winter. We had to take some small Jack Pine. Back then, nobody wanted to cut Jack Pine, it was considered a weed. They were small. Eventually, we all discovered that Jack Pine produced good lumber, but you couldn't have convinced me at that time. In any case, the Ministry of Forests said, "Try it." and they could call the tune. Walt agreed to cut Jack Pine but only if he could haul it tree length. The mill said, "Okay as long as you come in and buck it to log lengths." We hauled in about five loads of tree length before breakup. After we finished hauling everything from the bush, Walt said, "Well guys who wants to go and buck the pine trees into short logs?" Nary a word, silence, nobody wanted to do it. Walt said, "Ed, I guess you're elected then!" Well, what the heck, you can't win them all and work's work! So into the mill I went. These pine loads had been just dumped off and they were a mess. I just waded in and started cutting. A forklift came to help me. He took the bucked logs away and spread them out for scaling. Scalers are people who measure up the logs to determine board feet, a very important number when it comes to payment. There was a lady scaling that day and when I was done my job, I went over and asked her how my lengths were. She said, "Pretty good!" I thought, "Yeah, right." I hadn't measured a stick. This scaler's name was Frieda Tegart and she was to become my second wife.

Blaine and Barb, 1960

Jean, Joan and Shirley with niece Debby and Blaine, 1959

Author with Blaine and
their dog Pal, 1960

Son Blaine at three
getting an early start with a
Super 44 McCulloch
chainsaw, 1960

Author in 1964 with
his 1954 Ford

Sadie Carroll and Joann, 1963

CHAPTER 4

The First Deal

I had worked with a school friend, Garth Scott, on various jobs and after one particular job was finished he got married. Garth was a good guy, friendly and hard working. His new wife was going to teach school in Kitimat. He asked me if I would like to go up with him as he was moving a load of furniture and could use the company. He was going to find a house to rent and look for a job. It sounded like a good idea to me so I left Blaine with some friends who were willing. Blaine was seven and had started school in Clinton so taking him with me wasn't too easy anymore. The trip with Garth was a nice one and a good experience. We took the time to visit people we knew along the way.

One stop was in Quesnel on the way up to Kitimat. Our friends Tommy and Marion Francis lived on the outskirts of Quesnel, in a small house, and had two girls, aged 6 and 8. Garth and I commented on what a nice place Quesnel was and what a nice family the Francises were. When we got back to Clinton, I asked Frieda if she wanted to move to Quesnel. She said, "Yes," and we bought a 10 × 56 mobile home and moved it to Shiels Trailer Court and set up housekeeping together. I went falling for Don Sales, an independent logger with a good reputation, with Tommy Francis, out on the Garner Road. Frieda got a job scaling at John Ernst's sawmill. My job lasted until November when Don Sales moved to a blowdown sale on the Barkerville Highway. Then I was back to job hunting again.

I had seen a nice patch of Christmas trees at a ranch on the Narcosli Creek road, on our way to work. I phoned Emerald Christmas Tree Company in Kamloops, and talked to Bob Kershaw. He said, "Sure I'll buy trees but I'll need a carload, about 4000 trees." I said, "Okay, I'll try to get that many trees." I had cut trees in Vernon years before and it had been a good experience. Hoping luck would be on my side, I drove out to the ranch that had the good trees. It belonged to Pete Vogelar. I knocked on the door and heard someone holler, "Come in." In I went to find him working on a washing machine motor on the kitchen floor. His farm hand, Ralph Twan, was helping him. I asked him about Christmas trees and he said he wasn't fussy as some company from Williams Lake had been around cutting and not making a good job, leaving trees hanging on the stump, not cleaning up after themselves, etc. I said I thought the area he'd just logged along the road would be okay, mostly toppers, and I could slash it all down good or bad, seeing as he was going to clear the land anyway and it wouldn't matter if we made a mess. In that light, he said okay. A price was arranged and we went to work.

By the 10th of December we had our carload of trees. These trees had to be baled and tagged, the butts trimmed and inspected, then loaded into the boxcar. It was a lot of work. Each day as we finished work, we would load up with trees and bring them to town. We used Tommy's yard as a place to sort, bale and store. What a lot of trees! When we paid Pete for the trees, his share and our expenses, we made wages. It wasn't a big money job but it was very nice work, the bush is so fresh and the scent of the trees as you cut is just great. Our venture with Pete Vogelar was the first load of Christmas trees shipped out of Quesnel.

The one bad side to cutting trees in the fall is the rain. They don't break easily when they're wet, so it is better when you're cutting toppers (toppers are Christmas trees taken from the top of larger trees), and by cutting toppers you don't break as many branches. But cutting trees in the rain is very wet work, and when you get wet, you get cold. With something drier in mind, I went north to Prince George after Christmas. Blaine and Frieda stayed behind in the trailer on the outskirts of Quesnel.

Prince George was a good place to fall in the winter, partly because there weren't many good fallers up there. Because the area was wet and muddy, the logging companies had to wait to log until after freezeup. This meant lots of snow and cold weather. Then around the 1st of April the roads would start to melt and the logging would shut down until the next winter. Most outfits logging in the wet country only logged from November to April, and the crews worked mostly seven days a week. These were camp-based jobs with about 30 to 60 men in each camp. Most companies paid their fallers by the tree. I liked that system. It was a great incentive to work hard and make money. Each day you could rate yourself.

At that time, in 1966, most companies paid 55 cents per tree, and with the caliber of the saws at that time, a good faller could fall, limb and top an average of 100 trees per day. Fallers were a tough lot in the days before mechanized falling, especially in the north, where snowshoes and deep snow were the norm. Most areas east of Prince George had an average of 6 to 8 feet of snow each winter. That means snow pretty well every day from November till February; then it would begin to taper off. There was a lot of snow plowing on the job and to get to the job. February and March were the best months for falling. The snow was deep and our muscles (and balance) had become used to the snowshoes by then. Once the snow stopped falling, it packed down for easy walking. When that happened you could make good time. All the mess on the ground — fallen trees, buck brush, devils club, and such — would be covered up with snow, making a nice even surface. Sometimes in March, after a rain or thaw, it would get cold again and a good crust would form on the snow. This made for very good snowshoeing. You stayed right up on top. The snowshoes we used in those days were called Bearpaws, mainly because of their oval shape. They were 14 inches wide and 30 inches long and flat. They were made of wood frames with leather lacing in between and a harness in the middle front so when you lifted your foot the front of the shoe came up first. These short, rounded shoes were best for manoeuvering, and there were times when you needed to move really fast when falling trees. By the time spring came, northern loggers were pretty handy on snowshoes.

Every two weeks I would go home to Quesnel. On one trip home, a fellow working in the mill at Ernst told me he wanted to sell a piece of property he owned 20 miles south of Quesnel, at Narcosli Creek. His name was Jim Lyons and he was asking $1,500.00 for a parcel of 160 acres with some old buildings on it. I was very interested as trailer park living was getting pretty cramped. And, as always, I wanted some land of my own. I said, "Look Jim, I would like to buy this land, but I haven't enough money right now." He said, "I don't need the money until spring, so I'll give you a month to raise it." This sounded good to me so we made a deal! I had $600.00 and needed about $900.00. Back to work I went, and stayed in camp for 20 days until I was $1,000.00 ahead. I had to ask my boss a favour, to pay me up for my trees, and I explained the reason I couldn't wait. He was agreeable, and off I went to Quesnel to buy this property. Boy, was I excited. We closed the deal the next day and I owned my first farm. I called it a farm but in reality it was a stump farm. There was a water hole, a small meadow and about 50 loads of timber. Timber wasn't worth much in those days as most of the mills in town had enough Crown timber of their own to cut, but it was timber, and in my line of work, timber was always a good thing.

I was back in Quesnel by spring and started calling a few outfits for falling work, one of which was A.S. King Logging. I talked to Alf King, the owner, and he said, "Yes, we need fallers and as this is April we won't be starting until mid-May. When we need you I'll give you a call." He asked me the usual questions about my experience and such. He was pleased about the length of time I'd been falling. We said goodbye and he said, "I'll be talking to you soon." Around mid-May I got a call from Ted Kennedy, who ran E&K Logging. He was looking for a faller. I said that I was waiting for a call from Alf King, as he was going to call me to work in May. I said, "If he doesn't need me, I'll get back to you." I hung up and thought about that for a while. I decided why not work for E&K? He called first and was starting right away. I called Ted back and told him I'd like to take the job. It turned out to be a good job. Close to home and good pay. Ted was a good guy to work for; fair to his crew and he maintained his equipment well. At the time of this writing, 30 years later, I still have not received a call from Alf King. So much for that!

Working for E & K that winter was hard work. I had the falling contract myself and in order to keep trees ahead I had to work long days. Travelling time from Quesnel was one and a half hours so when I got home at night I was really beat. I got into the habit of lying down on the couch after supper and falling asleep. This bugged Frieda because she wanted to visit and I would be fast asleep. One night she decided to get even. She changed the time on the clock and on my watch (I had a Big Ben pocket watch then and it was easy to get at without disturbing me). She set the time at 6:00 a.m., made me a big breakfast and then woke me up. She shook me awake saying, "Ed, Ed, you've slept here all night and you're going to be late for work." I usually left at 6:00 a.m. so I would, indeed, be a bit late. I quickly washed and sat down to eat. I always had bacon, eggs, fried potatoes, toast and coffee back then. About halfway through this meal I thought to myself, 'I must be coming down with something. I'm not that hungry' but I finished up anyway. I filled up my thermos with coffee, grabbed my lunch and out to the truck I went. I started it up and let it run a bit to warm up, and turned the radio on. I wasn't able to get my usual radio station and thought that the station must be off the air for some reason. As I was sitting there, I noticed the moon. Something didn't seem right. Then the radio station I had found said, "Time for the news at eleven." I couldn't, for a minute or two, figure out what was going on and then I clued in — Frieda had played a trick on me! I should have realized something was wrong when she had breakfast made . . . I went to work earlier than she did and usually made my own breakfast. Boy, had she got me but good! I went back inside and she was killing herself laughing. The mistake I made was, when I realized what was going on, I should have just driven to work anyway and slept in my truck, pretending nothing unusual had happened. But, I didn't, and Frieda sure had a good laugh on me!

I had been working with crosscut and chainsaws in the bush now for 15 years. I'd worked mostly as a faller but had taken stints driving cat, skidding, building roads and landings, bucking logs, loading with a cable heel boom, skidding with horses, splicing cable, making chokers, etc. At each job I had I tried to learn as much as I could about that job and anything related to it. I was very open-minded and wanted to learn. One day working for E&K, the main skid cat broke its mainline about a foot from the end. Ted said, "We'll have to go to town for a new mainline." I was standing there and said, "Hey, I can splice an eye in that or I can tie a bowline in it." A bowline is a knot that leaves a loop in the end but does not slip. Ted seemed a little skeptical but let me go ahead. I proceeded to do just what I claimed I could. Other jobs had taught me it was always best to fix something up fast if you could so you could, at least, finish the day.

Another time we had a mudhole on the road in our bush. The pickups could not get through and the big trucks had to be pushed through. We asked Ted to fix it but he figured it would freeze soon and fix itself. Well, it didn't freeze and one weekend I was working to get a few trees ahead, and decided I had fought that mudhole long enough. I had learned to fix problems with roads down south and decided I would apply the tricks I had learned there here. I used Ted's cat loader and felled a few trees along the road. Then I bucked them into 16-foot lengths, laid them crossways in the road, placing them tight together and driving the cat on them as I worked out into the mudhole. About two hours later and about 30 logs, I had this mudhole covered with logs. A skiff of dirt on top to smooth it out and I was done. You could drive a Cadillac across it. This was on a Saturday and on Sunday it snowed about 6 inches, and covered everything up. Monday morning Ted said, "See I told you it would freeze and all would be well with the mudhole." I never said anything but I'm sure he could see the log ends sticking out at either side of the road. I was to use this corduroy method many times in later years.

E&K stood for Ernst and Kennedy, Ted Kennedy and John Ernst. As I said before, John Ernst owned a sawmill. He had one of the first chip-n-saws in the area. A chip-n-saw is a small log machine that takes peeled logs in one end and cuts boards as it goes through to the other. The slabs and corners are made into chips. This machine made small log sales really viable and it took lots of small logs to keep it going. John had been awarded more timber rights from the Crown and he was hiring logging contractors in preparation for the new cut. I went to see him and got a contract to log, load and haul from Milburne Mountain to the mill in town. I had bought a 1951 cat from George Wells; he was bucking for E&K at the time and didn't need it anymore. It was in very good shape. George had taken good care of it. He wanted $4,000.00 for it. I made a deal with him: $1,000.00 down and the rest in payments. I hauled the cat home and George gave me a pickup load of spare parts for it. I was in business!

I phoned my brother in Falkland and said I had a job for him falling. He said, "Okay, I'll be right up." I hired a bucker, Jim Klapatiuc, and a local guy, Wayne Lavally, who had a truck and loader. Jim was an older fellow and a chainsaw man. I hired him through the powersaw shop (the UI office for chainsaw men!). Wayne? Well, Wayne was a 25-year-old workaholic who came with a loader operator named Len Ecker. Len would go on to work for me, on and off, for the next 25 years. Finally I was away. I had my own logging outfit.

We started logging May 24, 1967, skidding tree lengths from the bush to the landing, bucking them into 16 to 20-foot logs, and hauling them on tandem trucks to the mill. We worked hard and by fall I was able to buy a rubber-tired skidder to work with my D4 cat. It was the first skidder put out by John Deere. It was a wonderful machine, so much faster than the cat. It was called a 440 John Deere and had 59 flywheel horsepower. We were able to skid wood now! I would start at 4:00 a.m. and skid until the rest of the crew arrived at 7:00 a.m. I would have the landing full of trees by then and would help the bucker while Roy took over on the skidder. As soon as the bucker got caught up, I would get on the cat and make trails, and fall and skid any tough trees. I hired a new faller when Roy took over on the skidder and then moved Jim from bucking to falling. Jim could put lots of trees down, but they were all over the place. He was always in too much of a hurry. I expected a lot from the fallers as I knew how it should be done, having done it so much myself. Spring and summer were okay; we worked the kinks out, and we followed up with a very good fall and winter.

The next summer was more of the same. We had the logging down to a science and, other than building roughly one mile of corduroy, we continued to haul logs throughout a particularly wet July. That summer the operation ran pretty well and nothing exciting happened. I had set up a system where I was the one building roads and landings and acting as spare man if anybody needed a day off or didn't show.

We had a bush boss, Gordon Durrell, who had been giving us a bit of grief for some time (a bush boss looks after the loggers who are employed by a logging company). As it happened, Gordon would tell the faller not to get too far ahead of the skidder, and then tell the skidder operator he had to finish one trail before he started another. This was a big problem because the skidder had to work the other side of a landing when a truck was in getting loaded. There were usually about ten trails to a landing and, when a truck was being loaded, the skidder automatically skidded from another trail. One time I had logged some right-of-way in the area and left the tops in the roadway. At the time we were required to bring limbs and tops to the landing to be burned. I had asked Ted Kennedy, the superintendent, about the right-of-way tops. He said, "No you can leave them on the right-of-way and when we build the road we will bury them." When Gordon Durrell inspected the right-of-way logging, he came and said to me, "You are shut down until you skid those tops to a landing." I told him what Ted had said but he maintained that he was the one in charge and those tops had to go to a landing. I said, "Okay but how about if I promise to skid them on weekends? Could we keep working on our regular job?" He said that would be okay. So, I spent five weekends skidding tops off the right-of-way to a landing. Nobody in the business had ever heard of such a thing! Gordon was just showing his power.

One day the same guy snuck up on our faller and was watching him. The faller was upset, said it was creepy, and came and told me. This was the last straw. We ran an honest operation. I found Gordon and told him that that was it! I didn't want to see him in my bush again, upsetting my crew and causing problems. He went straight to the mill and talked to John Ernst. John sent word to the bush that he wanted to see me as soon as was convenient. Not too long after, I went to the office to find John, knowing very well what he wanted to see me about. By this time I had cooled off about Durrell; I didn't like his way of doing things but I was no longer in a temper. When you arrived in John's office he never asked you to sit down. He always left you standing in front of his desk. He started talking to me about how Gordon and I were acting like kids, and what was he to do about it? I told him the disagreement was not my doing and that it was Gordon trying to be important and cause trouble. John and I argued back and forth for a while and finally he slapped his hand on the desk and said rather loud, "Look here, if you were so smart, you would be sitting here and I would be standing there, but that is not the way it is, so end of argument." I guess I was told, a bit like a parent saying, "because I said so," but I failed to see the logic in it. But, John was the boss. I didn't have to agree but he was the boss. I thought of getting him a sign for his desk saying, "The Boss is Always Right," but I didn't know how he would take it, so I chickened out. Mostly though, he was a fair man and I got along with him pretty good, considering. He had a way about him that I admired.

Later in the summer the sawmill had some shipping problems because the railroad was on strike. As a result, they cut the loggers' production in half. The slowdown was trying and left me with some time on my hands. I used to read the Cariboo Observer, the weekly paper, faithfully every Wednesday night. It was a great little newspaper and I especially liked the want ads. One Wednesday evening I saw an ad in the Property for Sale section. It stated: Need your own timber? 160 Acres never been logged! I was always dreaming of property and timber, and this ad really stood out. I called the listing realtor and got the particulars. It was very interesting. He told me he had just advertised the place today, and had already had numerous inquiries. Early the next morning I went and looked at the property. It was only four miles from my new place. There were already two pickups parked in there as I drove in. One was Gordon Durrell from Ernst Lumber and the other was Cy Patchett from West Fraser Mills in Quesnel. I thought, "Oh, oh! This must be good for the mill's men to be out." The property was two miles off the main road and had an old road running through it. The road had been used years before to get to a coal deposit along the Fraser River. The start of the property was well marked and the coal road went pretty well through the centre. The land was marked at the far end by a rustle fence. The whole length of the property was full of beautiful fir timber that had never been logged. I was getting pretty excited. I turned around at the rustle fence and drove back to about the middle of the property and stopped. I got out and walked a small circle on each side of the road, eyeing the same quality fir timber as I trotted around. I had seen enough. The time for a detailed cruise was not now.

I hurried back to Quesnel and looked up the realtor. His name was Fred Baxter and he worked for Quesnel Realty. He was very helpful. I introduced myself and told him that I had looked at the property and wanted to buy it. He said, "Okay, the asking price is $20,000.00." I gave him a deposit and went looking for financing. I had very little money myself, though the business was holding its own and payments and expenses were keeping me about even. Any extra money went back into the business for stuff like tools. I had moved the family to the farm and was fixing up an old house for us to live in and that process was using up any extra money I had. I went to my local bank, the Bank of Montreal, and asked to see the manager. While I was waiting, I worked out some figures in my time book. I had not met the manager yet as most of my dealings were with a loan officer and the assistant manager. This time I figured I had better see the chief himself. The manager came out and ushered me into his office. We introduced ourselves, his name was Bradshaw, and he looked pretty serious. He was a big man with a big presence, piercing eyes that looked right at you like he could see you in x-ray. He was very intimidating to me as I wondered how I should start. He asked me, "What can I do for you?" I blurted out, "I'd like to borrow $20,000.00," just like that. He looked at me, smiled and said, "Tell me more."

I explained everything to him and showed him my page of figures. I said I figured I could log the timber myself, cutting costs in the process, and just about pay for the property that way. And, I would still have the 160 acres. He looked over my figures, did some of his own and we discussed various things. He asked me about my logging. This was home ground to me. Logging was my life. When he was finished questioning me, he said, "Just a minute," and he left his office. I hoped it was not to check my account as I had only about $500.00 in it. However, my payment record was okay: the cat, skidder, mobile home, and my pickup were all on payments but everything was up-to-date. The only thing free and clear was my farm. Anyway, he came back and asked me some more questions, one of which was, "How much did you pay for your farm?" I answered $1,500.00. He smiled again and said, "Okay, here's what we'll do. You offer them $16,000.00 with half down." I explained I sort of figured we should pay full price, as I didn't want to lose the deal. I figured it was worth it. I went on to explain that there were two mills also interested. He was firm and said, "Look we'll present the offer right away and they can counter or they can accept, and until they do, it's our deal." I nervously accepted this and headed back to the real estate office. Fred Baxter wrote up the offer and, as soon as I signed it, he phoned the owners, who had moved to Blue River, 350 miles south east of Quesnel. They weren't home so I had to wait until evening. I was very excited and anxious. It was a long wait. Finally Fred got through to them and they said they would consider the offer and call back in the morning. After a mostly sleepless night, I was back at Fred's office the next morning, waiting for him to open. Around 9:30 that morning the owners called back. They would accept the offer! Wow! I thought, now I have something. Boy, all that nice fir timber. Over to the bank I went and relayed this to Bradshaw. He didn't seem surprised that the offer had been accepted. Apparently, the owners had bought the property the year before from a local farmer, Henry Thiessen, and had planned to log it. They were logging in Blue River, had fallen on hard times and were forced to sell it. Timber value was changing fast and it was hard to keep up. Anyway, they had bought with an assumable mortgage of $7,000.00, held by Henry Thiessen. Bradshaw said, "Okay I'll lend you $9,000.00 to pay the Blue River boys out and the bank will take over the mortgage." This is what we did. The realtor, the bank and the lawyer worked this deal out, I mean. I was to learn more about deals later on but at this time I was pretty much a rookie.

I couldn't wait to go back to the property and have a good look at what I had bought. I hadn't seen much of it but I had a feeling it was a good deal. It's funny but, for me, a property looks much different before you own it than after you own it. I spent the weekend roaming my land! I found it had two nice ponds, a small natural meadow and a rock bluff. And all this nice fir timber. I made big plans as I walked the bush and couldn't have been happier. When you walk through big fir timber, there is a definite energy amongst the trees. I didn't do it then but now I hug trees and feel their energy. By today's standards, there were certainly some huggable trees out there. This was 1968 and I was 32 years old.

I talked to John Ernst about buying the timber on my new property and we made a tentative deal. I would take a leave of absence from my job, as we were still cut back, and log private timber for the winter. I moved into the timber on this new property, and started building roads and landings. It was fun and exhilarating to be working without restrictions. I could build roads or landings wherever I wanted. I didn't have to have permission or a logging plan. Just good common sense. I finished the roads and landings in about a week.

While I was still working the mills timber (sawmills have their own timber sales to work on), a new salesman from B.C. Equipment, Wayne Holly, came to see me. He had a 175 Internation Drott. This machine had many uses. It was a loader, a skid cat, or it could be used as a directional faller if a shear was attached to the front end. A squeeze of the hand on a lever would force the shear knife through a tree and, once you had it cut, you could turn the cat and either back up or go ahead in order to throw your tree into the bunch. The concept was great but I was never able to figure out how to fall the trees where I wanted them. They seemed to have a mind of their own. After about half a day of trying, I had such a mess that I drove back to the landing and said, "Hey Wayne, take this machine back to town. I can't make it work." He said, "Do you have any other work for it? I have a blade for it you know." I told him I could take it up to my new place and build roads and landings. This is what I did. After I finished (it worked real well with a blade) with it, another fellow, Helgi Hanson, who also worked at Ernst's, wanted to try the shear head. So he took it when I was done. Wayne Holly wanted to sell these machines and that's why we got to try it out; it was a demonstrator model, I guess.

It was time to begin the new venture so I moved my skidder over to the new land. I started logging and selling the logs to Ernst Lumber. John Ernst had a unique way of encouraging good-quality logs to come to his mill. He graded your logs in #1s and #2s. He paid more money for #1s; any defect natural or otherwise made it a #2; and any length that wasn't up to specs was #2. So it was important to manufacture the best possible log from the tree. This property was easy logging as it was mostly flat ground and big trees and I figured I'd have mostly #1s.

After Christmas that year, the weather turned extremely cold. We had a rule, if it was colder than 20 below Fahrenheit, we wouldn't work. At that temperature it was too hard on the machines, and the men, too, for that matter (although you could work quite comfortably if you weren't on a machine and dressed properly). The first week of cold weather the thermometer was reading in the -25 range and then things would warm up in the afternoon to about 15 below. We decided to up our temperature to 25 below at 6:00 a.m. The first morning after this change, it was 45 below. Too cold to work. By this time I was chaffing at the bit, wanting to get going at something. I was always in a hurry in those days. The old saying comes to mind, and a lot of times it fit me, "The faster we go, the behinder we get."

Finally, the sun came out and it warmed up a bit so I decided to go and do some work. I got my cat started. It had a gas starting motor. You started this gas motor with a pull cord, like a lawn mower, and when it was going good, you engaged the diesel motor, letting it turn over until it warmed up some. Then, when you turned the diesel on, it usually started right up. This type of engine would start in very cold weather and was unique to Caterpillar. Once my cat was warmed up, I started snowplowing a pond I had noticed earlier. I thought it was a great idea: just plow off the pond and get a free landing. I was plowing away, glad to be doing something, when a bump and a strange feel in one of the tracks jogged me out of my daydream. Before I knew it, I had fallen through the ice. Most of the pond was frozen hard but I had hit an edge where some beaver had dropped a few trees. The logs had kept the water from a full freeze. It's hard to see much when everything is covered in snow.

Well, the cat didn't go down too far, the winch held it up at the back. It sat up on a log and the blade stayed up on the ice in front. Just the tracks were in the water. I jumped off and poked a stick in to see how deep it was there under the cat. Oh, oh! Around four feet deep with a muddy bottom. What a mess. I went home and called my skidder operator to come and give me a hand, and I went back with a propane tiger torch. I started warming up the oil in the skidder. You could take off an inspection plate from the bottom pan and get to the bottom of the engine. Then, by sticking a stovepipe with an elbow on the end, you could put the propane torch in the pipe and direct the heat to the oil pan. Twenty minutes to a half an hour and you had the engine warm enough to start. My operator arrived just about when it was the right temperature and we got the engine going. While it warmed up, we had coffee to warm us up. My skidder operator at that time was Mel Spooner. Mel was a good logger. He was young, a bit roly-poly, and really dedicated to his job. When the skidder was ready we drove it around some to make sure the winch was working. We had to warm the oil in the winch with the tiger torch as well. We backed up to the ice as close as we dared. We cut a log longer than the cat was wide, and jammed it through the blade arms so it was sticking crossways out on both sides. This was supposed to keep the cat from going through the ice. It took a good pull to get it out. Lucky for me there was a tree just under the water at the back of the cat; this gave us some traction, which helped the cat climb out. What a relief to have the cat back on solid ground again. I paid a price for my impatience, however. Ice formed immediately on the tracks and, as I was driving back and forth to break the ice, I heard a snap and one track came loose. I had broken the shaft in the front idler. What luck. Now I had to split the track and take this idler off to get a new shaft in. The whole procedure took me two days. I may as well have stayed home by the fire and kept warm. This cold spell lasted three weeks that winter, 1968-69.

One morning our oil furnace quit. I had moved our mobile home out to our farm and set it up. The stove oil had jelled and wouldn't run through the lines. It was about daylight and I went outside to warm this oil up with my propane torch (many uses for this propane torch in the North Country). As I walked around the trailer, I noticed something out of the corner of my eye (I was intent on my job and I wasn't paying much attention). There was a horse standing about 20 feet away. I thought my neighbour Carl Bergs' horse had gotten out. I hurried over to the tank, intent on getting some heat into the trailer. I was busy with the torch but, as I stood there warming up the oil, I said to myself, "Hey my neighbour doesn't have a horse!" A funny, creepy feeling came over me as I turned my full attention behind me. There about 10 feet away was a large cow moose. She had moved around the trailer as I did. We stood looking at each other for a while. The oil in the tank would probably run through the lines now as it doesn't take much heat to change it from gel mode to liquid. I slowly turned the torch off and eased myself back around the trailer. The moose never moved, just stared. I didn't make a sound and neither did the moose. Safely back in the trailer, I cleared off enough frost from the kitchen window and watched this moose for a while. She was very cold and maybe sensed some heat or shelter from the building. She stayed around till the sun came up later in the morning, then ambled off to browse in a willow patch in the back yard. She stayed around all through the cold weather. You have to feel for these animals in the cold weather. I know they are equipped for all kinds of weather, but when it is 40 below that's a bit much.

When the cold spell finally ended, we went back at work with a vengeance. The timetable I'd set called for finishing the job by spring breakup. We were selective logging this property, meaning we were leaving anything under 12 inches on the stump, and all patches of smaller trees. If a patch had a handful of bigger trees, we'd leave them standing too. At this time, I left the small stuff because of financial reasons; the mill wasn't interested in small timber. Later on, I came to realize the importance of selective logging on private land.

We finished up logging the property around the 15th of March and when I sat down to work out the numbers. I was shocked. I was able to pay off the property, the bank, pay all the expenses and I still had some left over! It seemed my gamble had paid off. What a great beginning.

Wayne Lavalley who hauled and loaded short logs for me, 1966-67

Brother Roy and author with brother-in-law, Alfred Bruneski
in Quesnel, 1966

Trailer in Quesnel, 1965

John Deere 440 skidder, 1969

Brother Roy with 1976 Ford

Doug Andrews with load of five fir logs, 110,000 lbs. G.V.W., 1971

I may be getting a ticket. Billy Barker Days parade, 1976

Brother Roy – lost his saw?

CHAPTER 5

Gaining Experience and Acquiring Land

*S*uccess is a powerful motivater! When breakup came, I decided to upgrade my equipment and traded my D4 in on an International TD20 cat, a machine about twice as big as the D4. This cat would do it all: build roads, skid, clear land, the works. I bought it from B.C. Equipment in Williams Lake, from salesman Bruce Hooker. They were rebuilding the cat at the time of the deal and Bruce said I could come down to the shop and work with the mechanic until the cat was finished. This was a good opportunity for me as I could familiarize myself with the machine as we worked on it. We rebuilt the track frames, rails, pads, idlers, sprockets and any other thing we could find that needed doing. The mechanic I worked with was Pearly Holmes. It was a great experience because, boy, there wasn't anything he didn't know about cats. He also was a nice fellow and I got along with him great. When we were done with this cat it was in excellent shape. The deal I wangled for it was this: my D4 cat as a down payment, and I financed the remaining $15,000.00.

I started buying private timber the following spring. I would approach a property owner and, if they were interested in selling their timber, I would cruise it, determining how many loads were on it, then make them a cash offer. This seemed to work the best as most owners were skeptical about "cut now and pay later" deals. The latter took a lot of trust and I was a newcomer. Gradually, I was able to build up trust with the landowners, a commodity that is a must for a small logger. I was very honest with property owners, which counts for a lot and tends to get around fast. One time I bought the timber on a 160-acre parcel and I didn't look it over well enough. It turned out to have more timber on it than I had first figured.

Even though I had paid a lump sum for it, I went back later and said, "Look, there was more timber on your property than I originally estimated. I have figured it out proportionally and here is a cheque for the difference." They were pleasantly surprised. These property owners were Jim and Tina Lyons, and they lived out the West Fraser Road at Narcosli Creek; over the next years, I came to know them well. With private buying though, sometimes it worked the other way; I would overestimate the timber and pay too much. This didn't happen too often though, and it's a good thing it didn't because then your profits disappear out the window really fast.

In my next step as an independent, I bought a clearing blade and breaking disc for the TD20 cat and then designed a stump splitter to go along with the unit. I registered my rig with the agricultural part of the provincial government, which allowed me to clear land for the farmers and ranchers in the area. This allowed me to trade land clearing for timber, preferably logging the land first and then clearing it. When I was able to log then clear, I could make big landings, and in some cases push the trees over first, then buck the stumps off. It is much easier to push over trees than stumps, and it is faster than falling the tree and then pushing the stump out.

I met some interesting people while clearing land with my TD20 rig. One colourful character was Chow Lee. Chow had a big ranch just south of the Marguerite Ferry and he arranged for me to clear and log some of his property. He liked me to stop in at the house on my way to work in the morning. Every morning, I would find Chow's wife and four kids having breakfast, and when I came in, Mrs. Lee would insist I have a plate of Chinese food. I tried to say no thank you and that I had had breakfast already, but I was always too late. She would have a place set and a plate of food down before I was half way into my explanation. After several mornings like this, I learned to leave home without breakfast so I could enjoy Mrs. Lee's really tasty food. Even though I was on the same job site for months, Chow would have me stop by each morning so he could lay out the day's work. The Lees were a very nice family.

I bought timber and logged a number of properties besides the Lees. Over a period of three years, I logged for Willy Fichtenberg, the Narcosli Indian Band, Mark Lepetich, Remo Lepetich, Pete Vogelar, Dale Teleford,

Roy Hawks, Jim Lyons, Joe Becker, Sig Koch, and Harvey Newman, to mention a few. I was selling my timber to West Fraser Mills at the time. They had done some major expansion-style renovations at their mill and were cutting lots of logs. They had cut more than their quota on Crown land and needed private wood to keep the mill running to capacity. One July, their timber buyer at the time, Gary Townsend, came to the bush and stated the following, "Clean up your jobs, Ed, and that's it until further notice." I was shocked; this was a big mill. But lumber prices were down and their yard was full. The owner, Sam Ketchum, had made the decision to stop buying private wood. We finished the deals that were in the works and I moved my machines home.

When I was selling logs to West Fraser, I got to know Gary Townsend fairly well. He was Woodlands Manager and he was also their private wood buyer. My friend, Don Howlett, wanted to sell his timber and I said I could probably get him a good deal with Gary. He asked me to handle it for him. Don had 320 acres of nice timber. I worked with Gary and got the very best deal I could for Don. Gary asked me what was in it for me and I said, "I'm doing this for a friend and I don't need anything for it." Gary said, "Well, that's nice and since you've been selling wood to us for a while, and after this good deal (Don could have sold to any of three other mills), I'll look into getting you a steady quota job with us." I told him that would be great and I'd really look forward to it happening. At that time, having a quota logging job for a mill was a real plum, especially for a big outfit like West Fraser. You could make plans if you had steady work like that and I thought through all the ways I might set it up. I planned the kind of equipment I'd need, the number of men I'd hire, and dreamed of buying, not renting, the equipment.

In any case, while I was dreaming away, I was also supposed to oversee the logger who West Fraser had put in to log Don Howlett's property. Don and his wife Nancy had planned a trip away just as the work was starting. Nancy's Mom and Dad had come in to look after their four kids, Carol, Kathy, Brad and Richi. One day I got a call from Nancy's Mom and she was all excited. She said the loggers had their skidders on the causeway and were washing them down using the lake water. Don had built a causeway part way out into a small lake on his property and had installed a pumphouse at the end of it in order to get a good, clean water supply. I drove out as quickly as I could and, would you believe, there were two skidders parked out on the causeway with their fire pumps out. They were washing down their skidders, with all the dirt and grease running into the lake! I ran over, shut off the pump and chased them away from there. Their skidders had started to heat up and they thought, "Well, here's a place to wash them." Talk about skidderman mentality, these two guys took the cake. It was actually my fault for not watching them more closely. Any project like that needs hands-on supervision. But who would think anybody would mess with this clean and tidy water system. It takes all kinds, I guess.

While the job was going on and after, I waited patiently for my new quota job but it never materialized. Gary was transferred to another West Fraser mill and I guess I was forgotten about. That's how things work out sometimes. To me this was a big thing, not to be taken lightly, and to Gary it was probably something just said in passing. I ran into Gary after that, he was back and forth occasionally between the different mills, but I never mentioned anything to him. When I think about it now, I realize I was never very clear with anybody. Rather than speak up and get things out in the open, I would do lots of thinking and keep things to myself. This is a good way to get in trouble — but it's how life is, isn't it? You learn your lessons as you go along. It seems nobody can tell you differently at times. You have to go through stuff yourself. Why we can't see the obvious at times is beyond me.

I had moved a vacant house to my farm, renovated it, sold the trailer, built some barns and sheds, selectively logged the property and cleared some land. I was quite comfortable although the property was a little too far from town for convenience. Blaine was quite a distance from school and Frieda had a long way to travel to work. After talking it over with Frieda, I began to investigate moving in closer to town.

I had heard of a piece of property owned by Tony Fillian, eight miles from Quesnel on the West Fraser Road. It was in three pieces, with the bottom piece situated over the hill toward the Fraser River. An old-time friend of mine from Silver Creek, George Needham, lived on the town side of the property. I stopped in at his place to ask about the boundaries, as I felt sure he would know where they were. His son Dale was at home and he said, "I can show the boundaries." After coffee, Dale and I walked along the boundary toward the river, finally coming to an opening that was the end of Fillian's property. The land looked really interesting and Dale told me it belonged to Jim Ramsey. It was 120 acres in total with three quarters of a mile of Fraser River frontage, two benches, some fields and some big fir timber. More importantly, it was for sale! I said to Dale, "This place is beautiful. I like it." He pointed out that there wasn't much of a road into the property and, obviously, he considered that a big drawback. The property lay along a steep bank that led down to the first bench. The owner had built a road down the hill, but it was narrow and fairly steep. I looked it over and said, "Well, with my cat, I can fix it up to be not too bad of a road."

Jim Ramsey lived on a second property, on the main road, up above the one I was interested in. We went up to see him and talk about his place. I introduced myself and said I was interested in his bottom property. He was amenable to showing me the boundaries, so we headed off together down the hill. The more I saw of this property, the more I liked it. I said to Jim, "You sure have a nice piece of property here." His eyes lit up and he replied, "Yes I think so too and I wanted to build a house here but my wife, Irene, doesn't like the hill. Too hard to get in and out, so we decided to sell." I told him I would like to buy it, and before long, we had a deal. They wanted $20,000.00 for it, with $10,000.00 down. This was in 1970. Jim and I went to the lawyers and had Alex Shkuratoff draw up the papers. In a short time the property was mine. I spent many an evening exploring this place. It had everything, seclusion, springs, the river, good bottomland, and I loved it. For me, the feeling that enveloped me when I walked around land that I owned was like being on a high. It was wonderful. My Dad had always said to us boys, "Buy a piece of property, get the deed and you'll always have a place to live." That advice sure stayed with me and maybe it is why property has been such a big thing in my life.

I moved on to this property and started work. First, I had to figure out how to get out a patch of big fir timber from the bottom bench. With a few trails and some work on the road, I figured it could be done. John Ernst was buying big fir and selling the timber would help pay for the place. Logging big timber in a tough place was a challenge I enjoyed; making good skid roads and falling the trees "just so" was a thrill. I reworked the road and logged the property, taking trees selectively and only from the bottom end. When I finished, the property actually looked better. It was more open and I'd been careful not to damage any of the trees that were left. Selective logging can make a place look like a park.

Frieda, Blaine and I couldn't resist the new location. We wanted to move. I went to Prince George and bought a 12 × 50 mobile home (instant housing) and moved it on to the top bench, overlooking the river. I planned to build a log house there later. We could live in the trailer while I built the house and then sell the trailer. Trailers were fine on a temporary basis but I wanted something solid and permanent. To get set up, I had to get hydro to bring power down to the site. Easier said than done! I had to jump through some hoops to get the power: among other things, I had 2,500 feet of powerline to lay, nine poles to position and some serious slashing to do. Then I built a septic system and tapped into a spring by the river for a water supply. I built a road to this spring and then used a backhoe to dig a ditch from the spring to the house, a distance of 1,000 feet. I built a pumphouse and waited. Finally the big day came and we had power. It isn't until you don't have electricity that you realize how much you depend upon it.

I had carefully cleared part of the land, built a road, organized running water and electricity; now the next stage could begin. We had horses at the time, so I built several corrals; then I built a fence to surround the trailer. Finally, Frieda, Blaine and I loaded up our stuff, put the farm at Narcosli Creek up for sale and moved into the trailer. The new property had been purchased in the late fall and it was now summer. From buying to moving had taken about eight months. After getting moved in, I went to Prince George to work for the winter.

A school friend of mine, Jack Hodgins, from Silver Creek, was running a job east of Prince George called East Fraser Logging, and he needed skid cats for the winter. I figured it would be good money for a winter's work. There were about 60 men in the camp, which was located at McGregor, 60 miles east of Prince George. Jack was a straight-up guy and ran a good show. He was tough but fair. You needed to be to look after a crew this size. This was strictly a winter show: we were logging wet ground and needed two ice bridges just to get in. An ice bridge is corduroy put across a river and allowed to freeze in. As long as you got cold weather, you were in business. Once these bridges freeze in and have some snow plowed over them, they are almost invisible.

These winter logging shows have a hustle and bustle about them that can't be found anywhere else. That winter, McGregor received a record amount of snow. I swear it snowed every day and the downed trees always had snow on them every morning. It was tough logging. The outfit had 12 skid cats, 10 fallers, 4 buckers, 10 trucks, 10 chokermen, 3 company cats, 2 D8 cats, one HD21 Allis Chalmers and two rubber tired skidders. The loadermen and buckers worked night shift with light towers, the trucks hauled day and night, and the company cats also worked nights. There was always something going on.

The owner of the outfit was Paul Winthers and he had an office trailer that we used to end up in after supper, a place where we could talk about the day's work, turn in our tree count, etc. One evening, the two-way radio barked to life, asking for Jack Hodgins. Jack grabbed the receiver. It was a trucker stuck on the hill, and nobody could get by him. He had spun out and wanted a skidder or grader sent to pull him up. There were two skidders on the job and one grader. Jack carefully asked him how bad was he stuck? Were his trailer wheels over the bank? The trucker said, "My trailer wheels are in the snow and they look a little over the bank." That's all Jack needed to hear. He sprang into action. He switched channels on the two-way radio to contact the company cats, which had radios in them. Contacting the HD21 operator, he said, "There's a truck stuck on four mile hill and he needs a pull. Drop whatever you are doing and get over there as fast as you can. Put it in the big wheel." This cat was four miles from camp in the other direction, so he had eight miles to travel; a long way for a cat. Jack knew a skidder or grader could not pull a loaded logging truck from a dead stop and it would take a big machine like the HD21. The 21 was equivalent to a D8, maybe a little bigger, and it was fast. In a while, we heard the cat go clattering by, its metal pads clanging and banging. Jack had directed the loaded trucks coming along behind to get into pullouts and wait until the hill was clear, to keep from causing a traffic jam behind the stuck truck. He also needed room for the cat to get through. Jack followed the cat up the hill. He saw what had happened. The trucker had failed to chain up at the bottom and had spun out. When he couldn't make the grade, he had tried backing down but the truck had slid and jackknifed a bit and the trailer went over the bank. Bingo, he was stuck. When they had him on top of the hill and out of the road, Jack said to him, "Hey Joe, you know you were supposed to chain up for that hill. Look at what not wearing them cost. Wear and tear on the cat, trucks backed up for four hours, not to mention lost production. All because you were too lazy to put your chains on. I would like you to go dump this load and, tomorrow, go to the office and pick up your time. You're finished here!" That was Jack. He ruled with an iron fist and as the saying goes "that's why they paid him the big bucks!"

Around February 15th, the weather warmed up and it started raining. The crew was sent home to wait for another cold spell as the roads and landings were cutting up badly in the wet. But it just stayed warm and kept raining and the snow plugged the creeks and the whole valley started to flood. I got a call from Jack to move out: there were major flood problems and there would be no more logging for this year. My son Blaine came with me to help me get my cat out. He was 13 and I took him out of school so he could lend a hand. It was unbelievable — there was water everywhere, over two feet of water on the road in spots. When we got to camp, it was deserted, sitting on a high spot about two feet above the water. We went on to my landing and couldn't believe it — the landing was completely under water. There were logs floating everywhere and the cat was in about 4four feet of water. This TD20 was a gas start machine that switched to diesel when it got going. The distributor was under water so the rig wouldn't start. One of the company cats was at the camp, high and dry, so we went back and got it going. Then we hooked the running cat onto mine, towed the drowned rig into camp, dried it out and got it started. We had already used up a lot of the day and were starving. Luckily, we found some bread and jam that had been left behind in the cook trailer and had a sandwich before starting out for the main road, 24 miles away.

What a trip. We hooked the pickup behind the cat, as Blaine was afraid to drive it through all that water. There were mile markers along the road and they were a godsend. I would pass one, then wait a while and start watching for the next one in the distance. I needed them to keep me on the road. I normally never drove my cat faster than third gear, the higher gears were much too rough and hard on the undercarriage, but before that trip was over, I was in sixth gear and running wide open. We had contacted a lowbed from Quesnel to come and pick us up at the McGregor turnoff. The lowbed was there, waiting, and boy was it a welcome sight. The driver's name was Glen Swaile and he drove for Smith Transfer in Quesnel, an outfit owned by Jimmy Johnston. We loaded up and stopped at the first restaurant we found and ate a big supper, then drove to Quesnel, arriving around 2 a.m. Glen was a trooper and took us right home that night and unloaded. He thought if we waited until morning we might find ourselves 'in the soup' again as there were road restrictions going up on the side roads and we'd probably get stuck in town. It wasn't a good winter for anybody, especially East Fraser Logging. They didn't get many logs out for all their prep work, camp setup, ice bridge construction, etc. The cold weather usually held until mid-April, and since they were on all private roads, could normally keep operating until then. Two months production lost to bad weather was a disaster for them. I wasn't that bad off: I just lost some skid time but no money.

I went back to clearing land and logging private timber that spring. I had my brother, Roy, running the cat one shift and I was on it for another short shift. Roy would start early, I would come in later and work falling and skidding until Roy finished his shift, and then I went on the cat for four to six hours. In the spring and early summer, there's about 16 hours of daylight and two people can get a lot done. Some hot days we did not run the cat, falling and skidding instead. It was nice working with Roy as he could do any job in the bush. We would switch off and spell each other. We worked well together.

Partway into the summer I had a call from a real estate agent, Darwin Watt, saying he had a property out at Woodpecker (between Prince George and Quesnel) that I might want to see. I went and looked it over. It was a 160-acre parcel, with a small cabin. One hundred and thirty five acres were covered in small pine timber, averaging around 8 inches at the stump, and the remaining 25 acres was a field that had been cleared for a hydro line. All this timber was tall and straight. I measured off one acre and counted 1,100 trees. It was very thick. The asking price was steep but eventually we made a deal. I paid $45,000.00 for the land and timber, but I could recoup most of it if I could find a market for the wood. The mills in Quesnel were not buying much private wood that summer and what they did buy they weren't paying much for. They controlled the private timber intake with their pricing system. We were selling the timber from our land-clearing projects at break-even prices, just to get rid of it. The mills would not pay any more so what could we do? No one wanted to waste the timber and if it sat, cut and decked, for very long, it would dry and crack and become almost worthless.

With no markets in Quesnel, I checked Prince George. Nobody wanted small pine but an outfit that made ties, poles and fence posts, called Domtar, was interested and gave me a price list. After figuring out the work and delivery costs involved in cutting small post material, it didn't work out, but the idea did interest me and I started scheming a way to peel and treat fence posts. I talked to Domtar about a post peeler, but they wanted only raw material so weren't very helpful. In fact, they were not helpful at all. I started phoning around and an outfit in Vancouver said that they dealt with a company in Kalispell, Montana, Rollies Machine Shop, and they were dealers for Morbark.

Morbark is a machine company that manufactures chippers, sawmills and post peelers. I called Rollies Machine Shop and, yes, they had one post peeler in stock. I said, "Hold it for me and I will be down to pick it up as soon as I can." I made arrangements at home and left for Kalispell, Montana. It was roughly 800 miles from Quesnel. I drove to Revelstoke that day and decided to stay overnight. At around 8:30 p.m., I checked into a motel and then went out for Chinese food at a local restaurant. Arriving back at my motel one hour later, I went to bed. I tossed and turned and couldn't sleep. Maybe it was the food or maybe it was the excitement of my project, or maybe a little of both. In any case, I got up, dressed and left for Kalispell. I got to the border at King's Gate Crossing the next morning. I asked them what their hours were, and they said, "No problem, we're open 24 hours a day." I arrived in Kalispell around noon and found Rollies Machine Shop. My contact man was out for lunch so I had to wait around a while. When he returned, we went and looked the post peeler over. What a neat-looking machine, even not running. It was impressive. This one didn't have a power unit installed but I figured this wasn't much of a problem. I would be able to install one back home. We agreed on a price and I paid him by cheque. This involved a phone call back to Quesnel to the bank. We dismantled the peeler and loaded it in the back of my ¾-ton Ford. He also sold me a pointer for sharpening one end of the post. This was like a pencil sharpener. We said goodbye and I was off. I wanted to get across the border before I stopped for the night.

When I arrived at the King's Gate Crossing, I told them what I had bought and they said, "Sorry, that's business and we are closed for business. Our business hours are from 8 a.m. to 5 p.m. and, as it is now 8 p.m., we are just open for passenger vehicles." As this was a Friday night, he suggested I'd have to go back to the States until Monday morning. I thought, "No way," parked and followed him inside. I said, "Look here I asked you on my way through what your hours were and you said 24 hours." He said, "Yes I did but you didn't say you would be doing business." I started arguing with him and finally I said, "Hey, to hell with it. I'll just drive through." This was the wrong thing to say. He hollered to somebody in another room, "Hey, Sam, impound this vehicle." So there I was, stuck at the border with a sticker on my truck, unable to drive it anywhere. I walked around some and cooled off, and went back to talk to the friendliest officer. I explained my situation to him saying I would be stuck for the weekend and needed to get back. He then said there was a way of doing it. I could go back to the little border town one and a half miles back, and find a bondsman. He would be able to post bond on my peeler. I located this fellow and for $50.00 cash he filled out some papers, allowing me to go to Prince George and have these customs people do the paper work. I folded up this paper work and walked back to customs (they would not let me drive as I was impounded). Showing this paper work to customs worked and they put a seal on my post peeler to be taken off at Prince George. They said, "Okay, you can go." I had to take the "siezed" sticker off my windshield before leaving. These guys have way too much authority for me. I was not used to being thought of as a crook. I stayed overnight at Cranbrook and had a very much needed sleep. Two mornings later I drove into Prince George and paid my duty on the post peeler. This was an interesting event in itself. I had phoned ahead and asked about the duty. Customs told me I would pay a percentage on the purchase price. I told him how much I had paid and he said okay, bring this much cash. Once I got there and he inspected my load, he pulled out his book on pricing. Everything imaginable was in that book. When he came to post peelers he compared make and model, and said, "You didn't pay enough for it. It says here it's worth "x" amount of money and you will have to pay duty on my price. And that means the total will be this much!" He handed me a paper with an amount on it. "Cash," he said, and I had to go to the bank. What a frustrating experience. After that I always seemed to shy away from buying anything across the line.

Back in Quesnel I contacted a millwright machinist to help me get this post peeler in operation. We set it up so a power takeoff from a tractor would run it. This worked real well as a separate power unit and using the tractor as a power source meant you could use it for other things besides the peeler. We hooked up a conveyor belt for the bark and shavings, and it was away. I towed it up to Woodpecker and set it up. Boy, what a neat machine. Poke a 4 inch × 7 foot piece of pine in one end and out the other end comes a peeled post. I set a tank for treating the posts with preservatives and soon we had a production line going. It took some time to work out the kinks, but soon we were making posts.

I hired a local logger, Walt Bradford, to log the timber. He also logged for Ernst and was able to put together a deal for this timber. He had a 175 Drott feller buncher that allowed him to sort in the bush. Anything over six inches at the butt went for sawlogs and anything under went for posts. In this thick timber it was nice to see separate bunches, row on row. Walt skidded the six and over bunches to his landing, and I skidded the six and under bunches to the post mill. Once these bunches arrived at the post mill, we bucked them into seven-foot lengths and decked them by the mill for peeling.

A company from Prince George was demonstrating a new mechanical grapple for skidders. You used it with two winches; and cables opened and closed the mechanism. They needed some bunched wood to demonstrate the grapple and contacted me. Would I set a date, let them come in and set up a demo, and find some loggers to come a watch? I said yes and they came out with a C8 Tree Farmer skidder and one of these new grapples. About 25 loggers from Quesnel and Prince George came to watch it work. It was quite an invention: one line opened the tongs and the other line dropped them over the bunch of trees. Then the lift cable closed the tongs around the bunch and lifted it off the ground. The advantage was you could let your bunch go if you got stuck, drive ahead and then winch it back up. It worked well but it didn't seem to catch on. I never did see many in use later. The loggers that came to watch the demonstration seemed more interested in the post peeler than the grapple. That was probably uncomfortable for the guy demonstrating the grapple.

We had the mill set up on the powerline clearing and we started losing tools and small stuff to thieves. After one particular big loss, we decided to hire a watchman, and have him live in a camper right on the job. I hired Dale Needham for the job as he was already working in the post mill. Dale was feeding the mill and he did an excellent job. After a few weeks he started going to the neighbours for milk and eggs, at least that's what he told me. One night he came back to his camper to find his chainsaw and radio stolen. We obviously had a persistent thief living in the area. What a shame to steal from a working man. What a shame to steal, period.

We ended up taking 130 loads of sawlogs and over 100,000 fence posts off this property. When you log a piece of private property it is essential that you make a nice job. It's important to leave trees around building sites, waterways and boundaries. They don't have to be big trees, just trees. Clearcutting is out unless you plan to go the whole way and plant grass. Leaving some cleared and some treed land is best. Then, when you go to sell it, the property looks and feels better. People like to see trees or patches of trees. Eventually I worked out a plan that took 50% of the trees out selectively, but taking trees that accounted for 80% of the timber volume. On a private property arrangement, this gave me both marketable timber and saleable land.

About that time I bought two more properties. One close to Quesnel and one out on the Barkerville highway, called Wingdam. Wingdam was a gold mining town in the early 1900s but was deserted as gold prices fell and wages increased. The place I purchased sat on 160 acres of deeded land and still had some old buildings on it. It was a nice property. The main highway and Lightning Creek ran diagonally through the centre of a narrow valley, and the steep sides had a nice cover of large spruce trees that continued on up a hillside.

The one close to Quesnel was an interesting deal. A friend of mine, Don Howlett, was working for Wall & Assoc. Realty when he came across the property. The owner wanted $45,000.00 with $15,000.00 down and the balance at $15,000.00 per year for the next two years. Another logger, Real Gamache, had made an offer on it that day. Real Gamache was in partnership with his brother and father in Phil Gamache & Sons Logging

Limited. Real was smart, hardworking, handsome, clever and athletic. Definitely competition but, we thought, what the heck, we may as well make an offer too. We followed the listing agreement to the letter and our offer was accepted. I had taken a quick look at this place and could see the potential. It was 160 acres with a 10-acre field and the rest in timber, mostly pine and fir. I decided to work the Quesnel property before the Wingdam one, and started in. West Fraser Mills agreed to take the timber. My son Blaine came and logged this piece with me. We had the TD20, a 175 International Drott loader and a 540 JD skidder. We spent the winter selectively logging. I did the falling and Blaine skidded. When the truck came in or when our landing got full, Blaine bucked and I loaded. What a pleasant winter. Just four miles from town.

Playing with horses, 1972

Dad with author's moose rack, 1967

Blaine measuring a large fir, 1972

Falling fir with Stihl chainsaw, Quesnel 1972

Author's equipment yard, 1974

Road building on steep side hill, 1973

Blaine skidding logs, 1972

Older D8 cat

Track loader

Skidder

Large fir logs from the Narcosli Creek area of Quesnel, 1975

CHAPTER 6

Friends, Family and Houses

I decided it was time to sell the Wingdam property, as I couldn't find a good market for the spruce timber on it. I put an advertisement in the Vancouver Sun. The caption read, "Town for Sale," and then the particulars. Jerry Van Haldren was reading the paper on his way over from Victoria on the ferry. He was travelling with a party of university students, of which he was one. He was taking his last year of law. The ad caught his attention and he turned to his companions, "Hey guys look at this, 'Town for Sale.' I think I'll go and look into this. There seems to be an opportunity here!" So about a month later, Jerry and his girl friend, Betsy, came to look at the place.

What a pleasure these two were. They were very knowledgeable about everything and were generally friendly and appreciative; quite the opposite of me. They were sophisticated city and I was country bumpkin. I loved them. We went and looked at the property. The old mining superintendent's house was just perfect for them and there was a brick block powerhouse, 40 × 80 feet, that had been used to power the mine. Now it would make an excellent shop. The close, burbling of the creek was awesome to them. They loved it and said, "We'll take it!" This was the beginning of a good friendship. They moved onto the property in September of 1975.

Jerry had a law degree, an economics degree and he was incredibly smart. He had two boys from a previous marriage and they were both smart like him. Their report cards were all "As." The youngest, Robert, showed an interest in an old truck I had and asked what I wanted for it, as he would like to fix it up? I talked to Jerry and he said, "Okay but you get Robert to work for you on the house for five days," a goods-and-services tradeoff. So later on, I had Robert come and help me on the house. He was 13 years old going on 25. There wasn't anything he didn't know. He continually corrected me on things until I started to lose patience. Then I thought, "Hey, what the heck, let him talk and maybe I'll learn something." He knew things I hadn't ever heard of. For example, around 3:30 one afternoon, I complained of being tired and away went Robert. He said, "When you get tired in the afternoon, your tryglycerides are lacking and you need potassium. You can either get it in a shot form from your family doctor or you can get it from eating bananas. I would suggest you try eating a banana every afternoon around 3:30 and you'll be surprised how much better you feel." I was out of my class. This is one of the many surprises Robert had in store for me.

I had many pleasant experiences with the Van Haldrens. Jerry was consistently polite; "old school" I guess you'd call it. He'd say, "Please hand me that hammer" or "Thank you" for that nail. I never knew him to swear but one night we decided to finish a wiring job and were installing a thermostat in the bathroom. When opening the package, a red card fell out saying, "You must have a double ground in the bathroom." We didn't have! Jerry was quiet for quite a while, then stamped his foot and exclaimed (in his heavy Dutch accent) "Gott Dammit, I'm pissed off!" I had to hide my laughter. We kept on working on the house together and time came to frame in the bedroom. I came in carrying an armload of 2x4s and my chainsaw. Jerry saw me coming and said, "Ed, please don't bring that chainsaw in here." He liked to have everything cut neatly with a skill or table saw. He didn't appreciate my rough chainsaw work.

It was about this time that I decided I was ready to build another log house. This had always been the plan for the Ramsey property and I figured the time was right to get to it. I went to West Fraser Mills and picked out enough logs for the house. I had drawn up a plan of a house with 12 corners. It looked good on paper but, if I had known more, I would have had four corners. I went ahead and bucked these logs to length, around 120 logs 20-to 24-feet long. I hauled them home, put them through my peeler, stacked them up in a dry pile, built a roof over them to keep them out of the weather and let them dry a bit. I then started on the basement (12 dumb corners again!). I dug it out with my TD20 and I hired my neighbour, who had owned the place before, Jim Ramsey, to help me.

Blaine was also there to learn and help. Jim was a very handy man. He was in his 60s then and had worked at many trades; he helped me a lot. We did the basement in about a month and then put in the floor joist. Two inches × 12 inches × 22 feet is an odd size. Oversized joists like these, placed at 12-inch centres, can, however, comfortably span 22 feet. The installation went well.

After the floor we started on the logs. This proved to be quite a challenge, as the only experience I had was the log cabin my brother and I had built in 1952. I had read a log building book written by Allen Mackie, and learned quite a bit about log building, but I couldn't get on to the technique of scribing one log to the other. Allen Mackie was teaching a course in Quesnel that spring and I decided to go and see how to do it in person. Jim said, "Hey, we don't need to scribe them," but I insisted, so off we went to town. It didn't take long to figure the process out as I was keen and had already started to learn by trial and error. We went back and the pieces fell into place. We began with 12 logs per round; but that soon got trying and seemed to take forever (we needed to get to eight feet high for the next step). As a matter of fact, it took all summer. I took a week off during a wet spell and had my tonsils taken out, they had been bothering me for some time (I haven't had a sore throat since), but that was the only house-building break. It was a wet summer and it was frustrating. Everything was wet all the time and there was no way to cover up the logs. It was a mistake to peel them ahead of time as they weathered badly, but how do you know?

Finally we got to the roof. I used a log truss system with open beam perlins and decking. I had to take a trip to the bush along my place, which was owned by Weldwood. I had seen some dry spruce in a swamp, which I thought would work for perlins and ridge poles. Weldwood of Canada is a large company and was a good neighbour. They didn't mind my taking some dry trees. I needed seven logs 55-feet long for this job. I found them and skidded them to the site and peeled them. We had quite a job getting them up as the loader would only lift 12 feet, but we somehow managed with cables and a comealong. I had read a book called *Grass Beyond the Mountains* by Rich Hobson. The main character, Pan Phillips, used to say about some impossible task, "all it takes is one man and a brain." I have thought about that a lot when faced with a tough problem, and applied that philosophy. Sometimes it puts a different slant on things.

Blaine and I made a trip to Vancouver to buy cedar for decking. I bought coloured aluminum from a local dealer for the roof. Once the roof was on things went easier. I had my friend Jerry Van Haldren come and help me with the inside framing, wiring and plumbing. I had decided to do all the jobs myself, plumbing, wiring and septic system. Jerry was a big help. He knew everything about building. He said, "You can do anything you put your mind to, never be intimidated by a job." Jerry was from Holland and he had learned the building trade at an early age. When I mentioned getting in a mason to do the brick work, he said in his pleasant Dutch accent, "Och, Ed, you can do this yourself. You know, in Holland this is the first job you learn to do when you are three years old, playing mud pies. Here, I'll take five minutes and show you how!" And he did! His attitude was catching, making me feel more positive about myself. After fighting the plumbing and wiring through to the end though, I decided this was the last time. I knew how to do it now, and in the future, I'd leave it for the professionals. I'd do my falling, which is what I do, and they could do what they did best, too.

As Jerry Van Haldren was encouraging me to do my own masonry, his wife Betsy was tangling me up with something else. A movie, *Klondike Fever*, was being shot in Barkerville, 55 miles east of Quesnel. Barkerville was a good choice because it had been a mining town in the 1860s and this movie was about the gold rush. The stars of the movie were Lorne Greene, Rod Steiger, Angie Dickenson, Gordon Pinsent and a few others. In any case, Betsy knew one of the coordinators for this movie and she was given a list of required extras and props. Guess who she recruited? They needed a horse and buggy in the film, and I happened to have one, and they needed big men (extras) for the saloon scenes.

This was during logging breakup and so I had the time. My involvement lasted about ten days and it was quite a thrill to meet actors I had known from TV and movies in person. I was in all the saloon scenes, in the background of course, but nevertheless still there. The climax of the saloon scenes called for a "honky-tonk" dancer to dance on the tables; I was in the crowd, clapping and jostling with the rest of the miners (actors and extras). My real job, though, was to catch this dancer when and if she fell. She fell a number of times as the tables were small and top-heavy, I had to catch her and I did, each time. She was a very brave lady.

These actors stayed in the small town of Wells, four miles from Barkerville. They were treated as ordinary people and they seemed to enjoy this. I remember one night in the Wells Hotel, Lorne Greene took the guitar away from Rick Meyers, who was playing music for the hotel, and entertained everybody for the rest of the evening, playing and singing. I talked to each of these actors and the only one who seemed uncomfortable, not quite natural, was Gordon Pinsent. A friend of mine, Mae Ramsey, asked me to get Angie's autograph. When I asked her she said "no problem." The actors were very professional and worked hard; and, in Barkerville anyway, they worked 12-hour days.

I have a copy of this movie and I watch it occasionally. It sure brings back memories. The movie crew moved on to Revelstoke for the next part of the movie and I never did get to use my horse and buggy. They figured there was too much snow in Barkerville for them to stay there. I could have followed them to Revelstoke but that life could get addictive and it wasn't for me at the time. It was sure fun though.

What's the saying, "How are they going to keep them down on the farm after they've seen Paree . . ." Well, tempting as it was (and brief), back I went to make the finishing touches on my house. The overall house-building experience was a good one and by November 25th, we were able to move in. I still had some finishing to do but thought, "Oh well, I'll do it in the spring." What a change to move from the trailer into a big house. The house wasn't that big but compared to the trailer, it was a mansion. When I made the plans to start on this house, my mother had said to my sisters, "I wonder why Edward is going to build a log house when he can afford a proper one." The log houses my mother lived in were usually low ceiling, dark, dingy, small and hard to keep clean. I guess she remembers no running water, no inside plumbing and, like me, remembered well the chore I had as a small boy of mixing chinking for their log house. Chinking consisted of cow manure, fox tail hay and lime mixed into a smooth paste and trowelled in between the logs. It could later be nailed without cracking. When my mother saw the log house I built, we had quite a good laugh over the difference and the lack of chinking.

My wife, Frieda and I were not getting along about this time. We had been married for eight years. She had never really accepted my son Blaine. She had her own ideas about kids and they sometimes differed from mine.

I felt she resented him. There was always lots of stress in the house. I think when I look back on it now, if I told the truth, it is myself I am upset with more than her as I let it go on far too long. Before I knew what happened, Blaine had had enough and he left home at 15 to live with friends. I didn't realize at the time that this was a pattern I knew well. That summer was the beginning of the end for Frieda and me.

Blaine was gone for two years. I didn't see him much over that time but I kept track of him. He was staying with friends and working on their ranch. Frieda and I continued to live in the house but pretty much went our own ways. After a while, I decided to build another log house on a five-acre lot in a new subdivision. Blaine wanted to learn more about building and I was happy to have him working with me, and it would give me a chance to be with him and maybe make our relationship better. We went out to a forestry logging area close by the subdivision and cut 65 large pine logs, 50 feet long, and hauled them onto the site. This hauling was done by a friend of mine, Doug Andrews. Doug was short and strong; what he lacked in height he made up for in personality, and he had a good wit and a way with a joke. Doug had been hauling logs for me for quite a while and he had a nice, new Hayes Clipper long log truck. I loaded him up in the bush and he said, "How are you going to unload?" I said I'd show him! "We'll take two lengths of cable and tie around each end of the load, leaving them done up secure, but fairly loose." We drove to the building site, turned around and I proceeded to tie the cables to the load. When everything was ready, Doug said, "Are you sure this will work, Ed?" I was confident and said, "Sure it will." We both tripped our stakes together and it started to unload perfectly, then one cable broke and left one end of the load still on the truck. Doug looked at me disgustedly and said, "Yeah Eddy, I can see it worked real good!" We had to walk down to a trucker's place two miles away and get him to come and help clean up this mess. So much for that!

My brother Roy wasn't working at the time so he came and helped Blaine and me build this house. It was a spec home on my part. I designed the house myself, a three-storey log house with open beam concept. We started on September 1st and by Christmas we had the roof on and the house ready to lock up. We then had a big wood heater brought in and started on the inside work. This heater was a godsend. The month of January that year, 1978-79 was very cold. The logging trucks only hauled 11 days that month. As we were beside the Nazko highway, we knew what days the trucks didn't move, and they didn't roll often. We were okay 'cause we'd just get our heater hopping and it kept us nice and warm.

I contracted the plumbing to Virgil's Plumbing and Heating, and the wiring to Quesnel Electric (I had learned my lesson about plumbing and wiring). Roy had moved back to his regular job when we reached lockup and so Blaine and I started on the drywall, cupboards and fireplace. We had located some big, white quartz rock in a deserted mine in Wells earlier that fall and now headed out with a skidder and lowbed to haul it. We parked the lowbed as close as the terrain allowed and then drove the skidder one mile to the site. We skidded the biggest rocks we could find, some four feet through. We skidded them right up and onto the lowbed and, when we had a load, we put the skidder onto the rig and headed back to the building site. We broke the rock up and then carried it into the house and put it around the fireplace to warm up. We roughed in the fireplace with cement blocks and then faced it with the white quartz rock. The fireplace was 32 feet from the bottom to the chimney cap. This fireplace, with its white quartz rock, was a real showpiece and worth all the extra effort.

When the house was finished, we had a house-warming party with about 75 people attending. My Mom and Dad came over from Calgary for the occasion. My Dad supplied the music. We never talked about my younger years; he just seemed to mellow and I was able to enjoy his company. About two years before this particular evening he had said, "Edward I wanted to give you this old violin when I passed on but I decided to give it to you now and maybe you will learn how to play and we can play together." He gave me the violin and I signed up for lessons. My teacher was Frank Hennessy from Quesnel. He was a good player and teacher. I took lessons from him at a school with about 10 students for six months, then went on to take private lessons from him for another year. Betsy Van Haldren also took lessons with me. Two people make it easier to play. Frank played for the Old Time Fiddlers when they played for dances, and later I joined him. It was easy playing with Frank, as he would cover up any mistakes I made. I entered a few fiddling contests and played as a guest fiddler with a band from Kamloops when they played at the Billy Barker

Inn in Quesnel. It is something you need to keep up with or you soon forget everything you learned. I also played with my Dad. He was fun to play with although he had a different style. He played by ear and I played by reading music.

Frieda and I officially separated after the housewarming. She stayed in the new house and I stayed at the original house. Blaine never did move home but he had a really nice girlfriend, Shaun Eglin, and they set up housekeeping. They got married that same year.

I took the rest of the spring and summer off to regroup and do some soul searching. I spent some time with my friend, Doug Andrews, just hanging out. It was a nice change. I had quit drinking in 1972 and was still adjusting to a different way of life. When I was drinking, after having a few, I could talk to anyone and felt comfortable most places. After quitting, it took me a while to realize that I could do these same things cold sober. It took me around five years to start feeling comfortable with myself. As well as drinking, I had quit smoking. Boy, I'll tell you that was hard to do. Smoking is a habit that becomes so much a part of you it is scary. Without even thinking about it, you plan your life around smoking: where and when to buy them so as not to run out, coffee breaks and pauses when you can have one, matches in the truck so you can light up when driving, etc. It's like you and your cigarette are the only people around. There are, however, non-smokers. I don't think I was very tolerant of non-smokers. I remember one camp I was working in way back when. I was single and had signed up at this sawmill to take a lumber-grading course. This other fellow and I were going to travel together. The course was two nights a week and after supper I went to get in his Volkswagon bus and he said, "Oh by the way, I don't allow smoking in here." This was in the sixties and I looked at my newly lit cigarette, looked at him and said, "Well, Bill, I guess you will be travelling alone." I couldn't see myself going 17 miles without a cigarette.

My self-imposed break to reflect and re-assess did me a lot of good. When fall came, I met a wonderful lady, Vicki, who was single and had two young boys, 8 and 10. We hit it off and soon became a family. We had a nice wedding in 1981. Vicki and I were to go through many challenging life experiences together.

Miners' shaft house on Wingdam property, 1978

Frieda in front of logs dry piled for the 12 corner house

2" × 12" floor joists dry piled for 12 corner house

The 12 corner house, 1974

Working on the 12 corner log house, 1973

Ranch gate that author built to 12 corner house

Dad and I playing a tune, 1979

On the movie set "Klondike Fever"

Driving my horse and buggy in the Billy Barker Days parade with
Highways Minister Alex Fraser in Quesnel, 1975

Author in Billy Barker Days parade with two young friends, 1975

Winword House Blaine and I built, 1978

Dad reflecting on the hearth of the quartz fireplace in Winword House, 1979

Vicki with Steve and Brian on our wedding day, 1982

Vicki, 1984

CHAPTER 7

Me and the SBEP

*I*t was the early '80s. My friend, Jerry Van Haldren, got in touch with me and said that he had heard of a new Forestry program called the Small Business Enterprise Program (SBEP) and that I should investigate it. The program was just starting up and was the provincial government's response to years of complaints by the small loggers. It was a way to appease the small independents who, until now, had had no access to any Crown timber. The Ministry of Forests saw this program as a way to give timber to the small guy and not upset the big guy too much. You had to register under SBEP and then, as timber licences were put up, you were allowed to bid on this timber. Until this time the only timber an independent could cut was either on private land or as a sub-contract on Crown land held by one of the major logging concerns. This new program was not supposed to antagonize the big guys too much because they still had automatic access to big swaths of Crown land and the SBEP licences would be for much smaller, "extra" parcels of timber.

I had Blaine and myself register for this program. I think the first registration cost $100.00 per year. It took a while to sort out the kinks, from both sides, but soon most SBEP registrants became familiar with the rules and procedures. When the program first came out, the timber licence was sold by open auction. This was a very stressful and exciting process. Some licences, about half, were sold by sealed tender bid, and others at auction. I liked the open auction, but the sealed tender bid was by far the most fair. You could bid against anybody and be equal. The open auction was more cutthroat as the big guys with their deep pockets could just keep on bidding up until they got it.

My first SBEP timber licence was located at Twan Creek, 30 miles southwest of Quesnel. It was a sealed bid sale and you could bid on each species. The fir had a $18.00 per cubic metre upset and the pine was at minimum, which was $1.10 per cubic metre. I bid a $2.10 cubic metre bonus on the pine and was successful. It was a low bid, but that was all the market could bear. The fir was overpriced as it was. This was the second SBEP sale to be offered in Quesnel. West Fraser Mills was buying timber and I went to see the woodland manager, Jim Spinks. He worked me out a price for the pine and fir. The pine price was okay but the fir price was a little light. I would have to log and haul for $15.00 per cubic metre. The pine worked out to $18.00/M³ to haul and log. Once the mills found out what you paid for your timber, they offered accordingly. They left you just enough to log and haul. If anybody made money, they wanted to make it. I decided to log just the pine that winter and leave the fir stand as long as possible in case the stumpage went down. Stumpage is indexed with the price of lumber; if lumber prices go down so does the stumpage.

We finished the pine by breakup, getting it all logged and hauled before the roads were closed, but we left the fir standing. I had until October to finish this sale. Well, wouldn't you know it, the farmers with their agriculture leases and woodlots had been making noises about the high stumpage on fir, and enough of them had phoned or written to the Minister of Forests until he decided to do something about it. Farmers stood to make a lot more money on their woodlots and agricultural leases when stumpage was low. The Minister announced that as of June 30th of that year (1980), all stumpage on small operators (including SBEP sales) would be reduced to the minimum rate, which was $1.10 per cubic metre. This meant my stumpage went from $18.00/M³ to $1.10/M³, a reduction of $16.90/M³. I thought, "Boy, it sure paid to wait, now I can log my fir and make some money at it." I went to see Jim Spinks to talk to him about deliveries and when I was going to start, etc. He said, "Well, Ed, your stumpage sure came down." I replied happily, "Yes, it sure did." Then he said that West Fraser was prepared to meet me half way, and pay $8.45/M³ less than they'd agreed to last fall as the stumpage had dropped $16.90. He said, "That way we'll both make some money." I couldn't believe what I was hearing; he wanted to pay $8.45/M³ less than the agreed upon price! I said, "Jim, that's not fair!" He said with a smile, "Take it or leave it!" I said, "Well I don't think you will be getting this fir for that price," and left the office. Jim was not happy but I felt that what I made on the timber had no bearing on what the timber was worth.

I called Barry Brown, who was timber buyer for Lignum Sawmills in Williams Lake. He said he would be interested in looking at the fir. We arranged a time to meet at the sale site and went for a walk together. The area looked good with all the pine taken out and just the fir left. Barry said, "Hey, this is nice timber. I'm interested and I will pay 'x' amount for it," which was $5.00 per cubic metre more than West Fraser's original price. I said, "You just bought yourself some timber." We agreed on a conversion and he said he would supply the trucks. As this sale was on the way to Williams Lake, the hauling wasn't that much more. I was very happy. We moved in and started logging. Barry Brown and Lignums were very nice to deal with. They paid me for everything I had coming and were happy to get the logs.

That summer I successfully bid on two more big sales, both located at Pantage Lake on the Blackwater Road, 35 miles from Quesnel. I sold the timber to West Fraser Mills again. The two sales comprised approximately 1,000 loads of long logs. We delivered an average of 20 loads per day. I hired my brother Roy and his partner, Roy Zerke (they called themselves Double R Contracting) to do one sale and an old friend, Vern Botkins, to log the other sale. They each put out around 10 loads per day. West Fraser was pretty impressed. Jim seemed to have forgotten our little disagreement earlier on. I hadn't forgotten, but was trying to work around it. We finished these two sales late in the fall, including cleanup. Landing burning and rehabilitation was our responsibility back then, along with slashing (slashing is when you cut down any leaners or damaged trees).

After finishing these sales I was enough ahead and had enough confidence to buy some more of my own logging equipment. I was in Kamloops to attend an equipment auction at Richie Bros., hoping to find something, when my wife Vicki called me and said that West Fraser was looking for me with a logging proposal. I was to get in touch with Jim Spinks, their woodlands manager. I called Jim and he said that West Fraser had bought Kersley Lumber, a small sawmill 10 miles south of town, with a 10,000 cubic metre quota per year. The mill was five years behind and in danger of losing a valuable timber cut. West Fraser needed to log it that winter in order to keep current. It was already December 15th. The West Fraser loggers were all busy and he needed someone who could produce a high volume that winter. The timber had to be cut and hauled into their mill by March 15th. I was definitely interested! I agreed to look at the site as soon as I got back to Quesnel.

When West Fraser purchased this mill and realized they had to log 50,000 M³ that same winter, the mill's forestry people had a meeting to decide who they could get to come in this late in the season. Jim Spinks suggested I was a good bet because I had produced 20 loads per day in the summer and that was the kind of production West Fraser needed to get this job done. All seemed in favour except Bruce McLean, who was a junior in the forestry department. Bruce McLean is my brother-in-law and he had a thing about any of his relatives working for West Fraser. (He went on to become General Manager of West Fraser Mill in Quesnel and is still against hiring relatives, even though most of his in-laws are a logging family. I still haven't figured that one out.)

In any case, Jim won out (I never did find out why) and, when I got back to Quesnel, he flew me out to the timber in a helicopter, as the roads were snowed in and needed to be plowed. It was nice timber but wet ground and would need a cold weather freeze-up to make it work. I said, "Yes, it looks good!" and we went back to the mill and talked price. Jim said they were paying $10.00/M³ loaded on the truck. It wasn't a great price, rather low in fact, but the timber was good so I agreed to take it on. I got right on it, as I would have to produce 20 loads per day and deal with a tricky weather season. Christmas was also in there, and I knew the job would be quite a challenge.

There was a logging road to the start of the block, with washouts along it, and no roads or landings in the block. The first thing I did was to hire a neighbour and friend, Remo Lepetich, with a D8 cat to come and build the roads and landings. My brother and his partner were still working for me, and took on the skidding contract. Roy also had a 175 Drott feller buncher, which we would use later in a patch of small pine. I then rented a TD20 cat and 640 JD line skidder from Wayne Holly of Coastal Pacific Equipment in Williams Lake. I rental purchased a 540 International loader from B.C. Equipment in Williams Lake and a 966 Cat loader from Finning Tractor in Quesnel. I also hired a local logger, Tony Kosic, who had two 667 Clark skidders, and was a good logger. My son Blaine and his friend, Paul Smith were doing the bucking. I had three steady trucks hauling for me at this time, Mackie Ramsey, Wayne Roch (my brother-in-law), and Hugh Christie. West Fraser would supply any extra trucks we needed. We built eleven landings and connecting roads, and we fought mud well into January before we had any frost to speak of. Eventually we got this mismatched bunch of equipment organized and started producing logs. I had numerous fallers that winter, including John Moore, Jim Klaptiuc, and Jim McLean. I did the odd falling shift when I had time.

Starting up this late in the season made it hard to find a good crew. Most loggers have their jobs for the winter. But the terrain was good and so was the timber. It was mostly spruce with some pine. The spruce was two feet at the stump, tall and straight. Once the frost hit in January, we worked seven days a week and every machine that had lights worked 10-hour days. The rest of the crew and equipment worked eight hours per day. This timber was approximately 30 miles east of Quesnel on Dragon Mountain. It was a very hectic winter and breakup came a little early. The weather dictated the last day we could work: we started hauling at midnight and worked all night and all the next day until 8:00 p.m., but we finished hauling. We had machines all along the road, wherever there was a mudhole too big for the trucks to get through on their own, waiting to push the haulers through. Gus Cameron, the yard foreman at West Fraser who was in charge of trucks, was coordinating his end. He sent word to the bush that he would be keeping the scales open until we were done. Gus was a trooper, working far beyond his regular shift. We were a happy crew when the last load left the bush. That last day we hauled 57 loads to the mill. We finished in the nick of time as the next day the main road was closed to logging trucks, though we were allowed to haul our machinery out over the next few days. That's how the Ministry of Highways handled the side roads in breakup; they shut the roads down to log hauling and left them open for two or three more days to allow everybody to haul their machinery out of the bush. We finished the job by the skin of our teeth and came in slightly over the requirement. We cut and hauled 55,000M^3.

Around Christmas time that same year, a small SBEP timber sale came up. It was 25,000 cubic metres or approximately 600 loads, at Strathnaver, 30 miles northeast of Quesnel. I did not have any work lined up for the summer and getting this sale would fix that. I went and looked at the stand of timber with Robin Grady, West Fraser's timber buyer. It was a nice spruce and balsam sale and West Fraser wanted the timber, so we worked out a price on what West Fraser would pay me for the timber, which dictated to me how much I could afford to bid. "Upset" is the term used for stumpage set by the Crown. It could be any amount depending on lumber prices at the time. Any amount over or more than "upset" would be the bonus bid. For this job, upset was $1.10/M³ on both species and I was going to bid $8.00/M³ on the spuce and $10.00/M³ on the smaller stand of balsam. Everything was agreed and we headed in our separate directions. The sale was in Prince George, a one-and-a-half hour drive away, the next day. Late that night around 10:30 p.m. I got a call from Robin asking how things were and was I still going to bid $8 and $10 on the sale. I said, "Yes" and went to sleep. I got up early the next morning and drove to Prince George with Vicki. We decided to forgo breakfast at home and eat in Prince George, in case some trouble came up on the drive there and we needed the extra time.

I had been feeling uneasy about something and I couldn't put my finger on it. As we drove, Vicki and I talked about Robin calling to verify the bid so late at night and suddenly it hit me. He was making sure what our bid was, maybe not for a good reason, and I didn't feel right. I had nothing to base this suspicion on except he never called late, and we had already worked the bid out earlier. I decided to change my bid at the last minute. A sealed-bid auction called for a certified cheque for 10% of the bid to be enclosed with the offer. I changed my bid to $10.00 and $15.00 respectively, worked out the extra security deposit, and then ran to the bank to arrange for a second certified cheque. The bank had to call my Quesnel bank to verify funds and, with one thing and another, we just made it to the sale in time. It started at 10:30 a.m. sharp. After that hour, no more bids were accepted.

I handed in my tender for the sale, they accepted it and we went and sat down. There were about 40 people in the room, including three MOF people, a secretary and the SBEP manager who conducted the sale. The closing of tenders was announced and the officials then checked the eligibility of each applicant. There were about 12 eligible bidders. As they started opening the bids, I can't describe the tension and the excitement. It was palpable. All talking stopped and you could hear a pin drop. The only sound was the rustling of paper as the envelopes were opened. Then, in no particular order, the name of the eligible bidders were announced. I was surprised to hear one of West Fraser's loggers, Art Provencal's, name called. I started feeling uneasy again. Finally, the actual bids were read. His was $9.00 on the spruce and $11.00 on the balsam. My distrust had been valid. It was obvious that West Fraser wanted the sale to go to their own logger and had done some manoeuvering outside our agreement.

More bids were read, but Art's was still the highest, and then they came to mine. The auctioneer announced, "Reierson $10.00 on the spruce and $15.00 on the balsam." There was lots of "oohing" and "aahing" as Robin and Art exchanged looks, and then glanced over at me. I was the successful bidder with Art Provencal a close second. After the paperwork was done and I was awarded the sale, I looked Robin up. I found him and exclaimed, "What in hell was going on, Robin?" He said, "Oh, I guess Art wanted the sale too." He looked very uncomfortable. I let it go; what could you do?

Later on that evening I received a call from Tony Novak who owned Dunkley Lumber at Strathnaver. He had heard that the Strathnaver sale had come my way and wanted to see me. He said, "Ed, I think it will be in your best interest." I said, "Okay, I'll be there in the afternoon." When I arrived the next day, and went into the office, Henry and Joe Novak, Tony's brothers who managed the mill, said hello and ushered me into a conference room. They asked about the sale and I said I was probably going to sell to West Fraser, although I hadn't signed up yet. _ We talked at length about the deal, with me trying hard no to be intimidated by their obvious expertise. We talked money and scheduling, but couldn't quite come to common ground. Through the following years we had many joint ventures together. It was fun but I had to be sharp. It took awhile to realize humour was part of their strategy for putting together a deal. In most cases it worked out favourably for both parties.

The sawmill controlled the SBEP prices. They would set the price ahead of time on a timber sale for, as an example, $50.00 per cubic metre. As an independent and as a bidder, you would figure out how much it would cost to get that timber to the sawmill. Using the same example from above, it might cost \$25.00/M³. That would leave \$25.00/M³ that you could bid. Wherever possible, it was smart to leave a dollar or two for landing cleanup and any unforeseen occurance. But these timber sales were very competitive; the bidding went to the wire. I sometimes had to bid into my logging costs in order to get a timber sale. When this happened, there was a lot of pressure to pull the job off without going in the hole. I know that on some sales I had to do the logging for less than the "going rate."

After a while, the Ministry of Forests started putting SBEP sales on the block with a requirement that a percentage of the trees to be logged were to be harvested with an overhead cable system called "high lead logging." This method was to be used when the ground was too steep or wet for conventional skidders. I had bought two sales with a total timber amount of about 35,000 cubic metres, and about 25% of it had to be cable logged. In order to do this I had to get a yarder of some kind. I found one down at Whistler. It had been working on the ski hill there. I talked to the fellow who owned it and we struck a deal. I agreed to pay his price, but only if he would come up with me for a week and show me how to do this particular type of logging. He agreed and we got it hauled to the bush and set up. It was a 45-foot tower on a D6 cat. It had enough oomph with the winches and cables to log a 1,000-foot strip and could skid uphill or downhill. Imagine a motorized clothesline: you just hook a log on the line with a choker and wind the clothesline in. No rocket science there.

The fellow that came to show me how to make this thing work was a jack-of-all-trades. I was agonizing over a bid on a timber sale one night and Neil came over and said, "Ed, what are you doing, can I help you with something?" I explained my system for bidding: get a price from the mill, then work it back, bidding as much as you dared. Some of these auctions were sealed bids, you only got one shot so it took some figuring. Neil said, "Okay, let's talk about this. I used to prepare bids for Highway contracts in the late 1950s and early '60s for a big road building company. My job was to win the bid first and then figure out the economics." I said, "How would this work? That's backwards." He said he'd show me how he would bid on this particular timber sale and asked me to get the bids for the last few timber sales in that area.

He spread stuff out and said, "Now let's see what the successful bidder paid for some of these sales. Let's take these last three winning bids and average them out. We'll say the number was $25.00/M^3$. Using my formula, my bid on this timber sale would be $25.50 or $26.00. This is how I worked out my highway contracts back then. The object is to get the job and then do your figuring. If you don't get the job, you have nothing to work with. For me this system worked. Whenever I worked out a bid on a highway job and didn't get it, I had 50 guys down on me; and when I bid high enough to get the job, I was their hero. The cost of these jobs was irrelevant." I thought and I thought about this method. It started me thinking differently about my bidding strategy. Actually, I really hadn't had a strategy, just dollars and cents. Integrating some of Neil's methods into my bidding system worked wonders. I also started averaging out my cost for timber sales. If there was a particular timber sale in my area that I wanted, I would use Neil's method and just get it. Then I would take the cost of my last three sales, adding in the cost of the last sale, and if the average cost of these four sales was workable, I was happy. I knew this "after the fact" figuring was strictly psychological but it worked for me.

By this time I was getting enough timber sales to be able to maintain a steady crew and steady trucks to haul my logs. I was logging these high lead sales and shipping my wood to West Fraser, and I was coming up a little short. I went to see Jim Spinks about a little more money for my logs. I had figured another 50 cents a cubic metre would make it a lot easier. Fifty cents a cubic metre doesn't seem like much, but if you figure over the whole two sales, it could mean as much as $17,000.00. Jim was a tough negotiator and I couldn't move him. He sighted all the obvious reasons. Lumber prices down, wages up, and West Fraser in it for the long haul. I reminded him that some other mills were paying more, and his answer to that was, "Well, they probably won't be staying in business very long at that rate!" He would rub his temples and look so down that you felt like lending him some money. West Fraser also had a quality control system that was very stressful. They gave you 50 cents a cubic metre extra if you had all your lengths within 10%, and penalized you 50 cents a cubic metre if you were over 10%. Also the same 50 cents a cubic metre for less than 10% bad butts, and the same penalty for more than 10%. This meant you could get a dollar per cubic metre more or a dollar per cubic metre less, depending on their perception of your wood (and I say their perception of your wood because of an incident that happened).

I was told I had two rotten logs in my load (I would call every day about lengths and rot), and when I heard this, I said, "Hold that load, I need to see this." We were very careful about rot. I met Gus Cameron, the yard foreman, and we went and looked at the load. They had it all spread out on skids and it was easy to inspect. I discovered that, during the unloading, they had broken a small balsam in half, and in the middle was a brown discoloration, typical of balsam. Both of our ends were sound. This was their idea of two rotten logs. The way they had it figured two rotten logs in a load puts you over 10% and you would be fined 50 cents per cubic metre. This was on your two whole weeks production, and then you started over again. This time, my case was easy to make, I just had to bring the oddity to Gus's attention.

Another time we were getting fined for wrong lengths. My son Blaine was looking after the bucking so lengths were his responsibility and he was efficient at his job. We decided to get to the bottom of the problem. We were cutting some big timber at this time and we taped every log carefully, starting at the shortest point on the butt, as we were instructed. If the undercut was cut out of the log, you measured from the top of that. Most of our undercuts were out of the stump but, on steep ground, some trees had the undercut out of the log. We kept doing this, being very careful with our measuring until one of the trucks came back and said his load was a company sample. (The company could sample any load at random.) I waited until the next day, called in to check on the sample, and sure enough there were five bad lengths in a load with 32 pieces, putting us way over our allowable 10%. Blaine and I headed for town to get to the bottom of this. We went straight to Jim Spinks' office and asked him if he would come to the yard with us. He asked, "What for?" and I told him we were having trouble with our lengths. "We have a sample spread out in the yard, and I would like you to come and check it with us." He agreed. We went and checked the load, finding no wrong lengths. We went right over to the yard office and he asked, "Who checked the lengths on this load?" Alfred Krause said, "I did," and Jim asked him for the paperwork. Alfred gave him his clipboard with the page in question, showing five wrong lengths. Jim said, "Alfred, I personally checked this load and I get no bad lengths, so let's go out and do it together. Obviously I'm missing something." Alfred was very defensive, saying he had carefully marked down each length and were we questioning his ability to read his tape? Jim was patient but firm, and insisted we go and check this load. Alfred came although reluctantly. Jim held the tape on the butts and Alfred marked the lengths down. Nothing wrong. Alfred was getting uncomfortable as he was getting a new set of lengths. He said, "How can this be! I am always careful to mark down the exact reading on the tape." Jim said, "Who helps you with this measuring?" Alfred said it was his yard bucker. "Go get him," Jim said. Alfred rounded up his helper and Jim said, "Okay you guys measure these logs." This helper was measuring from any place on the butts. If it was a crooked cut, he held it in the middle of the cut. If the undercut was cut out of the log, he'd disregard that and measure from the longest point, which was the big, flat cut (which in his defence, was where most buckers started from) and, of course, the measurement was different in each case. Alfred could read the tape on his end perfectly and it would be wrong if it wasn't held in the right place on the butt. Jim asked the helper about this and he said hotly, "What do you expect me to do, get down on my knees to inspect these butts?" Jim replied, "Whatever it takes to do the job right." He said thank you to Alfred's helper and sent him back to his job. Then said to Alfred, "This is not the helper's fault, Alfred, it is your responsibility to see that he knows what to do. Lord knows how many more lengths you've screwed up with your system. You were there when it was decided where we would measure from in order for everyone to get the same number. I will be working on this and will get back to you when I have thought it over." Alfred looked very sheepish as we went back to the office. I had to hand it to Jim. He took my side in this and was not easy on his crew when he got to the bottom of these different lengths. He was more than fair.

When I could see no movement in Jim and West Fraser regarding log prices, I went to Dunkley Lumber. They were closer to the timber I was working and maybe they would be interested. Their log buyer, Blair Mayes, said yes they were interested. It was their kind of wood, big spruce (anybody's kind of wood, really). Dunkley philosophy was, "good timber equals good lumber" and they were not afraid to pay for good timber. They agreed to pay more money for the timber than West Fraser, and the trucking would be less as it was tree length, off highway, right to their mill. That made the deal very attractive. I agreed to ship the rest of the cut at this price, and thereby started a long relationship with Dunkley Lumber.

Dunkley's had no penalties for lengths and rot. They felt if your overall quality was good, all was okay. A little here and there balanced out in the long run. It sure took a load off everybody's shoulders, buckers, truckers and the loaderman. Before, they had to be exceptionally vigilant doing their job. I'm certainly not suggesting we could just load anything up; we couldn't. We maintained a certain quality standard. But there was no measuring when we hauled tree length, which was a big plus. We had some very long trees one time and Blaine called in to ask about lengths etc., if he was to cut them in half or what? Dunkley's yard foreman and quality man, Bob Buxton, was sent out to the bush to help us with this problem. Arriving at the bush landing, we had a number of long trees set aside, waiting for bucking. Bob looked them over and then stepped to approximately the centre of them and said, "Blaine, you can buck them off right about here," and he pointed off handily to the middle of the trees. Hey, that was our kind of bucker. We gave Bob the thumbs up, and carried on.

Blair Mayes was Dunkley's private wood buyer at that time. I would find timber, phone him and we would go and look at it. Blair worked in the forestry department of the office. Any time he got out to look at timber he enjoyed it. He liked to walk and make a day of it. It seemed like we would look at every tree on the sale. One time we went to look at a sale in mid-winter, on James Mountain. We snowmobiled in and had a tough time walking, as the snow was a good three feet deep. After struggling through about a mile of this, we came to the sale boundary. We followed some strip line ribbons to a plot, which is a predetermined spot on the strip line to count trees. These sales have a grid like number of strip lines and plots put in, in order to cruise the timber (when you cruise timber you are determining the amount of timber in cubic metres). With a map made to correspond to all the numbered strip lines and plots, you can tell where you are on the sale at all times. On this particular sale we followed the strip line to a plot and inspected it. The numbers were wrong according to the map. Further inspection revealed the sad truth. We were on a different timber sale. One that had already been sold or hadn't come up yet, we didn't know which. Not that it made any difference. I teased Blair about that one. I said to him, "Blair, I thought I was safe travelling with an R.P.F. and now you have gotten us lost." Blair was Woodlands Manager at that time and he went on to become General Manager of the sawmill. I don't think this incident had any thing to do with the shift!

There were a few years, when I was selling to Dunkley, that were good. They were paying more money for logs and this made it easy to buy timber. There was more room to compete. My new method of figuring out bids was working well. I would get the averages of the SBEP sales of a particular area, and if the sale was one that I particularly wanted, I would add a few dollars to it and, usually, get it. Sometimes I got fooled and paid too much. With sealed bids you never knew; anything could happen. One case in point happened in Prince George. There were two high lead sales that came up one winter and I wanted them both as they were in my area. At the first sale I was the only person to show up and I was able to get this sale for the upset price of $1.10/M^3. When the next sale came up, later that week, only one other person showed up. His name was Jim Hankins and he was a high lead logger based in Prince George. I knew him slightly and I spoke to him as we sat waiting for the sale to start, "Hi, Jim. Are you here for the sale?" He said no, he wasn't interested in it himself, but had just come to watch and see how things went. I was prepared to be the only one interested in this sale, as before, and thought I would get it for the same low bid. When they called the sale to order, we both went in. We were the only ones there, other than the forestry personnel conducting the sale. The forestry officer asked for bids. I waited to see if Jim was going to bid anyway; afterall, you never know! When the auctioneer called for bids for the third and last time, I got up and handed in my token bid. As soon as I had done this, Jim stood up and, from under his shirt, he brought out the winning bid. I was very upset with him. I waited outside for him and when he came out, I went to him and said, "Jim, why did you lie to me about not being interested in this sale and then submitting a bid?" He said, "Well, when you're competing with Dunkley's you need to be that way." I countered with, "Oh, why is that?" He replied, "Well a few days ago I got a call from somebody who worked for Dunkley, asking me if I was going to the sale and if I was interested in it. He wouldn't give his name and I didn't like that. So this is why I handled it this way." I hadn't known anything about this, before the fact, and I thought to myself, "well, another lesson learned."

In the course of the SBEP, I have had some 46 timber sales. Some of these sales were sealed bids and some were open auction. Sealed bids were different because that method allowed you to compete with your colleagues without conflict: you figured out your bid, handed it in, and waited for the results. These results were written in stone: the bids were there for all to see and if you weren't successful, all you could do was shrug and hope for better luck the next time. Sealed bids also let you see where every other bidder was and determine if there was an emerging pattern. Knowing previous patterns might help you in your next attempt.

The open auctions, on the other hand, were a very different process, and much more exciting. The bidders (or the people you suspected might be bidding) and the interested onlookers (the auctions were open to anybody, including spectators) would gather in the auction room. The MOF auctioneer and, usually, two secretaries, were the officials. The auctioneer would read off the qualified bidders and ask for the first bid. Someone usually bid upset (the stumpage set by the Crown) and the bidding would be underway. Unlike the sealed bid system, at an auction you could see your competition and their reactions. Sometimes there would be angry moments over "too high" bids and sometimes a bidder would wait and wait and then wade in and pick up a sale at the very end without even letting anyone think they were going to bid at all.

It was interesting to see the posturing behind the scenes. Some bidders would look for a sign from a partner or log buyer. Others would be figuring fast and furiously on their calculators, seemingly unattached to the sale, only to look up, bid, and then return to their figuring. I sometimes had paper and pencil in front of me, but not to figure but to doodle and seem inconspicuous. I always admired the bidders who were good losers. They always seemed the same, and when they lost they had the strength to smile and say "Good Luck" to the successful bidder. I, on the other hand, was a very poor loser. When I had bid my limit and a little more (which was usually the case with me at open auctions), only to have someone take it away with a higher bid, I would take it personally. I wasn't able to be gracious at all. I would sulk off and be mad at the world, maybe even for days. Two very gracious bidders were the Novak twins, Cyril and Metod. They would smile, shake hands and say congratulations to the sale winner. They were that way with most things, polite and cheerful. They are true gentlemen, and worthy of copying.

Doug Webster with load of fir

Steve Sheldon on a plantation where only one tree grew

Earl Olsen hauling tree lengths to Dunkley Lumber, Stephenie Creek

Earl Olsen hauling road lengths

Blair Mayes

Fir timber at Twan Creek

Landing ready for bucking

Skidding trees with D8, Quesnel

Lumber, wrapped and ready to ship

CHAPTER 8

Expansion and the Ministry of Forests

*T*he timber sales I acquired in the Slender Lake area were too far away from town for a daily commute. Working the sale was going to require a camp for the men. This was a different ballgame. A trailer camp in winter, in the north, is quite a challenge. I learned that the first couple are the hardest to set up and that practice helps. You have to arrange for running water, a septic tank, a generator for power and countless other things. My pattern was, usually, to arrange for three 12 x 60-foot trailers; I'd set them up side by side and hook them together. One was used for a cookhouse, with living quarters for the cook; one served as a wash trailer, with showers and bathroom facilities; the third unit became the crew sleeping quarters.

That first year I sure discovered just how much work there is to maintaining a camp! I hadn't planned on hiring anyone to look after the camp itself so, if a problem came up, I became the designated problem solver. And there were lots of problems! I'd worked in camps but didn't realize that in order to keep one running smoothly, a full-time handyman was needed to look after all the odd (problem) jobs. It seemed like every time I turned around, there was something: a plugged toilet, a broken water line, a power plant that was out of fuel or broken, snow to be shovelled, groceries to buy for the cook, hot water heaters to fix, water lines to unfreeze, and on and on. In that first camp job, I don't think I got any of my own work done. I was supposed to be building roads and landings, doing payroll and generally looking after things. Without my son Blaine, things would have been a real mess. He handled the day-to-day things in the bush and made that part of the show somewhat easier.

After that first camp experience, I made sure I hired a handyman full-time. One of the men I hired was Wes Unrau. Wes was a carpenter with a mustache, thick glasses and a quick smile whose regular job was mostly in the summer. Camp set-ups were wintertime only, so the work fit his schedule really well. Winter camps were ideal for him. Wes was good at all kinds of stuff. He would build us porches and shelters, or run to town for things as they were needed. He made my life a lot easier. One time we were setting up a camp and were putting in water lines. I noticed that Wes was not putting clamps on the joins. I asked him about this and he said, "Oh no, I've got these new plastic couplers and they don't need clamps." I was doubtful but Wes was adamant. I shrugged and said, "Okay, I guess you know what you are doing." Later on, as we turned the water on and plugged in the heat tape, some of these new couplers popped apart. One morning about 3:00 a.m., I awoke to a splashing sound under my trailer. I went and looked and, sure enough, one of these fittings had come apart. I ran over to Wes's bed, shook him awake and said excitedly, "Wes, Wes, wake up. One of your new couplers has come apart and we have a flood going on." Poor Wes; but it was his choice and he needed to take responsibility. Normally, once he got an idea into his head, it was hard to change his mind. After the flood, Wes put clamps on all the waterline joints the next day and we had no more problems after that.

Having a camp with 20 to 25 men is a job in itself and I always seemed to find out things the hard way. I learned early that there are really no shortcuts or easy ways. The "domestic" side of a timber sale is rough! Some of the things I had to deal with in those first camps were plugged septic tanks, frozen water lines, an inadequate power plant, one trailer short, no camp cook, and too small a fuel tank for the power plant. In order to have a smooth running camp, you need enough room to hire extra men, a good camp cook, a handyman on call, a good power plant, snowplowing equipment, and a good water supply. Any time we worked close to a town where they had motels and meals, I found it easier and less stressful to board my crew out. The cost was a little more but the reduced responsibility was worth it.

One time our camp cook, Maryann Moir, couldn't start for two weeks. She was completing a first-aid course. When I told my wife about this, she said, "No problem. I'll take her place until she comes back." My wife is an excellent cook but a camp is different than home. We both thought that she would have time to get organized because it was the weekend and the crew wouldn't need to start being fed until Monday (in the cookhouse). The groceries, dishes, pots, pans and cutlery weren't there yet and the water hadn't been run in. We arrived around 3:00 in the afternoon and Vicki started unloading. By 5:00, 18 men, hats in hand, showed up for supper, and she had nothing prepared and was in a panic. Back then, Vicki got rattled more easily than she does now. She sure had to scramble around, semi-hysterical, to get those men fed, but it did get sorted out. After supper, there was a mountain of dirty dishes, and no hot water. Oops! The next morning, I asked if I could help with breakfast. "Sure!" was the response. She had bacon and eggs cooking in pans, and was planning to cook hotcakes on the griddle next. The first thing I did was to stir the lumps out of her pancake batter. Big mistake! Four o'clock mornings were not Vicki's best time. I still hear about that. What I learned from having my wife come to cook in the camp is that the safest place to be is in the bush. The crew sure appreciated her cooking, though. Vicki's meals were very home cooking style; Maryann was a good cook too but in the traditional camp-cook style. No matter what, a good cook in a camp is very important. People who are working hard and stuck in trailers off in the hinterlands need to be fed well, and being without a cook a couple of times sure makes you realize that real quick.

As Dunkley improved the cutting capacity of their mill, they had to buy more private timber. Their yearly cut of Crown timber was 150,000 cubic metres and their facility could handle up to 300,000 cubic metres per year. As they expanded they hired more men. One man they hired to purchase private wood was Steve Sheldon. Steve worked with Blair Mayes until he was familiar with the system and then he was on his own. Blair had been promoted and was working the mill end of things. Steve was fun to work with. We often met for breakfast on a day we were heading out to look at timber. We would discuss markets and prices first, then go over stumpages, and then go to look at the timber, usually making a day of it. He had a good sense of humour and we got along well. He seemed to think I needed to know a few different words to beef up my loggers' vocabulary so he started teaching me a new word and its meaning each time we went out. He got the biggest kick out of that. Some of the words he taught me were ungulate, riparian, eclectic, indiginous, etc. I noticed he stayed away from words like, retroactive or negotiate. I always enjoyed a day out with Steve. Steve saw issues from both the loggers' side and the mill's side. Dunkley's was real hands-on, and they gave their people the responsibility to act on deals more than most places. Dunkley Lumber was good to me. If I needed help on a deal that I felt might be too big for me to handle, they were right there to help with advice and encouragement.

Woodlots were coming in at this time and I applied for one. Woodlots are mini tree farm licences with a yearly cut of approximately 1,000M³. These woodlots were offered up to appease the small logger and to create a means of utilizing unuseable private land, land that was not suitable for agriculture but would benefit from reforestation. Private land was included with your woodlot and, after some tree planting, the province would benefit from increased growth. The woodlot program was administered by the Ministry of Forests and, in Quesnel, our woodlot man was Paul Kennedy. There was a woodlot put up close to town on the Ernst Road. Several people, including me, applied for it. Applications were rated on a point system: "x" points for bush work experience, "x" for private land contribution (called Schedule "A" land), and "x" points for your overall project plan. As they added up the points at the opening, I had more points than anybody else and was awarded the woodlot.

The next day, Paul called me to say that there had been a mistake and he had added up the points wrong. Could I come in and see him? I went to see Paul and he said Ted Kennedy and his partner, Marty Zadorozny, had come in and complained that they hadn't gotten enough points for their private land. They said Paul had missed one parcel of land they had put up. Because of his mistake, Paul explained he would have to award the woodlot to Kennedy and Zadorozny. As a consolation he offered me a woodlot out at Alexandria; it was 45 miles from town and not as good. I should have stood my ground and said "No" but I thought, at that time, that he was right. I said okay, but I didn't want to put up all my private land towards this woodlot. Paul said no problem, that I could delete some. We agreed on what land to delete and I was awarded the second woodlot. Paul stalled long enough with the land change that it never happened. They held me to my original application. I should have had it in writing. I have always thought that there was something going on that I was not party to, on that first woodlot. I think some extra private land was added in after the fact for Ted and Marty to end up with more points. Woodlots require so much paperwork with cutting permits, road permits, cruising info, logging plans, boundary upgrading, roads built to specs, wildlife studies, archeological studies, management plans, silviculture prescriptions, etc. etc., that it is a very frustrating process. The ordinary logger has a difficult time wading through it all and usually ends up hiring a forestry consulting firm to look after it. And then, with all the logging restrictions, it can be a very uneconomical venture. I know for myself; I almost gave it up many times. The sawmills have the same problems, but they are big enough to have a forestry staff to do this work as part of their job, where the ordinary farmer or logger gets overwhelmed with the never-ending paperwork, letters and applications.

I was working for West Fraser when a new project came up. The MOF had built 20 kilometres of new road into Nyland Lake, 30 miles east of Quesnel, and were putting up the timber for bids. They had logged the right-of-way first and then built the road. The logging was done poorly. It had been felled and then skidded into large piles, and pushed up on the first half of the right-of-way with big machines. Some piles were on the low side and over a hill. When the road work was done, mud had been pushed into the decks and, in some cases, big ditches had been dug in front of them with no thought to how the wood was going to be moved. The second half of this right-of-way was done better than the first. Large openings had been cut out of the right-of-way to put the timber in. It was still a mess but at least you could get at it. MOF had sent a scaler out to block scale the timber. The ministry had contracted and paid for this right-of-way and had set the stumpage upset to include the cost they'd paid to have it done. The mills were not happy with the state of the wood or how it could be accessed. Weldwood and Bruce McLean of West Fraser had gone up to inspect the wood and both said the volume stated by the MOF was not there, and that they were not interested in buying it. Weldwood contacted their people and me, and said they had talked to the rest of the mills and had arranged not to bid, and let the MOF wear this one (as they put it). If nobody bid, the MOF would have to sell at upset without adding their extra costs. The mills, led by Weldwood, were so worried that they were paying for this poor logging job, they failed to realize that if the MOF had left the logging out and just started at upset, the bidding would go over the added logging cost anyway. The mills always wanted timber for nothing, and until programs like the SBEP came in and enlightened many people, myself for one, they usually had their way. I had spent my life in the bush logging for mills and was very much in the dark as to the workings of stumpage, roadwork, Section 88, reforestation, etc. As the SBEP came in and I became more informed, I began to realize how much timber was being sold for little or no money.

Anyway, back to this sale. I decided to go for it. I had figured beyond the first few landings and said to myself, "Well, somebody has built a road right through some logged trees, which can be reached from the road, and they felled the trees too." Looking at it this way, I was gaining in two areas — I would have no road building and no falling costs. Figuring the price of timber then, I knew I could bid considerably above the starting price, including the contentious logging that the mills were so steamed up about. The sale day came and I hadn't slept the night before, anxiously awaiting it. I was there early with my homework done. All the mills were represented. Lloyd White from Quesnel Forest Products, Robin Grady and Jim Spinks from West Fraser, Hugh Goodman from Weldwood, and Graham Long from Weiers Sawmills. Ernst Lumber had a man there also, though I don't recall who he was. The wild card they hadn't figured on was Blair Mayes from Dunkley Lumber. They hadn't considered Dunkley as this wood was on the far side of town from Dunkley. It didn't seem to make sense that Dunkley's would haul through town to their mill, since there was still some semblance of territory being honoured. Each mill stayed in their own area; if Dunkley went for this they would be encroaching on Weldwood's area. Anyway, this was not a SBEP sale. It was an open auction for anybody. The advertisement for the auction implied that it would be a sealed bid sale but, when I inquired, I learned it was to be open bidding. When they called the auction to order, and asked for the first bid, Blair Mayes stood up and moved to the front of the room, handing in a sealed bid. They opened it and read it out, and said this would be considered as the first bid. It was a lump sum bid with the upset and logging based on a MOF block cruise that was close to $90,000.00. Blair's bid was $115,000.00. The auctioneer called for any more bids and not a word from any mill. They just sat there, taking notes, doodling with their pens and paper, or just trying to be inconspicuous. When I realized the mills were not bidding, I said, "Reierson bids $135,000.00." Blair was under the impression that this was a sealed bid so he was not prepared to bid higher. I was awarded the sale. It was another exciting day for me. Now I had quite a challenge.

It was October and I had until March to get this wood out. I planned to reskid all the wood to proper landings in order to manufacture it properly, so I hired my brother and two of his skidders for the job. I realized there would be lots of loader work involved (moving, sorting and loading) so I brought in my two 966 cat loaders, one with a snowplow blade. Since we needed landings and were in a snow belt, I brought in my D8 cat, a machine I had purchased from Finning Tractor the year before. That cat was one of the best purchases I had ever made! The D8 could do pretty much any job. It was equipped with an angle blade and a winch. It was my baby.

We were the only logging show using this road so we had to look after 30 km of snowplowing. Many a night Vicki and I plowed, me on the cat or loader and her with the pickup. We had a plow on the pickup for plowing our own lane at home and it worked fine if the snow wasn't too deep. We had a lot of snow that winter with plenty of cold weather, which was good for this job. As soon as we turned off the main road, there was mud under the snow, because the snow had fallen before full freeze-up. Because of this, any new part of the right-of-way had to be plowed so it could freeze in. I bought a large nylon tent and set it up about half way along the sub-road, so that I could park machines overnight or repair anything, out of the weather. The irony of this sale was that it was nice timber and, before the sale, no mill in Quesnel wanted it, but after I bought it, they all wanted it. I ended up selling to West Fraser.

This was a very busy winter, and fulfilling. I accomplished a great deal in a short time. I don't think anybody realized how important or nice it was to have your main road built to every landing ahead of time. Especially in a soft ground, wet-belt area. Well, it was our gain. My son Blaine, the bucker, wasn't too pleased with all of the mud on his trees. Some of the decks on the bottom side of the road had mud sticking them together and had frozen. In some cases, the mud had flowed into the deck like dirty water, freezing the trees together. We sometimes had three or four trees stuck together. The good news was the majority of the decks were okay.

Altogether, there were 67 decks of logs along 21 km of right-of-way. The loaders, skidders and cat worked seven days a week that winter on that job, and the cat sometimes plowed snow all night. One particular day, I was plowing snow on the right-of-way, ahead of the crew and I stopped for lunch. I backed the cat off the road into the standing timber a ways, to get out of the wind. It was very windy and cold that day. I shut the cat off to enjoy a little peace and quiet. After about 20 minutes, I saw two wolves coming down the unplowed section of the road, about a quarter of a mile away. They trotted effortlessly through the deep snow, sinking down about six inches. When they got close to me, they didn't seem to see me, or look up, or anything. They just, all of a sudden, leaped sideways and dis-appeared into the bush. They didn't wait for anything. I would have thought they would have stopped and looked me over before leaving, but no, they just dashed off without a sound.

The forest officer from Quesnel looking after this job was Paul Tataryn. He was very good to work with. Friendly and obliging, always ready with a suggestion or agreeing with a request. It was a pleasure to have him as our forest officer. He had a lot of common sense and helped to make this job workable. Sometimes forest officers in charge of sales can be dangerous. I mean, whether they help or hinder you. They can hold you up with red tape, permits and verbal okays with no followup or, worse yet, no verbal go-aheads allowed. Each sale was different and a different forest officer oversaw each sale area. When you are on a deadline, a forgotten road permit, an unsent letter to a trapper, a logging plan with one too many landings or a missed detail of another sort, can be a big problem. The forest officer has it in his power to make you wait, or let you start and dot the Is and cross the Ts as you go. Anyway, with Paul Tataryn as our forest officer, we moved along nicely and finished up in plenty of time. The volume was also right on so this turned out to be a very profitable venture.

Speaking of forest officers, I had purchased a small timber sale at Antler Creek, 15 miles east of Wells. I was finishing off another sale at the time, on the other side of Quesnel, and so I sent Blaine and Kelly Vipond, our feller buncher operator, to get started with roads and landings on the new site. We had drawn up the logging plan earlier on and it had been ap-proved. I stopped in at the MOF office a few days later to let them know we were starting work on the sale (notification was a requirement). The forest officer for this sale was Andre Kikkert. I told him our plans and he said, "Oh by the way, I can't okay your startup until you put in a 600m culvert in the creek crossing, at the start of your sale." "Andre," I said, "this is after the fact." "I know," he said, "but I overlooked this. It has to be put in before I can give you the okay." He explained to me carefully again, the reason and importance of the culvert. I was seething inside but I kept my calm and said, "Okay, Andre, I'll personally go out and install this culvert tomorrow and since it's so far out there, could you give me a verbal "Okay" to start up? Later you can come and inspect it at your leisure." He said, "Well, I don't usually do this, but in this case, I will. Okay you can start, and I'll see you out on the job." Boy, I got out of that one! Blaine and Kelly had been there with the cat and buncher for three days. I wondered how they had gotten across the creek. Blaine hadn't said anything about it, and I usually talked to him every evening. I hurried out to the sale to look for myself before buying a culvert, especially one so big. Arriving there two hours later, I drove into the first landing and then the second landing, and there was Blaine and Kelly having lunch. We exchanged greetings, and I said, "Hey guys, looks good. You will be done soon. Two landings built and the road completed." "Yes," Blaine said, "the weather was perfect. Cold enough to freeze everything in nicely." I said, "Good, by the way, how did you cross the creek? And where is it?" Blaine said, "Oh, there was an old creek bed, but it is dry. We just filled it up with snow." There was about two feet of snow covering the area. We went and looked and it was hard to find this creek. If you didn't know where it was, you wouldn't have been able to find it. I told them about Andre's message, and we had trouble figuring that one out. As this was a relatively small sale, we finished it in about one and a half months. Everything went smoothly, we bunched our landings for burning the next fall, and on our way out, I pushed the snow out of this dry creek bed in case of runoff in the spring. Andre and a helper had been out to the bush one cold, windy day, stopped at the landing, rolled their window down, and said, "How are you guys doing?" Of course we said, "Fine, Andre." They drove around some and left. I still can't believe he didn't check for that 600m culvert that just had to be put in.

Shortly after Christmas, I was in the MOF office, to start another sale in the Wells area. Andre was looking after this sale also. He said, "Oh Ed, I have some bad news for you. I'm sorry I didn't make it out to your Antler Creek sale for final inspection." I said, "Oh, it turned out okay, and what is your bad news?" He said, "You know that 600m culvert I had you install out there?" I said, "Yes," and he said, "Well, we have a new policy and you have to remove it before breakup." I said, "What?" and he said, "Yes, I'm afraid you'll have to take it out." I replied, with a long face, "Well, if I have to, I suppose I have to." He helped me out a bit when he said, "Oh well, you can probably use it again." I replied, "Yeah, well okay, Andre, and thanks a lot. We'll see you out in the bush one of these days." "Okay Ed, see you." This was one of those times when something worked out, but it shows you what you're dealing with at times!

Some officers had no bush savvy whatsoever. In their defence, they should not have been given such an important job without the proper background. It was a little better as time went on because finally the MOF created supervisors who could give direction to an officer if he got stuck or didn't know something. With any job, if you expect more from your men than their training allows or if you don't know their capabilities, you will usually be disappointed in their work. With forest officers, the ones that understood logging practices a bit were okay, and the ones that didn't caused the logger grief. You also had personalities involved, and lots of time a sleep-deprived, short-tempered logger was hard pressed to understand some forgotten piece of paperwork, insisted on by the forest officer. And, if you ever got on the wrong side of one of them, they could make your life miserable.

We had another timber sale on the Ernst Road, 12 miles from town. It was a partial blowdown sale. We had paid $32.00/M^3 for this timber and had started in on roads and landings, etc. The forest officer, a young fellow from Salmon Arm, came out and said to Blaine, who was working that sale, "Hey, you have the wrong culvert size in this crossing." Blaine said, "Oh, oh! Okay I'll change it." The forest officer said, "Yes, you will! You are shut down until that happens." Blaine dug out the culvert and replaced it with a different size and went back to work. This fellow wasn't satisfied with anything. He said we were supposed to log the blowdown first, which is what we were doing. We had handfallers go in and cut all the blowdown and leave the standing trees, then the feller buncher came in and bunched the downed trees into piles and also felled whatever standing trees there were in the patch. When the forest officer left the site, he saw all these bunches and shut us down. He came back with his boss, Gary Horley, and the Assistant Manager, Al Moi. I took them into the patch and started to explain that most of these were blowdown trees. Gary Horley said, "No, anybody can see these trees were all standing as they are in bunches." I said, "Hey look at the butts, where they were cut off, these are mostly chainsaw cuts and look here, this is a buncher cut." We had a Roto saw head and it made a rough wide cut. Gary looked me in the eye and said, "That's your story." Al Moi just smiled and said nothing. They said, "You have to clean all the felled timber up before you can go into the standing trees." This is what I had planned anyway. If they had just paid attention to what was going on, all would have been okay. This was my sale and I had paid good money for it. I would be completing it one way or another, but sometimes they, the forest officer in this case, were just impossible to get along with.

We had a steep draw going through the middle of the sale and we requested a road to go through this draw. This forest officer said, "No way! You can haul around by the bridge, the one that is already in. This draw is too deep to build a road through and it has a creek in the bottom." So we had to haul around this draw. It meant two miles of more road and a steep hill that we had to push every load up. When we were about halfway through the sale, Tolko Forest Products (they had bought Ernst Lumber) were going to log a sale behind ours and they had to go through our sale to get to theirs. They asked how we got over that draw? We said, "We don't, we have to go around." They said, "That's ridiculous!" and proceeded to build a road across this draw. Well, it made our job easier, I'll say that.

These loggers for Tolko were very arrogant about their area. We were there first, had fixed up the road, and put our radio frequency on the start of the road as required. One day I drove in and just about ran into one their trucks. As we went by I shook my radio at him to signal that his was not working. He stopped and I went over and said, "Hey Bud, your radio is not working. I heard no miles called." He said, "I called all my miles." I said, "Well I heard nothing, so something is definitely wrong. Let's see if we can figure out the problem as you can't haul until your radio is fixed."

Well, what we discovered was that they had changed the radio frequency on us and were on a different channel. I went to their boss, in the bush, and asked what was going on? He informed me that they always used this channel on the road. I said that that would have been okay, but why had he not notified me. He said he didn't have to, that's why! I said, "Well, you are lucky we haven't had an accident because of that, and from now on we will be going back to our channel, and if you don't like that, you can stay off the road until we are finished this sale! I have a road permit for this road. If you had come to see me, I would have agreed to change channels but after this, no way." When I got to the mouth of our road I saw my radio frequency signs torn off the tree and one of theirs put up. I changed them over again and then phoned the woodlands manager at Tolko and explained the problem. He said, "Don't worry, Ed, I'll get to the bottom of this." Apparently he did because I heard no more about it and we kept our own radio channel. Talk about gall. Some of the quota loggers were that way when a SBEP sale came up in their area. Thank God they weren't all like that. Most of the quota loggers were very helpful and pretty easy to get along with.

Anyway, the next time we had a problem with this forest officer, Blaine told him, in no uncertain terms, to get out of our bush or he'd have to bury him there! I had to do a lot of damage control over that one. I got to be the "man about town" when it came to negotiating or smoothing something over with the MOF. It had taken quite a bit of learning for me to be able to do that.

I realize the MOF needed to police loggers and their practices in relation to the environment and to look after the public's interests. For the most part, they did a good job. I came to believe that some of the forest officers got a lot of grief from some of the major players and took their frustrations out on the littler guy whom they could handle. A lot of rules were set in Victoria and had more to do with other interests than forests or logging.

Some of the people that stand out at the MOF, who were helpful and easy to work with were Edith Fellman, Art Knauf, Paul Tataryn, Dale Bubela, Allen Kohlen, Doug Flintoff, Al Moi, Phil Hunter, Becky Anderson and Bill Rose. Bill was from Williams Lake and is a wonderful fellow. Most of these folk are still living in the area, carrying out their lives. Al Kohlen has retired.

Large spruce tree at a timber sale in Wells, B.C.

Deck of spruce logs

Blaine with 966 cat loader picking up landing, Webster Lake

Load of fir logs heading for the mill, selective logging area

Earl Olsen loaded and ready for town — Abbott Heights

Tree length load, Stephenie Creek going to Dunkley Lumber, 1989

CHAPTER 9

Big Cats, Big Roads, Big Business

I have been logging for a long time and have handled my share of foulups, breakdowns and general mixups. Through it all, however, one of my biggest nightmares is the thought of getting stuck with a cat, especially a big cat like a D8. It is scary because it is almost impossible to find a machine big enough to pull a stuck cat out of wherever it's mired. I once had to haul in a TD25 International to pull me out of a swamp. Another time I had four skidders hooked on to the stuck cat with their winch lines, all pulling on me at the same time. What a picture that would have made with those four skidders all spread out in front of me! Once I started to move they all revved up, smoke pouring out, and all pulling together in a cloud of blue.

The best combination in the bush, in wet country, is a mid-sized cat and a big cat, like a D6 and a D8. The smaller D6 does all the doubtful areas, not caring that much if he gets stuck because the D8 is always there to pull him out. The D8 can then follow along and work the safe places. One important lesson about getting stuck with a big cat is, *don't try to get yourself out!* It's your first inclination and it's a bad idea; you end up going back and forth and, of course, you just get in deeper. If you are working in standing timber, the best thing is to hook your winch line to a tree, drive and winch at the same time. If you're not too far in you can usually get out.

I always like to have an angle blade and a winch for developing (building roads and landings). Some loggers use a cat equipped with a ripper instead of a winch. I always thought that was a poor choice for developing timber sales. If the ground is good, though, a ripper is a good thing. Some guys would use nothing else. I guess I never tried one enough to realize its worth. The saying "what you don't know" comes to mind.

154

Excavators are used a lot for road work but I didn't start using one until quite recently, when I promptly realized this was certainly a better way to go. In building roads, the excavator lets you put stumps and rubble in your wet part and then walk on top, always staying out of the mud. A cat has to get in the mud to push a road together. I like cold weather to work wet ground: whatever you do today freezes tomorrow. If you can find a bank or high ground hump, you can push the dirt from it on top of areas that are wet, covering everything with two or more feet of dirt. It's not good to push trees out in wet ground; it's better to fall them, cutting the stumps as low as possible, and then cover the stumps over with fill. When it freezes it makes an excellent base. When I encounter a creek, I build the road right to the edge of the creek, wait until the next day and lay the culvert in (sometimes it's necessary to slash out the creek by hand) and then push new fill over the culvert. If, while you do this, your cat isn't on a firm or dry base, you can break through the crust and then you are in trouble. This method is strictly for winter roads and would not be conducive for summer use. All-weather roads require a different approach. Most of my roads were temporary ones, as these SBEP sales needed a one-time-only road.

I have always been stuck on getting things done. Set a deadline on a timber sale or a logging job and I'll move heaven and earth to get finished on time. If cold weather hits, I'll get a generator to heat any machines with plug-in heaters, and leave the ones without running all night (if you shut a machine off overnight in -40 degree weather it will not start without help). If more snow comes than expected, I bring in another big cat for trails and snow plowing. If you have a sale to finish in deep snow, it's possible to keep logging by making trails in the snow with a D8, for example, close enough together to be able to fall the trees on the trails, then skid them to a landing. I have done this in up to eight feet of snow. Once the trails are made and kept open, you can carry on. If you began from scratch with a January start up, with that much snow, if would be difficult. You need to start in November and get your roads and landings built, your trails in and then frozen in, and then carry on. If it looks like there is more timber left than anticipated around February, then you bring in more machines, either by hiring or renting,or if those two options are unavailable, by buying. Anything to get the job done. When conditions get tough I get my back up and keep going.

One time on a timber sale we had trouble getting anything frozen in, as there was no cold weather. Mother Nature just wouldn't cooperate. Rain in mid-winter creates mud. We had finished three landings out of nine, but the rest didn't have enough ground to be able to work in wet weather. I made the decision to try and corduroy the remaining landings. We skidded trees, end to end and touching each other, and then covered each landing. I drove around on the surface with my D8 until the trees levelled. We then found some dry dirt from a pit (dug from a bank) and covered the logs with a thin skim of dirt, smoothed over by the cat, loaders and skidders. We ran every machine we had around on these newly covered landings in order to pack them down. Each landing took around 150 trees but they lasted the rest of the winter. With a base this solid it only took a few degrees of frost to tighten them up. We had extra skidders to pull and push the trucks so they could keep hauling. These landings are still there. It is not a method the MOF likes these days but these were built long before the procedure was frowned upon.

Another time, working on Dunkley's tree farm, we were brought in to help finish a large sale as the company loggers were behind due to wet weather and deep snow. We were assigned four tough landings in mid-winter. We moved in our extra equipment as we were also logging our regular block. What equipment I didn't have, I rented from Finning Tractor. Realizing we would have trouble finishing before breakup, I put on a night shift skidding, and worked day shift seven days a week from daylight until dark. Whenever I had a tough sale as well as our regular sale, I would use Blaine and myself (and it usually took both of us alternating between day shift and night shift) to keep things going. Many a cold night I stayed in the bush plowing snow and keeping machines running, only to have to work days when we would be somebody short. It's a good thing breakup came around March 15th, as everybody's nerves were starting to wear thin and everyone was pretty tired. Family lives went short in winter for everybody on these logging jobs. I've often wished we could have worked the whole year on a regular shift rather than the hectic winter pace and then three months off during breakup. Myself at breakup, I would schedule repairs, new purchases, acquiring new timber sales and/or property with timber, and generally doing the stuff to get ready for another year. It's a good thing my hobby was walking through timber looking at property, as this was pretty much what I did on my time off.

I was building skid trails on a SBEP sale at Slender Lake. This sale required a partial cable operation because one portion was very steep. I was at the top boundary building a trail down, keeping it to a grade we could manage with skidders. I was working an area that had already been logged. It was covered with roughly four feet of snow. The idea was to take a small amount of dirt from the high side, mix it with snow and make a base hard enough to support the machine. It takes patience and care to work this snow and dirt into a solid base, being very careful not to get too far ahead of yourself. This particular time, I ran into a piece of rock and I had a hard time finding any dirt to mix with the snow. On a steep slope you need dirt and rubble to mix for a base; just snow is not enough. I had gotten too far ahead of myself and I slid off the rock and down the bank. I managed to get the cat straightened out and headed downhill. I eased it up on a couple of stumps until it was fairly level. I took out my lunch and thermos and decided to eat while taking stock of the situation. The hill I was sitting on went pretty well straight down for about 200 feet and then slowly levelled out. I had no way back up to my trail and had nothing big enough to pull me back up. My only way out was to go straight down. I didn't know if I was brave enough for that. I was feeling very anxious at this time. If I hit a stump on the way down and turned sideways, I would surely roll over and if I kept my blade up there was no way to slow down. I agonized over what to do as I ate my lunch. I looked down on the camp in the valley bottom far below. This was the weekend and I was the only one in the bush. Vicki was in the camp and Steve and Brian were slashing in the bottom. I finally decided I had only one choice and that was to go down the hill, head first. I had heard from some other cat drivers that if the hill was too steep to go forward, then you should back down. I was never comfortable going backwards and could not see the benefit of this method. I manoeuvered off the stump I had put my front end on and lifted my blade as high as it would go and started down with my heart in my throat. The cat started to slide and I couldn't keep my feet off the brakes. Soon the tracks were stopped and the cat and I were freefalling down the hill. I couldn't see much as snow was flying all around. I prayed and hung on to my levers for dear life as we careened down the slope, finally slowing down as the slope lessened. I then had to keep the cat moving through the deep snow, as I didn't want to get stuck. Finally I broke out on the main haul road far below. I thanked my lucky stars that I had made it. Now I had to travel about a mile and a half around to get back on the trail I had been working on. I certainly would take it slow and careful from now on. I always seemed to say, after the fact, "Boy, I won't do that again," and before I'd know it, I'd be right back at it.

Any time we had a main road that gave us problems, we would use corduroying, sometimes doing up to 3 km. of road. This corduroy works wonders with culverts. You put your culvert in and then about 100 feet of corduroy on both sides of it. This way, you have no mud problems on top of the culvert. Sometimes this was the only way to be able to keep hauling. In summer you looked for good ground to make landings for wet weather but you couldn't always put your roads in good ground. You had to go pretty much from A to B, sometimes through swampy ground and over creeks. There were times when things looked pretty much impossible, but if you looked at it from two or three different angles, you could usually find a way

Sometimes the MOF was your biggest problem. Deadlines or steady production didn't mean much to them. If you were having problems in mud or deep snow and going broke, they seemed happy. It's like (subconsciously maybe) the MOF, the big mills and others expected the small operator to go broke and so didn't help, and maybe even unconsciously worked toward accomplishing that very thing. The MOF shut you down if your camp was in the wrong spot, your landing was too close to a creek or too close to a bank, if your road was too muddy. The mills gave you the poorest timber and kept the rates low and, generally, just put up roadblocks. So much of it was unnecessary. One time working on a SBEP sale at a place called Stephanie Creek, 50 miles east of Quesnel in the Prince George forest district, the conditions were 60% high lead (cable logging), and 40% conventional logging. One day the MOF forest officer came out and said, "Okay guys, you have your 40% conventional logged; the rest will have to be logged with cable." I explained that as we had our tower set up and had been logging both conventional and cable, it would be impossible to determine how much of each was done. He took out his map and made some calculations and stated, "You are to cable log everything that is left and that is that! And I will be coming back to see that it is done." This was in September and on a Thursday with Labour Day weekend coming up, making it a long weekend. I moved in two extra skidders and put all our skidding machines, including cats, skidding. I assigned a faller to each machine and we started logging this cable ground on Friday morning, knowing that the MOF would not be out on a Friday before a long weekend. We worked everybody we had Friday, Saturday, Sunday and Monday, finishing up on Tuesday, knowing the MOF would not be out on Tuesday after the long weekend. They would usually do office work on Tuesday or take a sick leave day. By Tuesday night we had pretty well finished all our so-called cable ground. This was accomplished without making trails (the ground in question was not very steep) and without causing very many ground disturbances. I went around with my cat and smoothed off any ruts or rough ground after logging. I had taken matters into my own hands and did what had to be done to get the job done.

Three MOF officials came out, including our forest officer, the next week and commented on our good job of cable logging. One guy said, "Boy that sure didn't take you guys long." Of course nobody clued in about our finishing by conventional methods. If anybody from the MOF had come out on the weekend and seen our five machines skidding on cable ground, we would all have been locked up. My point here is that no matter whether it makes sense or not, the MOF will stick to their guns, not caring that it might create a hardship on a small operator or put them under. In this instance our forest officer tried to make this job impossible. Why some of them used little or no common sense is beyond me. Rather than trying to work out a workable plan, they would stick to the book. I think in some cases it was a power trip. The little guy could be pushed around. Any time this was tried with a big operator such as the mill loggers, the mill would step in and, if warranted, go over the forest officer's head. The officer's superior would tell him to back off. In my 15-year involvement with the SBEP I witnessed a two-tier logging system: one set of rules for the small guy and one set of rules for the big guy.

One winter we were logging in a snow belt area and the snow started getting deep. I went to the MOF and asked if they could clarify the stump height for us. I was told by my forest officer on that sale, Arthur Knauf (a good, sensible guy and a friend), that for this winter, due to heavy snow the stump height would be the snow line, for everybody, mills included. That means the trees could be cut off at the snow depth. Say there were four feet of snow, the stump would be four feet. This is what I instructed my fallers to do and the following summer, Al Moi from the MOF called me in and said to me, "Ed, we have a problem out at Stanley." I asked what the problem was and he said, "High stumps." I explained our problem and told him I had come in and discussed it with Art. He showed me the tender package for that sale which he had underlined in yellow marker, the part that said "stumps must be cut at 30 centimetres." I said, "Oh, come on Al, this would not be fair." He said, "Well this is what the contract reads and I'm going to stick to it." I said, "What about my conversation with Art, and his approving snow line falling?" "Do you have it in writing?" he asked. Of course I didn't and so the MOF took scalers out to the sale and had them scale all the stumps that were over 30 cm. high, which I might add was pretty well all of them. They then slapped me with a waste bill, which can be as high as one and a half times the stumpage. In this case, it worked out to be in excess of $30,000.00. Blaine and I spent a week that summer taking pictures of other companies' stumps in that same area. Both West Fraser and Weldwood had been in there at the same time as we were. Weldwood was the worst with some stumps as high as 15 feet, where the buncher had reached from the bottom side of the trail to cut the trees. Most of the stumps on both these operations were as bad or worse than mine. Also, their sales had lots of good wood left on the ground, and on Weldwood's sale, they had left pretty much all the balsam standing, to be slashed and burned. Their landings had at least 20% good, merchantable wood on them. These unwanted, standing trees that were left would have been assessed as waste on a SBEP sale and the owner would not have been able to get another sale, ever.

We documented this and took the pictures to the MOF. We were told they would certainly look into the matter. I figured this discovery would surely negate my fine or at least make everybody play by the same rules. But nothing was done. The explanation given was that the major licensees looked after their own logging and they would assess the situation themselves, and do the appropriate thing. As if they would fine themselves! When I checked on the West Fraser and Weldwood sites later, both companies had slashed and burned, including the good trees, and had left lots of unskidded good trees and more good wood was left on the landings. I went to see Al Moi about this and he just smiled at me and said, "Don't worry, Ed, this is being looked into." I then asked for my pictures back and he said, "I'll get them for you, they are around here somewhere." Naturally they did not turn up. You had to either give up and get out of this situation or put it out of your mind and carry on. This is what I did. I tried to put it out of my mind and keep going, but looking back, I feel as frustrated now as I did then.

In my years of involvement in the SBEP many good, young operators went broke and had to quit. Sometimes because of inexperience but lots of times because of these unfair situations. There were a number of things the MOF did to help these loggers go broke. If a sale wasn't finished by dead-line date, it could be cancelled and the deposit forfeited. If the sale bid turned out to be too high for current market conditions, no extensions would be granted. If it got too wet, the MOF would or could shut them down. If any trespass happened, they would be shut down, fined and in some cases, jailed. Yes, jailed! Some small operators could be and were jailed for offenses that happened all the time with the big licensees, with no penalties for the big guns. Colleagues of mine went to jail for trespass-ing in some beetle wood that needed to be logged, and was logged later on by a big company, and for no stumpage at all. Sometimes the small inde-pendent failed no matter what . . . whether because of inexperience, poor management or lack of capital. But, for the most part, the 25 or so SBEP operators were pretty enterprising guys and most went on to make an okay living. Some were successful, if you can call being a logger successful.

One year we had a beetle epidemic in the west of Quesnel. In order to clean up this problem, the MOF increased the A.A.C. (Annual Allowable Cut) in this area and gave extra wood to the majors (major licensees) and also some extra wood to the SBEP. The majors with this extra wood needed to hire extra loggers. I took a contract with Weiers Sawmills to log their extra cut of 75,000 M³ per year for five years and other loggers were hired for the other mills. Most of these loggers were the SBEP operators, and the mills got together and decided to pay their new loggers a rate of $8.50/M³. A regular rate for the majors at that time was $11.50/M³. When I complained to my new woodland manager for Weiers, Al Whitmore, I was told, "Oh don't worry, Ed, this is just temporary. We will make it up to you next year. The regular rate we will pay will be $10.50/ M³ and we will make it retroactive back to when you start." I took this in good faith and the following year I went to the mill only to discover they had changed woodlands managers. Graham Long was the new man in charge. I explained my situation to him and asked for this back pay and a new rate. He looked at me, smiled and said, and I quote, "What do you think I am, a cabbage head? You get nothing." I wasn't long in stopping my company logging career. There was never any money paid to me in this case. I don't think the rest of these extra loggers received any money either, although I had heard Weldwood paid their logger, Tom Sword, $11.15/ M³ for logging this beetle wood.

The guys that worked for these mills as logging superintendents were for the most part good guys. One fellow, who was my company foreman, was on our case, or maybe just trying to be important. One morning he drove up to our landing, jumped out of his truck and ran over to the deck of logs. He marked "cull" on about 10 butts then jumped back in his truck and drove off. Blaine was looking after the bucking at that time. He came and got me, and we went to look this over. We had bought a feller buncher with a fast saw head, and it made the butts look different. This foreman had not looked close enough to see if the butts he had marked were rotten or not, he just saw something different. I decided to teach him a lesson. I cut two inch wheels off these butts marked with his "X"s, drove 60 miles to the mill, piled them on the woodland manager's desk, and said, "This is your foreman's work and would you please straighten him out as I can't." These wheels I brought in were all sound wood.

Another time the same foreman came to the bush one morning, stating he was going to time the truck cycles in order to set the rate for Reierson trucks. He always talked too much on the radio and we all knew before he got there what was happening. He waited until two of our trucks left the landing loaded and started out ahead of them so it wouldn't be too obvious. Partway out one of the company loggers called him and asked to see him. He asked them to switch to their company radio channel and then told this logger he would come and see him but he was timing trucks and didn't want us to know so he wouldn't be able to stay long. Of course we had switched channels too and heard all this. My two truckers stopped along the road and waited until they heard him on the radio coming back.

They then leisurely carried on some three quarters of an hour later. He didn't seem to catch on because later on he told my trucks he knew how long it took them to make a trip. He started to pick on one of my truckers, Earl Olsen. Earl was the wrong guy for him to pick on. One day he came up to Earl and said, "You will be hauling in #3 position tomorrow." Earl was usually in #1 spot. Earl said, "I don't think so." The foreman said, "Yes you will, you are working for me now." "I don't think so," smiled Earl, "if I am working for you then you can take your job and shove it!" The poor guy didn't know what to do as Earl stood right up to him. Earl just moved to our small business side and kept on hauling. We were all happy when we got out of the situation with this company.

This small sawmill was having management problems. The owner, Herb Weier, had moved to a healthier climate and had difficulty running his company from away. A company that is struggling should have careful "hands on" management. (Actually, all companies are better for that approach all the time.) When I worked for this company, I observed one thing that was significant: their mill yard was full of poor-quality logs. Dunkley Sawmill was about the same size as this other company and their yard was full of good-quality logs. Poor-quality logs means poor quality lumber, and it seemed to me, management was responsible. Poor-quality logs were cheaper to buy all right, but sometimes cheaper is not better. This mill had to purchase a large part of their logs privately as their quota was too small. Also, their regular logger was not closely supervised and would deliver poor-quality logs. It all summed up disaster. Weier's sawmill was purchased shortly after my stint with them by Quesnel Forest Products, for a rumored $11,000,000.00. The mill was adjacent to Quesnel Forest Products and, though little was changed, it thrived under the new management.

One payroll day my accountant, Paul Westwell, who at the time worked for Rigsby Lea Barr & Co., said to me, "Ed, I got a call from your bank to give you a message that they want to see you." I said, "Okay," and later on that day went to the bank. This was in the early 1980s when things were tight (when aren't they for loggers?) at the banks because of poor deals they were making at the time. (I remember hearing of a Canadian bank that loaned 70 million dollars to Mexico and Mexico said, "Sorry, we can't pay you back." The bank had to eat this loss.) Anyway the banks had sent in men from outside to tighten up lending policies and were making it even tougher on the little guy. This particular fellow was from Toronto. He introduced himself and explained the reasons the bank had brought him in. He was sort of a troubleshooter kind of guy. I said, "Okay, yeah, we do that too." He fidgeted around awhile and then finally said, "Mr. Reierson I have something rather unpleasant to say to you and I don't know how to begin." I replied, "Well, I have this friend, Dave Vosper, who is manager at Finning Tractor, and he says anytime you have something to say, you just blurt it out," and I smiled at him. He looked at me as if to say "this is serious stuff and I don't see anything funny." I just stared at him. He finally said, "Well it's about your bookkeeping and paper work. I have been looking over your file and some of the forms that you have filled out are incorrect or not filled out at all, and these loan application wordings — what does 'approximate standing timber value' mean? And Finning — 'approximate mean equipment value'? Everything is very disorderly. And what are all these cheques written out, marked 'cash' for? Anyway Mr. Reierson," getting warmed up to the subject, "your bookkeeping is atrocious! Do you have an explanation?" I said, "Well, you are not telling me anything I don't know. It is terrible isn't it? You see this is why I have Rigsby Lea hired, to look after my books. You may as well know, I am not good at money management either, and that's why I have the bank look after that end of it. My legal knowledge is not that good, so I have a lawyer hired to look after that end. No, I'm a logger and that is what I'm good at, so that is what I try to do." This poor guy didn't know what to say. Being a city banker from Toronto he was not used to Cariboo loggers and their philosophies, mine at any rate. He said, after he'd had a chance to compose himself, "I'll be reviewing your account and you will probably be hearing from me."

He was right, bookkeeping was not one of my better subjects. If it got too complicated I would shy away from it. I knew the simple things. If I bought a property for $100,000.00, logged it carefully, then resold it and the timber and land had brought in $100,000.00, employed some men and paid all expenses, I was making money. If I bought property for $100,000.00, logged and resold it for $75,000.00 I would not be making money. I always used round numbers; it didn't have to be exact. Some years if there wasn't much left at the end of the year, you just had to try harder. Getting back to the banks, it always amazed me that they wanted $500,000.00 worth of security for a $100,000.00 loan. They mostly treated you like an enemy rather than somebody who paid their wages, in a roundabout way.

One time I bought a new piece of equipment from Finning Tractor and I asked my accountant, Paul, to figure out the best way to finance it. After a few days he said, "Ed, the bank has a lease policy that seems the best. They buy the machine from Finning Tractor and lease it back to you." I said, "Okay," and he set it up. After a month, we finalized this deal and I paid lease payments to the bank. After a year, we realized this machine was not for us. We took it back to Finning Tractor. They had a man in Mackenzie who needed it right now, and they shipped it out to him as a rental purchase. In order to rental purchase to him, they had to own it, so they gave me a cheque thinking I was the owner. The cheque was in excess of $300,000.00. I deposited it in my bank and waited to see what would happen. When Finning went to register it, they found out the bank owned it. They talked to the bank and explained that they needed some papers signed. The bank asked Finning to come in and pay them out first, and Finning said, sheepishly, "We have already paid Ed for it." "You what!" said the bank, and Finning said, "Yes, we just assumed that Ed owned it." The bank of course panicked, contacted me and asked for an explanation. I hammed it up, saying, "Well, you know, it's just one of those deals. You win some and you lose some." I let them stew for a few days, then said, "Just kidding!" and paid them out. I never tried to see what the legal implications were but I think, if the truth were known, the bank would have been out this money. It was nice to know they don't always have the upper hand. This was fun for me.

Digging out the hitch on the 966 loader

Moving fuel tank

Truck on its side

Spilled load of logs

CHAPTER 10

Chainsaws and Other Useful Things

*A*s far back as I can remember I have been fascinated by chainsaws. When I first started working in the bush, most loggers were using hand, crosscut saws. My brother and I had bucked eight foot ties for Dad with a thin bladed swede saw. Before that, when we were five and seven years old, he had made each of us a small bucksaw to cut fire wood with. The first chainsaw I saw was when I started working in the tie mill at Ewings Landing. It was a two-man McCulloch. A two-man saw has two handles on the engine end (like a garden rotovator), one of which has the gas feed. The operator controls the sawing from this end. On the other end of a long bar is another handle, a handle through which the chain runs. The handle is far enough out to allow a helper to guide the chain into the tree. The two-man saws could really cut when you got them going and they were very heavy. I was paired with another guy and I got to hold the handle end of the bar. It was a real shock to discover that the only way to turn the saw off was to grab the spark plug . . . and then to learn that that was the "line" the new guy was always fed. The fellows at Ewings had a good laugh at my naiveté. There was, actually, a ground wire to short the saw out and shut it off.

The first chainsaw I ever owned was an I.E.L. swivel bar that I traded a 303 Enfield rifle for. The guy I traded with knew it didn't run but didn't tell me. He gave me a story about it needing a carb kit and a new plug before it would run. As it happened, the main bearing was shot but I was too inexperienced to tell. I never did get this saw running. Any place that I worked at that had a chainsaw, I was the guy nagging to run it. Once I got permission, I kept at it every chance I got; falling, bucking, and trying different things until I became quite proficient with it. I would practise falling trees and making different cuts. By the time I was 18 years old I could pretty well tear apart any chainsaw made and fix it. I could make them all run: I became good at chain care, and I could file a chain to make it cut smooth.

Pretty soon, using a chainsaw, I could fall trees with the best of them. I would make a game of it. I would fall trees against the lean, swing them around corners, hit imaginary targets, practise different stump cuts, run the saw left handed, run it with one hand limbing and topping. I tried just about everything with a saw. I could adjust the timing on a saw so you could shut the ignition switch off, and when the motor just about quit, turn it on again, causing the chain to run backwards. This worked well for any cuts that had dirt on them. You could cut the dirt off with the backwards running chain and not dull your teeth. A flip of the switch and the motor would be running right again.

My brother and I would enter chainsaw contests at Loggers' Sports Days. These events were especially popular in the 1950s. This one sports day, in Enderby, we entered the Open Sawing, where anything goes - you could use any saw you had. We had a big one man McCulloch. A gear drive, model 73, equipped with a 30-inch bar and chain on it. The teeth were filed from the back until only the front of the tooth was left. It would have been dangerous for ordinary use but for a few cuts at a contest it was okay. Anyway, doing this gave us as much kerf (width) as was possible. We cut the depth gauges down to 50 thousands and we had a mean cutting saw. The open category meant making one down cut and one up cut in a 25-inch white pine, set up on skids. We pretty much won every category that day. What a rush it was. Engine tuning and chain filing was important but technique was a big thing as well.

In the '50s and '60s the chainsaw companies had travelling representatives advertising their brand of saw. The main ones were McCulloch, Pioneer (I.E.L.), Homelite and, later, Stihl. These reps could handle saws. One time some fallers were giving this rep a bad time, ribbing him about being a salesman and not a saw man. He challenged their best man to a cutting contest using the same saw. They laughed and said, sure let's go! They found a two-foot log out back of the saw shop and one of the fallers grabbed his saw and said, "Okay, time me." He got it running and waited above the cut for the signal. As the timer's hand came down he started cutting fast and confidently, after all, he had years of practice and knew he could do it well. These private contests were usually just one down cut, slicing in anyway you saw fit. He finished with a flourish, shut off his saw and said to the rep, "Beat that!" The rep grabbed the saw, started it, held it about three feet above the log and kept the engine wide open. As the timer's hand came down, the rep slammed the saw into the log in one fast downward motion and did the sawdust fly. He beat this experienced faller by a good margin. This method is hard on both saw and man, and sometimes the chain will break or the saw will stall, but the guy proved his point. You didn't have to be a logger to be good with a chainsaw. I used to have a standing joke with these different reps - if they could beat me doing one cut, I would buy their brand of chainsaw. I ran McCulloch at this time.

McCulloch were probably the best saw out at that time. A bit finicky, but if you could keep them tuned, they were good. A nicely balanced chainsaw. One day a new saw came into play called Stihl, a German saw. It was supposed to be good. The Stihl rep brought one of these saws out to the Pondosa Pine, where I worked as a faller at the time. Pondosa Pine had eight fallers in the bush at this time and it would be a feather in the Stihl rep's cap if he could get an in. Pondosa Pine was known as one of the better outfits in the area. If you worked for the "Pond," you were pretty well set. This rep showed up in the bush at noon one day, and of course I mouthed off and gave my usual spiel. "Hey, I'll buy your saw if you can beat me cutting one cut in a two-foot log." He was nice about it and said he didn't really want to take advantage of me and why didn't I take his saw, use a tank of gas up and see what I thought. I said, "No way, unless it can cut faster than mine, I am not interested." He was giving me a way out but I failed to see it. He said, "Okay, but will you buy it if I beat you?" "Yes, of course," I bragged, in front of my friends. He even gave me a further chance to save face by suggesting I cut one cut with my saw and then one with his saw, and time each cut. I would have none of it and insisted he would have to cut with his own saw himself. He agreed, we found a log and I made my cut confidently and with many exaggerated moves. I set my saw down and said, "It's all yours." His saw seemed quite awkward compared to the McCulloch, but he started it with a little flip of the starter cord and it idled quietly. It had a muffled, hollow sound, different from our Macs. On our McCulloch we would remove the baffle plate from the muffler, to get a bit more power, and it had a powerful cracking sound. He walked over to the log and, without any effort, made his cut. We compared the time and I said, "Hey, there must be some mistake here." He had beaten me easily without even half trying. I tried again and again, using every trick I knew, but I could not cut faster than this nicely dressed rep with his Stihl chainsaw. He then said, "Take it out and try falling with it." I did this and, although it seemed a bit awkward compared to what I was used to, it cut rings around my McCulloch.

I hated to admit it but I came back and said, "You certainly won fair and square. This saw is a cutting fool. I will buy one!" and I did. I have owned Stihls ever since, to this very day, some 40 years later. I bought my first Stihl in 1960. It was called a "lightning" and the McCulloch I used at that time was a "'Super 44A." My friend, Art Smith, and my brother Roy used to tease me about my new unbalanced saw. They would say, Ed has to fall two trees together so he can walk down one to limb the other. The bar on the Stihl saw was built on the side of the motor, which meant you could fall a tree at ground level (a European thing). It made the saw seem a bit unbalanced. The Mac, on the other hand, was better balanced because the bar was attached to the middle of the saw. I took this ribbing with a smile, knowing my new saw didn't need the constant tuning the Macs did, and knowing, too, that it would cut a lot faster. This was the first saw I used that forced you to slow down as you came to the end of your falling cut or you would cut the tree right off. It took a while to get the feel of the new saw, but pretty soon I was handling it with confidence.

I was always trying to get my falling work done faster each day. I would set a goal for the day (a certain number of trees) and then I would work like crazy to reach this goal in the shortest time possible. I always liked to work contract price - that way I got paid by the tree. I would challenge myself to fall one tree and, as it was being finished, I would look to another tree close to me. If I spotted a suitable candidate, when my tree was cut up and starting to fall, I would jerk my saw out and run to the next tree and start cutting, trying to get this tree down before the first tree fell. And so-on and so-on and so-on. Sometimes I would have two or three trees on the go at the same time. It was exciting and dangerous falling. One time, with a helper carrying gas and oil, I dropped 285 trees in four and a half hours. Just dumping them, no limbing or topping. I don't do any of this anymore and I don't recommend it. Young and foolish isn't always best.

I did, very early on, plan my jobs. I'd plan what I wanted to get done in a day and then go for it with gusto. I wonder if this trait started when Dad would tell Roy and me, when we were doing our weekend chores, that we could go off and play but not until we'd finished all our work. If we were digging post holes, he would give us a number; if it was fire wood, he would make a mark between two trees and when we reached the mark we were done. Anyway, I still work this way today. I think I would go crazy if I had to work in a plant where you never got finished. A different kind of work to be sure and I suppose, if I had to, I could get used to it.

◆ ◆ ◆

The person who invented the chainsaw sure made my work easier. As far back as I can remember I was always thinking about easier ways to do things, or different ways, whether it was piling wood or sawing wood with a buck saw, way back when I was small or later on when I was older. Being lazy helps I think, or what is called lazy. I'd like to think another word for lazy is innovative. My inventions always came about because I needed another way of doing something.

I designed and built a stump splitter for a land-clearing cat I owned. This cat was a TD20 and was a little small for the job. I needed something to help with the bigger, more stubborn stumps. This splitter was built to attach to the drawbar in back and was held in place with the winch line. When not in use, it was drawn up into the winch drum, and when the winch brake was set, it stayed out of the way until you needed it. It was 10 feet long, the body one-foot square with the splitting end tapered back from centre, creating a long wedge-like shape. The point was sharp and when it was pushed into a stump it would split it. A big stump could be split into four pieces. It did this job pretty well, and once the stump was split, it was easy to dig out of the ground. It also made piling and burning easier because you didn't have to deal with a mud ball at the bottom of the stump. The only down side to this splitter was its position: because it was on the back of the cat you had to turn and look behind you, and that's hard on the neck. Looking back while working levers is harder than looking forward and doing the same. I gave some thought to figuring out how to attach my stump splitter to the front of the cat but I could only think of a way to do it using a different blade. To change the blade each time you wanted to split a stump wasn't practical. When I got a larger D8 for clearing land, the splitter was no longer necessary; the D8 could split stumps with the piling blade teeth. It always amazed me how strong these teeth were. They were long and slim and, you'd think, easily bent or broken; but you could push and lift with all you had and they'd take it! Nothing damaged them. It was always hard for me to understand the different strengths of steel. To me steel was steel.

Another time I thought I had invented a tree cutter with an accumulator attachment. This contraption had long scissor like blades with teeth cut in it, much like a hand saw. These blades were held together by a big spring and had a "V" shaped front that would allow the blades to open as you moved into the tree. The pressure on each side of the blades from the spring would cause the blades to cut into the tree. After the tree was cut it would remain standing in a gate-like system while you backed up to where you wanted it to fall. You'd then lift the blade of the cat, which had this cutter attached, and the tree would overbalance and fall. This thing worked well in a controlled area but not in the bush. Uneven ground, cut stumps, bucked branches, anything that was in the way of the cat that would cause it to change angle in mid-cut would cause problems. I ended up leaving the thing somewhere in the Nazko area. To make it really work I needed the means and the time to do a bunch of cut and weld work; without that it got to be a headache. It didn't help much to have my brother running our new 227 cat feller buncher alongside of me.

One invention that didn't get past the drawing board was an attempt to make spring-loaded grousers for cat pads. If it had worked, when the track was on a hard surface of rock, the grousers would have retracted and made a smoother ride, and yet retain some bite on slippery surfaces. Too bad. It was a good thought because if a cat with solid grousers travels over a hard or frozen road, it is very rough.

An idea I wanted to try but didn't get around to was to put another set of wheels on the blade of a skidder, the same width as the outside of the blade. These wheels would be lifted up when not in use and pushed down for skidding. It would be useful primarily for downhill skidding on steep slopes where you could push down on your blade wheels and level out your machine a bit. It would be virtually impossible to tip it over, also you would have six wheels for braking power. An idea, but never used.

Another time I planned a way to build a road along a steep sidehill without making a cut in the ground. I planned to cut a right-of-way through the timber and leave the stumps on the low side (high up) and put logs on them in a long line, making a grade up the hill. I could then put 12-foot logs on top of that runner, in corduroy fashion, stretching from the runner to the bank, keeping it level as I went. You'd need a machine like an excavator moving along as you were building. When the road was finished, I figured you could haul your timber out and then dismantle the road . . . and you wouldn't be able to see where you'd gone! Seemed like a good method for areas along creeks or other sensitive places where conventional roads would not work. It would be something like the old wooden oxen roads built years ago. Sometimes we get ahead of ourselves and forget some of these older methods. My philosophy has always been "whatever it takes to get the job done."

As Pan Phillips, who ranched in the Chilcotin years ago, once said to his partner, Rich Hobson, "Rich you can do anything you set your mind to. All it takes is one man and a brain." I think about this whenever I am by myself and some difficulty arises. It will surprise you what you can do when you stop and think about it. I say to myself, I wonder what Pan would do? Some method usually presents itself.

Bucking fir with two-man crosscut saw, 1950   BC ARCHIVES PHOTO: F-08954

'73 McCulloch "contest saw," 1958

Two-man McCulloch saw, 1952

Original two-man saw demonstration   BC ARCHIVES PHOTO: NA-07137

Popular 430 McCulloch, 1956

"Lightening" Stihl, 1960

176 McCulloch chainsaw, 1965

Author bucking logs with Stihl chainsaw, 1972

Brother Roy's chainsaw collection

CHAPTER 11

A Big Leap of Faith (and Fear)

I was buying private timber wherever I could get it. I preferred to buy the land and timber, but that was not always possible. I bought one nice piece of property on the West Fraser road, known as the "Hill Place." It was 240 acres with a mile of Fraser River frontage, and had Narcosli Creek running through it. A pioneer family, the Hills, had owned it for years. I saw the ad in the *Observer* and phoned the current owner, Brian Upton. We met at the place and took a nice walk around. I had been aware of the property for years and had always been partial to it. I didn't need to see much of it because I knew I liked it. Brian said he wanted $110,000.00, and I asked him if he had anybody else interested. He said, "No, not really," so I said, "Okay, I'll take it," and I offered him full price. I gave him a deposit right there and suggested he come in to see my lawyer, Gary Quinn, the next day. He said, "Okay," and we shook hands. It was a deal.

This was a one-of-a-kind property, only 12 miles from town but with all the privacy of the country, and a nice creek and the river too. It was about as good as it gets. I estimated about 125 loads of timber on it. I moved my logging outfit in right away, but after putting in some roads and seeing the beauty of the place, I didn't have the heart to log it. I shut my crew down, much to their dismay. When we first moved the feller buncher in, Blaine said to the buncherman jokingly, "Hey, Kelly, move down to the creek first and get it cut before the Chief gets here with his ribbons." I would ribbon out any area I didn't want logged, usually creeks, draws, wildlife shelters, windbreaks, etc., on most private property that I bought. My crew would groan whenever I came around with my ribbons.

We called the property by its old name, the "Hill Place." Somebody had told the man who owned the adjoining property, Remo Lepetich, that Ed was his new neighbour. Apparently, Remo commented, "I don't know why Ed would buy that property as it only has 37 loads of timber on it." I know where this figure came from because, when Brian Upton had owned the land, he'd had Mike Sarabyn, a private wood buyer from Weldwood, come and cruise it. Apparently Mike wasn't impressed with the small wood and just gave it a lick and a promise. Brian told me he just made a small circle on the top side of the property and said the timber on the bottom was too small anyway, and he could probably get 37 loads from it. The advertisement in the *Cariboo Observer* even said "240 acres for sale with 37 loads of timber." I found it hard to figure that one out. What Mike was figuring I don't know. You wouldn't have thought he'd be that careless. We had logged only 40 acres on the top side and had taken off 45 loads! The bottom 200 acres would easily have had an excess of 100 loads, even by careful, selective logging. But I decided to leave the bottom alone until I had time to do some planning.

While looking at a 160-acre parcel on the Ernst Road, above Quesnel, I was having trouble with one boundary, so I phoned the real estate listing agent, Ivan Malinosky, whom I had known for a long time. He answered my questions and said the Lands Department were doing some survey work up in that area and were building some roads. That was why the boundary looked different. I thanked him and found my problem easy to solve. After looking this property over and making a note of it, I drove around until I found this new road B.C. Lands had built. It was a nice job of roadbuilding, culverts and ditches, the right-of-way cleared, and the stumps and brush buried. I wondered what was going on, as I found survey ribbon and corner pins all along this road. I thought I might as well phone them and find out. I called B.C. Lands in Williams Lake, right from there in my truck, and talked to one of the Lands people who was looking after this project. I was told they were putting up six parcels of land, approximately 200 acres each, for public auction, in about a month. They were still cruising timber and finishing up some paperwork. They said if I was interested to come down and they would give me the package on it, which would be ready in a few days. I was told that this land was being sold at public auction as so many people had expressed an interest in it. Timber and land, I thought, hey right up my alley.

These parcels all joined and this land was on a flat above Quesnel, five miles from town, and covered in timber. I drove along the new road, looking at soil types in the ditches and timber types along the tree line, where there was water, etc. In a few days the package on this project was ready and I drove to Williams Lake to pick one up, and discuss it with them. It was a thick package, outlining the plan for these properties. These six parcels were to be sold as Crown land Ag Leases (an Agriculture Lease is Crown land that is more suited to agriculture than tree farming. It is leased to a suitable applicant who must then clear, seed, farm or whatever. Once the work is done, the land is then sold to the leasee and becomes private land.) and could only be titled after certain improvements were done - specifically, clearing and cultivating 50% of each parcel. The timber was to be sold under the same plan as the SBEP, and stumpage was going to be charged as the timber was logged off. MOF would handle the timber part of this deal. I commented on the low stumpage and was informed that this stumpage was based on the average stumpage the mills paid for that area. No wonder the mills are making money, I thought. Inquiring about the eligibility, I was told any individual who was a Canadian citizen, did not have a timber quota, and was over 21 years of age would be eligible to bid. I thought, good, that includes me. An equal chance to compete was all that I asked.

The land system, in many cases, seemed to me to be wrong. I had seen a lot of abuse, especially when the farmers in northern B.C. were given land and timber under the Agricultural Lease Program. If you had a farm or ranch in the area, and had cattle on it, you were eligible to apply for a parcel of land under the Ag Lease program. The majority of the farmers then proceeded to log the land and sell the timber, which had minimum stumpage on it ($1.10/M^3). This timber money was theirs to keep and keep it they did, with often little or no improvements to the land. This was definitely not a fair system. If everybody could have taken out an Ag Lease to get started, I could see it. But to have this land given to only the established ranches was always a contentious issue with me. I used to have some hot discussions with my neighbour, Barry Higdon, about this very thing, as he was a benefactor of these Ag Leases. I would say, "Why should the government give you land?" He would always reply, "They don't just give it to us. We have to clear some of it, fence it and all that," and I would say,

"Yes, you do have to do that but the money from the timber more than covers that." He would say, "Yes, that's right, but we need something for our trouble and we are doing good for the country as we are adding to our farming base." I would explain to him that yes that was all true, but the fact remained that once you had the land cleared (and not necessarily put into production either), fenced and bought with timber money, you could sell it anytime, and the money was yours. He would laugh and say, "We could but we don't." Barry Higdon later sold the Higdon family farm and all its Ag Leases, and is now retired down in the warm south. Another rancher, south of Quesnel at Narcosli Creek, Bob Walls, had come up from Kalispell, Montana in 1976 and bought an established ranch belonging to Dick and Ed Gliege. When he realized that he could get more land under this program, he applied for and got 640 acres and then proceeded to log it. Rumour has it that he pocketed a cool million after selling the timber to Weldwood. Shortly after this he sold out and moved to Vancouver Island. I always had a problem with this kind of thing. How dumb was our government to allow this to go on? There is still evidence of "cut and run" projects, from Williams Lake in the south to Vanderhoof in the north. I am not saying all farms and ranches were doing this. Some are very conscientious and stable, and do all things required, but the fact remains, they are getting land for nothing. Our young people, just starting out, if they went to the government and asked for a piece of land they'd be told, "No, the government does not sell or give land away!" But they do, sort of, but only to people who already have land.

Another case in point is an old, established ranch south of Quesnel owned by Mark and Lloyd Lepetich. They own in excess of 5,000 acres and have been getting Ag Leases ever since I arrived here in 1965, and were still getting Ag Leases as late as 1994. First, you would wonder why would they need more land, and second, why would the government think they needed more timber money. They haven't logged much, if any, of their private timber (and they have lots). I know a lot a young people who would jump at the chance to be able to get 80 or 160 acres and have the opportunity to make good use of it, but they don't have a chance. I think the government is finally coming to realize their folly, as less and less marginal farm land, covered with timber, is being processed without someone questioning the why and how.

When the Abbott Heights auction (for the 1,200-acre, six parcel pieces of land off Ernst Road) came about, I heard lots of comments by the farmers in the area, like "Why are the loggers allowed to bid on this land?" It's so ironic, once a farmer gets a timbered Ag Lease, he then becomes a logger!

In any case, as I studied the Abbott Heights package I found the timber cruise to total 80,000 M³ on all the parcels. As the sale date was a month off, I had ample time to do my own cruise and study each parcel separately. This was definitely a beautiful property. It had a small lake, numerous ponds, two creeks and some natural meadows. Some areas had been logged in the 1960s and had grown back to thick pine, 20 feet tall. Not merchantible, but definitely a nice plantation. I spent pretty much the whole month cruising, exploring and studying these properties. On sale day, I wanted to have all my bases covered. I checked with the mills to try to get a price for logs, but the timing was wrong. The United States was challenging Canada's softwood stumpage policies, saying that Canada was subsidizing the sawmills with low stumpage, and as this allowed them to sell their lumber cheaper, it was unfair to U.S. producers. The irony of this was that it was true — our government was giving our timber away to the big mills. Anyway, rumour had it the U.S. was going to charge a 37% tariff on any lumber shipped across the line. So with this doom and gloom over the industry, no one wanted to commit to any long-term private timber deal until the problem cleared itself up. If this tariff was imposed, private timber prices would dry up. In times of trouble in the mill industry, private timber purchases were the first thing cut back. I agonized over the issues and outcomes and decided to disregard the impending problem and pretend it would not happen. I was selling to Dunkley Lumber at the time and I knew what today's price of timber was. I would use that as a basis, take the gamble, and if any of my bids were successful, I would hope things would stay the same and prices would hold. This would be a time when my old cohort Neil's philosophy of "you have to get it before anything can be worked out" came into play. Although if a deal this big backfired, I would be in serious trouble. But I planned on giving it my best shot.

Finally the long-awaited sale day came. It was being held at the Elks Hall in Quesnel. You had to register before the sale and have a deposit of

$2,000 for each parcel. The sale was being conducted by Egan Wager, the Land Manager from Williams Lake. The auctioneer was senior land man, Wally Bergan, and two more secretaries were there to keep track of the bid prices. The hall was packed, with standing room only, and the air was charged with energy as they started explaining the rules of the sale and how they were going to conduct it. I had worked out a page for each parcel, outlining my very top bid, and if it went for more I would be out. I was nervous as I looked around at some of the people I knew. Money people. Paulette Ernst, Real Gamache, Ted Kennedy, Blaire Mayes, Richard Glassford, Quesnel Redi-Mix, Tony Bensted, George Needham, Bob Falloon, Terry Givens, to mention a few. The first parcel came up. It was 250 acres and had 11,000 M³ of timber on it. The auctioneer asked for a starting bid. I don't remember who started it, but I held back to get a feel of what was going to happen. When the bidding slowed down, I stepped in and started bidding. Now it seemed to be between one other bidder and me. The auctioneer was saying, "For the second time are there any further bids?" and I wondered if I was the last bidder. Was that my bid? I couldn't remember, so I held up my card. The auctioneer said, "That's your bid already." I was anxious and excited as the bidding had stopped way short of my listed top price. Finally the auctioneer said, "For the third and final time. Sold it to Ed Reierson!"

He then started on the second parcel, which was 180 acres with 24,000 M³ of timber, definitely the best parcel. I immediately took what money I had left over from my top price on my first page, and added it on to the next property. I would be able to bid this extra. The bidding started again, I settled down and tried to be more aware of what was happening. When the bidding hit $80,000.00, the auctioneer said, trying to be funny, "If anybody bids $100,000.00, I will jump off this stage backward." I immediately stuck up my card and said, "$100,000.00." He was shocked! These land people never dreamed this land would go so high. You'd wonder where they had been. Everybody else knew the value of the timber. I guess the farmers and ranchers had preached to them for so long about ag land not being worth anything, they believed it. They got their eyes opened this sale day. Anyway, the bidding had slowed down again and I realized I still had plenty of room to keep going. Finally not being able to get any more, the auctioneer said again, "For the third and last time, any further bids? If not, I've sold this parcel to Ed Reierson." Wow, I thought, I can't believe this! I had never expected to get this last one with all that timber, but it happened.

I now had the first two and, when I used my leftover money to add on to the third parcel, I knew I would be hard to beat. It kept happening, and I ended up getting the first five parcels. The last one was the only one I had to pay slightly more than I originally priced. Overall I had paid a lot less than I had been prepared to pay. The last parcel went to Ted Kennedy and was next to his private land. He had been bidding on most of them. I felt sorry for him and let him have the last one. I was on top of the world. I can't begin to explain how good I felt. I had just bought 1,200 acres with 70,000 M³ of good fir and pine timber on it. I just sat in my chair as people started leaving, looking at my pages and trying to take it all in. I noticed somebody standing in front of me. I looked up and it was Paulette Ernst. She didn't look happy. She said, "Ed, I'd like to know who you are fronting for." I replied, "Paulette, you know me, I've always been an independent." She gave me a flip of her hand and walked away. I don't think she was too happy. Her ranch was very close to this property on one side.

Egan Wager, the auctioneer, came over to me and explained the system to me. He had totalled the bids for the five parcels, gave me the individual sheets, the grand total, and then he said, "Ed, you have seven working days to come up with the money." The total cost of this land and timber was over $700,000. He said they would come back to Quesnel on the seventh day and meet me at the MOF office by noon. I signed some papers and said, "Okay, I'll see you then." It took me the rest of the day and that night to get my mind calmed down. The next day I realized I now had my work cut out for me. I had to try to raise this money within the seven days. I probably could raise $250,000.00 myself but I was going to need help with the rest. I went to my bank and was told they could help me some but under this tariff situation, they were reluctant to cover it all. If the tariff was imposed, I would not be able to sell this timber and would not be able to pay the money back. I then went to Dunkley Lumber. They would put a third of the money if I committed 30,000 M³ to them at $30.00/M³. I agreed as I knew if they invested in this timber, tariff notwithstanding, they would take the timber. I then went back to the bank and showed them that Dunkleys was willing to participate and that gave them the push they needed to come up with the balance. Even though I had plenty of property to cover this loan, the bank always wants more. I had never dealt with a money institution, like a bank, that needed so much collateral. I always had trouble figuring out their reasoning. I guess that's why the three big banks make over one billion dollars profit last year. We should be in that business.

On the morning of the deadline, I got the money together and went to the MOF office. I had heard that a piece of land sold in Williams Lake the previous month, under this same system, for $600,000.00, had had a bit of a problem. The rancher who bid it up had no intention of buying it and was prepared to lose his deposit. The deposit was only $2,000.00. Pretty inadequate deposit for so much land. Of course, the land department didn't dream it would go for such a high price. Anyway, I had heard that this rancher came in and said he needed more time to raise the money. He was given more time. I didn't find out how much time.

As I walked into the conference room of the MOF building, there were three people from Williams Lake. Steve Mazur, being one of the lands people, and two MOF people to answer any questions about the timber. I decided to have a little fun as everyone was so serious looking so I said, in a deadpan way, "Oh by the way, I have a small problem with the money and I wonder if I could have some more time as I heard a rancher with a similar deal was given more time," and I let that hang for a while. There was dead silence as they looked at Steve Mazur, the senior man there. He really didn't know what to do with himself for a time. He started to say, "Well, maybe if you have a letter of guarantee from a bank . . . ," I didn't let it go any further than that. I said, "Just kidding," and pulled out my money. There were some sighs of relief in that room and we all had a good laugh and cleared the air.

I had done it! Or, at least, I had done it to this point. Abbott Heights was mine and now I had to get to work.

Hill property "Fraser River"

The author at the Hill property – birch clump

Sister Ines in a cranberry patch, Hill property

CHAPTER 12

Truckin' and Stuff

*T*his Abbott Heights deal was to be a very exciting and profitable one. First, though, I had a 55,000/M³ SBEP sale, 65 miles out east in Prince George spruce country, that was being sold to Dunkley's, to finish. This sale was a winter sale, meaning it could only be logged in the winter, and it was 75% blowdown. The timber was a real mess. I had to take the best men and equipment out there to be able to finish it before March 15th. It proved to be quite a challenge. Everything had looked good in the fall before the snow. As the snow came, and got deeper and deeper, it turned out to be quite a nightmare. I had two D8 cats, two 966 cat loaders, and eleven cats and skidders, some of my own and some hired. We had a terrific thaw in January that melted most of the snow and that saved our bacon. It took a while to figure the best way to get this blowdown out of the snow. We tried everything. One fellow I had hired to run a D8 had just pushed trees at random and broke everything up. He worked about a week before we realized what he was doing. It took some time to clean up all those broken pieces. We finally ended up getting the blade of a D8 under and along the downed tree, lifted the stump and then pushed the whole tree, stump and all out to an opening in the snow. It was then cut off and skidded to the landing. Projects often work better in hindsight — after you're done you realize how you should have done it, but it's not so bad if you look at these things as a learning process. This blowdown project had taken up all of my time and I didn't get back to my Abbott Heights project until spring.

I moved my brother, Roy, to Abbott Heights in the fall, to start logging and shipping as part of our Dunkley commitment. He had a nice start by breakup. By this time the U.S. tariff scare was over. It had been decided that Canada was not subsidizing its timber industry and it was business as usual. Private timber prices had risen in the wake of this, about $15.00 a cubic metre and as soon as I had the 30,000/M^3 logged for Dunkley, I would start to make some money. Over the course of the next two years we were to log most of the timber and clear some 500 acres and build eight miles of fence. I was still getting small business sales and logging them in conjunction with the Abbott Heights project. So it was a busy time for all. As we logged and cleared this property, I saved timber around all creeks and draws. I had wildlife shelters, wind breaks, trees around ponds and left any thick, small, nicely started trees. I worked closely with Williams Lake Lands department as we cleared the land and fenced.

Clearing and seeding 50% of the land was required but fencing was not. We did that on our own. I wanted to have it all fenced. We had quite a fencing crew. One D8 clearing a 30-foot right-of-way, a 966 loader pushing posts in and a crew following to string wire. We used this high tensile, smooth wire with posts 16 feet apart and two droppers in between. For droppers (stays), we used two treated 1 × 3s, four feet long, on each side of the wire and screwed them in place with drywall screws. It made a nice looking fence. I used this smooth wire purposely to protect wildlife. We had always had horses and barbed wire is a problem at times. Before they get to know about wire, some of them end up getting badly cut. The smooth wire, in theory, is supposed to stop them without hurting them. I know the deer appreciated it as they could either jump it or go through it. The grown deer mostly jumped it but the young ones crawled through without a scratch. I grew to hate barbed wire over the years: it cuts horses and cattle, and though you don't see the cuts on wildlife you do see the hair stuck on barbs and know that a cut happened. You have to feel for the wildlife — no one is caring for them and treating their cuts and scrapes.

One winter we had twin moose yearlings hanging around one of our landings. They grew quite tame. There were lots of moose and deer on this property. As I didn't hunt myself, I had a "No Hunting" rule for anybody that worked there. Once we had it all fenced we were able to keep outside hunters out as well. We had quite a game reserve going. We had one young fellow working for us at the time who was an avid hunter. His name was Lance Wilkins. Lance would get real excited whenever he saw a nice buck with big horns. He had asked repeatedly if he could shoot one, and the answer was always the same. One morning he asked Blaine if it was okay to shoot if they were outside the fence. Blaine replied, "No, Lance, they are still our deer, they've just jumped outside to go to the bathroom." Lance laughed but was pretty frustrated with us.

As we were selectively logging this property, I learned through trial and error which were the best trees to leave and which we could safely cut. If you leave all big trees, chances are they will blow down during a storm, and leaving just the small ones doesn't create the desired effect. I found the best route was to thin out a patch, taking out approximately one third of the bigger trees and leaving the rest. That way you still had a good stand left. By taking out the bigger trees, the rest were not apt to blow down. As I studied the wildlife, I found they liked these thinned out forests. They still had their shelter, but there was more grass and shrubbery on the forest floor after some of the larger trees came out. Also, the thinning let more sunlight in. I'd like to see the whole province maintained this way where possible. It would keep the whole forest growing and create jobs for all who wanted to work, also providing the log fibre to keep the mills going. This would eliminate the need for clearcutting all the closest timber. I imagine a tomato patch and compare it to a forest. You need to thin the plants as they grow; pick the ripe tomatoes as they are ready. It's the same theory, only instead of a yearly thinning with tomatoes, it's a 100-year thinning with trees. If we don't keep the forest thinned and healthy ourselves, Mother Nature will come along and, as it gets old and thick, will burn it down with fire. There goes all the woody debris that the environmentalists talk about. Some areas are not suited for selective logging. Pine forests, for example: the aged trees stop growing after about 100 years, which is the time when they have reached the end of their cycle. Compare this stand to an alfalfa crop. The alfalfa crop is ready to cut each year and, as you cut it, it grows back. If you don't cut it, it will grow so thick that it will eventually become rootbound and not amount to much, producing stunted and unhealthy plants. It's the same with a pine forest. It should be cut at around the 75 to 100 year mark since, after that, the stand will start to go downhill. Rot, bugs and dead trees will be the result, with eventually fire finishing it off. We may as well take it and get a new crop started. Everything thrives in a new growing forest. As for replenishing the soil, leave the woody debris on the ground floor for the next crop. Eventually we will probably be pumping our waste chips and maybe treated sewage back into our forests. When you see a nicely thinned pine plantation, it is a thing of beauty. It is so alive. One such plantation on the Barkerville Highway, between Quesnel and Wells, is a case in point. It is about 25 years old and around 10 miles along the highway, bordered on all sides by a mature forest. In winter, guess where all the moose are? That's right, mostly in this newly planted forest!

As we worked on clearing, seeding, fencing, thinning, leaving shelters and windbreaks, the Lands people would bring tours out to our property to show what could be done with a piece of forest. They were proud and appreciative of our project. Most of the Lands people were amazed that Crown land and timber could be bought for that much money and still be a workable project. They had been told for years that the farmers needed to get the land and timber for nothing to be able to make it work. In the farmers and ranchers defence, I think they would get their Ag Leases, in most cases, and spend years getting it developed, using the timber money to live on while they were doing it. For example, if it took a year to profit $50,000.00 from your timber, and it cost you $50,000.00 to live for that year, you would say you broke even, and didn't make any money from the timber.

I've heard the odd farmer, someone who has benefitted from an Ag Lease, condemn people on welfare, who get maybe $12,000.00 per year from the government. Compare that to $50,000.00 worth of timber and you begin to get a different view. I don't believe anyone should get something for nothing. I'm not saying we should do away with our social programs. Anybody who needs help, single mothers, people unable to work and older people should be helped; that's what it's all about. But I hate to see the system giving able-bodied young people steady welfare. When someone is between jobs or going through a tough time, I think social assistance is a wonderful thing. But people can take advantage of the system. I had one young fellow working for me, doing odd jobs, feeding cattle and doing some carpenter work. He didn't work too steady, and he had some story for why he wanted to get paid in cash. A story about going bankrupt. I never really paid attention until he was renting a trailer I had and asked for rent receipts. I said, "What for? I thought we were trading work for rent." He said, "I need receipts to get my rent money back from

Welfare of course." I said, "You are on welfare?" I couldn't believe it. Here was a perfectly healthy, young, single man taking advantage of the system. We soon parted ways.

Some people were always complaining about the government yet this same government was feeding them.

Some of the Williams Lake Lands people that I worked with and found to be very friendly and helpful were Steve Mazur, Egan Wager, Linda Sontag, Heather Knesovich, Dave Lutz, Wally Bergan, Martin Sills, Sharon Whitely, Duncan Williams, Lorraine Russel and Pente Lepenun. These people, as I said, were helpful and friendly, and also went out of their way at times to accommodate me in many ways. Eventually these Lands people got wise to this Ag Lease policy and tightened it up, closing some of the loopholes to stop this mostly timber grab. I always felt that all lands and timber owned by the Crown, including large timber quotas, should be put up for public auction. This would keep the system fair and would give everybody an equal chance to own land or be able to buy some land, or just have steady work.

The Abbott Heights deal was a success on many levels and so when, three years later, the Lands Department put up some more land and timber sales, I was interested. I bought another 1,500 acres of land and timber. This time it didn't come cheap, as there was no tariff scare or anything like that. This gave us another 1,500 acres and 120,000 M³ of timber to log, and another 500 acres of land to clear. We used this private timber to log in summer as it was all summer ground. We tried to save it for when we were out of Crown timber. We logged SBEP sales where possible. My three original truckers, Mackie Ramsey, Wayne Roch, and Hugh Christie had long log trucks, not tree-length rigs. When I started shipping tree length to Dunkley, they stayed on with West Fraser and I hired new trucks. I hated to lose those three. They were good, dependable truckers.

One of my new truckers was Earl Olsen. Earl was an enterprising young fellow. When I first hired him, I heard that somebody had found his fuel key and was helping himself to Earl's fuel. It took a few months to get to the bottom of the disappearing diesel and catch the thief. I heard about this before I met Earl. Anyway, Earl drove into the landing. I was working on the road with my cat. I stopped and went over and introduced myself and then asked with a straight face, if he had a spare hose and could I get some fuel from his truck? He didn't catch on right away and asked if my cat was out of fuel? I smiled and said no but I'd heard he was supplying fuel to people. He laughed and we joked about that. Earl went on to look after all our hauling, mostly using his own rigs to haul our wood. Earl kept a tight rein on things, and kept our wood hauled out.

We had a SBEP sale out at Hagen Creek one winter. Three of us, Fred Critchlow, Quesnel Forest Products, and myself opened up a new road for the winter, to save both time and frustration. A road existed but just for limited four-wheel- drive traffic, and it was only open in the summer, too. We took in our equipment and straightened the route out, put culverts in the creeks, snowplowed the surface and we were in business. There were too many trucks on our regular road. The new route was a lot shorter and some trucks figured the rate would be lower. So they decided to haul on our regular main road and go in empty on our new road. These were not our trucks, they were the main body of trucks hauling for the mills in the area. I thought, "Boy, what gall. Our own road that the three of us had paid $60,000.00 to open and improve, and they were going to tell us how to travel on it." Our plans were to use the main road empty and haul loaded on our new road, thereby keeping the haul rate the same. (Usually, the mill set the haul rates and the independent loggers used them as a guide.) This would take some pressure off the main road. There would be about 50 trucks on the new road for the winter. We sent our first loaded trucks out as soon as this road froze in. As this was a new road, fresh dirt and unpacked, it needed some good 10 below weather to freeze it in.

The truckers always stopped in Wells for lunch or coffee. Wells was about halfway to town. Not long after the new road was operating, my haulers were taking a break in Wells when they were approached by some Quesnel truckers, led by Sam Cork, who was the head of their organization. Sam informed them, in no uncertain terms, that they could not haul loaded on this new road! Earl stood up, looked him in the eye and stated, "Look here, I don't work for you guys! I work for Reierson. He signs my pay cheque and when he says — haul loaded on his new road, I haul loaded on his new road!" I was real proud of Earl sticking up for his outfit like that. Earl was very loyal and was a major part of our company for many years, participating and helping out where he could.

One of Earl's favourite pastimes was talking to quota trucks in town, on the radio, about things like, "Oh, aren't you guys hauling yet? Oh no, we have been hauling for two weeks already, we gravel our roads or corduroy them." He liked to bug them. We always tried to start hauling early in the summer. Having summer ground was important. It was a nice luxury to be able to leave any summer ground for the summer and log some place else in the winter. It wasn't always straightforward, though. One spring, around the 24th of May, we started hauling to Dunkley's and three trucks showed up only to find that the scales for weighing the loads were being replaced. We had mixed up the starting date and had started one week too soon.

One haul we had, east of Quesnel, had a very steep hill in the road. I would hook on to the trucks at the bottom of the hill and help pull them up with my D8. One morning I hooked on to Earl, let about 50 feet of mainline out and away we went. Well, my winch lever got stuck in gear and, unknown to me, was winding in. I was looking straight ahead and didn't notice anything. I looked around for some reason and here was Earl, about to go right up my winch! I had an arch on the back of the winch and the line was through it, making it about eight feet high. I pulled Earl's truck right up to the top of this arch before I noticed, through the noise of his horn blowing too. I had pulled the front of the frame apart and lifted the front part of the truck away from the rest. What a mess! We spent the rest of the day welding and fixing. I don't know if Earl ever forgave me for that or not.

Another humorous incident happened that winter out at Hagen Creek. Next to our timber sale, another outfit from town, Specialty Trucking, had a sale. The three partners in the operation were Terry Givens, Tony Bensted and Bill Poole. They had lots of trucks and, because it was so far from town, the trucks sometimes came back to the bush to discover there were no logs left. This happened quite often when trucks were hauling from several sources. Sometimes a hauler would have time to go to a different place for one load. It made it hard for the logger to know how many trucks to expect. Bill Poole and Terry Givens came to our camp one evening and talked to Blaine, who was in camp that night. They asked if they had any extra trucks come in, and they didn't have enough logs for a load, could they send their overflow to us? Blaine said sure, as long as we have logs. Terry then said, kind of uncomfortably, "Oh by the way Blaine, one thing. Our rate for our trucks is $13.75/M³ and we would insist on keeping it at that. So if you could pay us that much, it will be great." Blaine said he'd talk to the Chief, but he didn't see a problem. They started hauling off and on for us whenever they were short of logs. One day one of the trucks said to Earl, "Boy, this is a good rate we're getting from here." Earl said, "Oh, what's that?" and he replied, "$13.75/M³." "Yeah," Earl said, "that's pretty good. Almost as much as I'm getting!" "What!" the trucker said, "you're getting more?" "Yes," Earl said, "Ed anticipated some trucking difficulty cropping up with all this wood to move, and he set the rate at $15.50/M³." They couldn't believe it. Bill Poole came over later and said, "What's going on? I hear you're paying $15.50/M³ and we are only getting $13.75." "Bill," I said, "you insisted on getting your own rate. You just assumed that our rate would be lower than that. So hey, I don't see any problem." For some reason or other, they didn't haul much from us after that.

We hired another truck to come and haul for us that winter, from Salmon Arm. The driver was Butch Toukko. Butch was a good trucker, always able to keep his truck going and never hesitant to put on his chains. We had some great truckers working for us around that time: Doug Webster, a young friendly fellow who was always on time; Calvin Lee, a dedicated worker with a sense of humour; Rob Taylor, a young guy with a big smile; Gary Inwood, a short stocky man with a brush cut and a fleet of 20 trucks; Doug Andrews, who always had a joke; Pete Coe, when he wasn't trucking he was a team roper; Byron Cotter, a man who could keep absolutely anything running; Helmut Schults, who never failed to come back for a load; Abel Garcia, who was always ahead of us and waiting for a load; Dwain Suave, an enterprising owner with a fleet of trucks whose steady haul was with E & K; and Les Johnston, a steady soft-spoken young man who was always ready to help.

This sale at Hagen Creek was fairly high in elevation and so it got very cold in winter. One morning we woke up to no water. The taps were dry. Investigating the next day, I discovered the loggers on the next sale to ours had skidded through the little creek we had tapped into for our water supply, it had frozen solid and stopped running. I had to dig our well deeper. What a job that turned out to be. Water for a logging camp was definitely a must. Water is important any time, but when you have 15 or more men depending on it, then it's imperative. Doing stuff like re-digging wells in the middle of winter was always harder for me that falling a tree or fixing a cat or laying out a hauling pattern with a trucker. Oh, well, it all came with the territory.

Abbott Heights fenced with barbless wire

Aspen leave strip, Abbott Heights

Fir leave strip

An air overview of 1,200 acre Abbott Heights project

Earl Olsen of "Siea Ent" with a new truck

"Hauling"

Loaded truck at the weigh scale

"Track Arch" for skidding out logs

Earl Olsen with a load from Stanley, B.C.

Scaling yard, Dunkley Lumber

Earl Olsen with tree length load from Slender Lake, 119 feet of wood

Author's pine plantation

Author checking growth in fir plantation

Building the riding arena, hoisting up the roof trusses, 1983

Inside the completed riding arena, Quesnel, 1984

CHAPTER 13

Cows at Abbott Heights and Other Adventures

*B*y now I had a few properties, some of which boasted some hay land. With hay at hand, I decided to buy some cows. I'd had a few cows off and on over the years, but this time I planned to get around 100 mother cows. I contacted a friend of mine, Larry Bell, who had helped me with cattle before. Larry had a nice ranch situated on the Quesnel River and was a cattle buyer. I explained to him what I wanted to do and he said, "No problem, I'll find you some cattle." This was in early summer. I then figured out how much hay I would need and bought some serious haying equipment from Huber Farm Equipment in Prince George (it was a good excuse to get more machines to play with!). I bought a swather, baler, and a rake. I already had tractors of my own, so now I was in the haying business. When the hay was ready, a bush friend of mine, Dempsey Quinn, said he wanted to help me with the haying. He was on holidays from his regular job. I borrowed Blaine from the logging project and the three of us started haying.

Dempsey did the swathing, I raked and Blaine ran the baler. It was sure nice to hay with new equipment. I'd had some older haying equipment in the past. At the time I was using it, it was a difficult to decide which was harder to fight, the weather or the old machinery. This time, however, I had a run of good weather, and we put up hay for 14 days in a row. It was sure different than logging but we worked at it like loggers. We couldn't start too early in the morning because of dew, but we worked until we couldn't see at night. When we finished we had put up 1,100 round bales. We stacked these bales in different yards, and I figured at least we had lots of hay for winter.

Larry located 135 bred range cows from a ranch in the Chilcotin that was overstocked, and hauled them to Abbott Heights. We had this place newly fenced and just turned the cows loose on 1,200 acres of pasture. It was ideal for cattle, with creeks and ponds for drinking, one small lake and lots of shelter with patches of timber left and lots of natural brush and willows. To be ready for winter, I installed an insulated, self-watering tank, and built some pens and calving sheds. Then we went back to logging, leaving the cows on their own until winter. Cattle ranching seemed pretty easy. I could drive around on weekends and look the cows over. Other than putting salt out and keeping gates closed, there was little or no work involved.

Around the first of November I started feeding hay to these cows. Boy, they sure had appetites. I would take the ties (netting) off the bales and roll them out. I had a total of 135 cows and they were all due to calve in spring, and they sure could put away the feed. At first it seemed like no big thing, this feeding, but after a while it got to be quite a chore. I had temporarily moved a mobile home on to the property and was living, by myself, at Abbott Heights. I had arranged for hydro and phone, and had put in the water and sewer system. I was quite comfortable there although fairly lonely. I would come home after work and feed cows every night. They ate every day, no days off for them. Then on weekends, I would haul hay from the stackyards.

One weekend, my feller buncher operator, Kelly Vipond, and I were hauling hay from one yard to Abbott Heights, a distance of about five miles. We had a trailer that would haul about 12 bales. We couldn't get into the stackyard with the pickup, so I would haul them to the main road with the tractor and a farm trailer. I would pull this trailer to the stack, unhook, load up and then hook up and head for the road. Kelly would haul his trailer away once loaded and unload at the other end. We made a game of it, each trying to beat the other. It seemed that Kelly would be back before me no matter how hard I tried. I would hurry but before I could get out and unhooked, he would pull in. This one time I figured I had him. I was out on the road and unhooked, had a bale up and was waiting for him. I thought to myself, "Finally I've got you!" I waited and waited and finally I could see a white car trimmed with blue coming up the road. It pulled up and Kelly got out. I wondered what happened? Lots of things went through my mind . . . did the load tip over, did the truck break down, did he run out of gas? Then I saw the driver and I thought, Oh, oh! This guy had a uniform on. It was Jim Syvertsen, the D.O.T. man. I got down from my tractor and Jim and Kelly came over. Jim said, "Hi, Ed," and I returned the greeting, wondering what Jim was doing out on this back road on a weekend. I didn't have to wait long to find out. Jim laid out the problem. An insecure load (not tied down), no safety chains on the hitch, no brake setup, no lights, and no licence plates for the trailer? I said, "Come on, Jim, this is a back road and there is no traffic. We're farmers now, just hauling hay." He said, "Well, you still have to be legal!" He explained to us that we couldn't pull a farm trailer with a pickup. A tractor, yes, and the trailer had to be licensed and the load tied down. "You guys know the rules. I let you get away with one last summer, Ed, when you crossed the main road with the buncher, but this time I'll have to fine you." (Blaine and Kelly had crossed a paved road earlier in the year with the buncher. They had used tires for the crossing but had not stopped traffic. When Jim happened along they were just taking the tires off the road and brushing off some of the dirt lumps. "Moved the buncher across the road, eh?" Blaine said, "Yes, we did." "Where are your signs? You need somebody out with stop signs when you do this," Jim barked. Blaine said, "Oh, Jim, you just missed the Chief (that's what they called me). He loaded up the signs and headed to town." Jim replied, "Well I don't know if I believe that, but I'll let you go this time. Tell your Dad he just missed a $150.00 fine". This time he didn't let me get away with anything, he handed me a $75.00 fine. He said, "Be sure you get legal now and stay that way," and he walked to his car.

I had always had this quirk about this legal thing. I was always close to legal, but not quite. I knew better but I guess this was my half-hearted attempt to fool the law. I don't know why I had to do this. I would get a kick out of driving around with different licence plates on vehicles. This would really get Vicki going. One time I was going to move my log loader from Finning Tractor in town to the farm on West Fraser Road, a distance of about 10 miles, to do some fencing. I waited until after school, and then said to Brian (Vicki's youngest son), "Would you come and help me move the loader from town?" Brian liked machines and I knew he would jump at the chance. Vicki said, "Wait a minute, do you have a permit to move that thing?" "No," I said, "but it will be okay." She said, "No way, not if Brian is going with you. You will have to be legal." I said, "Okay, we'll go ahead and get started, and you go get us a permit." She said, "Okay, I'll do that; why you can't be legal is beyond me." I just smiled and mumbled something, and Brian and I drove away. We got to Finning and by the time we had the loader ready to go, Vicki was there with the permit. She said to us something like, "See that wasn't too hard, was it?" and went on her way. What she missed was who was going to drive the pickup home? Brian, of course. I drove home, proudly displaying the permit for the loader, with Brian following, with his flashers going and a pillow under his seat so he could see over the wheel. He was around 12 or 13 at the time. When we arrived home, Vicki looked the situation over. It dawned on her that the truck and loader showed up at the same time. She said, "How did you ————————? Oh God, tell me Brian didn't drive the truck home! You guys, I tell you ————————!" I made myself busy real soon, thinking how is Brian going to learn how to drive? How did she think Blaine got to be such a good driver before he turned 16?

Another time, a friend of mine, Burt Prest, wanted to borrow my boat and motor to go fishing one weekend. I said sure, and away he went with the outfit. Wouldn't you know it, he got stopped by the RCMP. They asked him for the trailer registration. He said, "I borrowed this trailer from my boss, and he didn't give me one." "That's okay," the officer said, "have him bring in the registration on Monday." Burt said, "I'll do that." When he got back from fishing and told me that, I laughed and said, "Gosh Burt, I borrowed that licence plate from Vicki's horse trailer." Burt said, "Oh no, now I'll be in trouble." (For some reason, everybody else wanted to be legal.) I said, "No Burt, you won't be in trouble. I'll straighten this out for you." He said, "I bet you will." I said, "No, seriously Burt, I will bet you I can straighten this out. Monday morning we'll go in together and I'll show you." Burt didn't look too happy but he said okay. What could he do? Monday after work saw us down at the police station. I had taken Vicki's registration for her horse trailer so the plate number would match. Burt said, "Look, how is that going to work? We are really going to be in trouble." I told him to leave it to me and that if we got fined, I'd pay it. "Don't worry," I said. He was worried though. We walked up to the desk and the desk sergeant said, "Can I help you boys?" I said, "Yes you can. My friend Burt here got stopped with my boat on the weekend and I hadn't given him the registration for the trailer." I handed him the blue slip that Burt had gotten, telling him to bring this in, and also the registration papers for Vicki's horse trailer. He was friendly and looked everything over carefully. He said, "You were hauling a boat?" He looked at Burt. Burt said worriedly, "Yes, I was going fishing." The desk sergeant said, "Yes, but this registration says horse trailer," and he looked at me sternly. "Yes," I said with a straight face, "it used to be a horse trailer, but I took the box off and put the boat on. Now it is a boat trailer." I could see Burt looking at me like I had lost my mind. I looked straight at the desk sergeant. He looked back at me, seemed satisfied and said, "Okay, but this registration should say that." He then crossed off "horse trailer" and marked in "boat trailer." Burt couldn't believe his eyes. I said, "Burt, it's all in the presentation." He retold this story for years.

In a similar vein, another time, later on in Salmon Arm, Vicki's sister Brenda and her family were down visiting and we went looking at tractors. Brenda's husband, Robert, wanted to buy a farm tractor and they decided to make a little holiday out of it. In order for us to have enough room for everybody to travel together, we went looking in my crewcab. They have three kids, Ashley, Eric and Mitch, and with Robert, Brenda, Vicki and me, we had a truckload. I noticed my licence plate had expired but figured, oh well, we wouldn't be going far and it would probably be okay. Well wouldn't you know it, going through Armstrong, there was a seatbelt road check. I was not wearing my seat belt. The officer said the usual about the importance of seat belts, and I kidded him about just giving me a warning. He said, "Nope, I'll have to give you a ticket." He looked in and saw everyone sitting there solemnly, took his ticket book to the back of the truck, put his foot on the bumper, and proceeded to write me out a ticket, writing my licence number on the ticket. I said to Robert, "Oh, oh, I'm in trouble now, my plates have expired." I heard Vicki say, "Oh God, not again!" I thought, "Oh well, I'll just have to take my medicine as it comes." The officer came back, handed me my seatbelt ticket, and said, "Here you go, now make sure you buckle up from now on." I said, "You bet I will," and drove away. Robert said, "You're BSing me about your licence plate being expired, aren't you?" They of course figured that because the officer had written down the licence plate number, he would have noticed something this blatant. I said, "No kidding guys, my plates have expired, I'll show you when we get home." Sure enough when we arrived home, everybody got out to look at my plates. And yes they were expired . . . over two months before. Robert laughed nervously. Vicki said disgustedly, "E.W. is up to his old tricks again." How this officer missed this is beyond me. Just one of those days, I guess. I wasn't long in getting the problem fixed.

This quirk with insurance, plates and permits has been with me for a long as I can remember, and will probably be with me for the rest of my life. I was hoping age would work for me, but I seem to still get as much satisfaction, if not more, out of some of these antics. I certainly do not recommend any of this to the rest of the world; it's a rather expensive and potentially dangerous risk. I will probably have to be on my best behaviour now as I have a new neighbour; Ernie Dechant moved next to me and a nicer young fellow, you couldn't meet. But, you guessed it, he is an RCMP officer! But, back to my cattle feeding.

One night I was later than usual getting home to my cows. When I arrived in the yard they were all standing around the waterer, milling around and looking at me. I thought, "Oh, oh, what's happened here?" It didn't take long to find out. This automatic, insulated, trouble-free, fancy new waterer was frozen solid. It was -33 degrees, with a wind blowing. Jeez! Just the kind of night you need to have water problems. The first thing I did was phone Vic Rhodes from the Co-op Farm and Ranch Supply. I called him at home using the phone in my pickup truck. I said, "Hey, Vic, guess what? That fancy waterer you sold me froze up! You said that would never happen." Vic was sympathetic and responded with the usual, "I have more than 50 of those out and I haven't heard of any one of them freezing up." I replied, "Well, now you have one frozen solid." I had just called him to whine a bit. I knew he couldn't do anything about it right then . . . I would have to do that. It bugs me when these guys sell you something, saying "oh yeah, this works great," and then you find out different. It was sort of my fault though, because when we were installing it, my water man, Fred Bartel, (who has been doing this type of backhoe and water work for years) said to me, "Ed, where is the electric wire to hook up to this waterer?" I said, "Nowhere Fred, this is a new insulated waterer and it is not supposed to freeze." He looked at me in disbelief and said,

"Reierson, you mean to tell me that when its 40 below in the Cariboo this thing is not going to freeze? You've got to be kidding!" Well I was thinking of Fred now and wishing I had hooked up an electric cord to keep it thawed out, but that wouldn't help me now.

I looked the situation over and planned my course of attack. This waterer was a four-hole waterer with two holes on each side of the fence, so that when I had cows in the pen, they could also drink. I checked the water with a metal bar. It was definitely frozen solid! I took my chainsaw and cut the section of fence apart that was over the waterer, built a frame around the waterer and covered this frame with some 6 mil. plastic I had at the trailer. Then I got my propane torch going inside this shelter. It was big enough for me to get in also. It didn't take long to warm up in there. I had to build a small fence around it as well to keep the cattle away while I was thawing out the waterer. Just like cows! If you wanted them they would be long gone and when you didn't want them, they were all over you. I left this heater going while I went up to the trailer, 500 feet away, to shut the water off and warm up. Minus 33 with a wind blowing is darned cold. I went back to the waterer and, with some wrenches, took the thing apart, and carefully started chipping away at the ice. I heated up anything that wasn't plastic. Finally I had it thawed out and put back together again. I turned on the water and made sure everything was working properly. Then I tore down my plastic shelter, put my fence back up, and let the cows come in. The problem turned out to be the flap that the cows had to push on to get water. In the extreme cold, it would slowly freeze. When cows drink they slobber, and the flap would get wet. It would freeze a bit, letting the flap stick open, allowing the cold air in. If it was left for any length of time, everything would freeze. If the cows drank fairly regularly, they would keep it open. The problem was they would all drink and then head for the bush to get out of the wind. I eventually solved this problem by building a windbreak around the tank. If it wasn't windy, things seemed okay. After getting this water problem solved and the cows fed, it was the middle of the night. I was sure glad to have a warm place to go to. I wasn't long in getting to sleep that night. I fell asleep wondering what on earth possessed me to think cow farming would be easy.

Whenever it was real cold like this I wouldn't be able to start my tractor and I would just pull these round bales through the gate with my pickup.

I'd put a rope around them, hook it to my bumper and away I would go. Whatever works, I thought. When spring finally came and I had to face the calving problems as well as the feeding routine — I was feeling great sympathy for all cattle ranchers. Did I once think they had an easy life? I know better now. Summers weren't bad, but with the thought of another winter coming on, I phoned my friendly cattle buyer, Larry, and said, "Sell my herd." It's not that I didn't like the cattle thing; it was that it took away from my regular job. Neither job was getting done properly and I was not getting any time off. Instead of haying after that, I rented out my fields for pasture. That was much easier. When the grass was gone, the cattle were gone. I had a different appreciation for ranchers after a cow-studded winter at Abbott Heights.

Cows at Abbott Heights

Twin calves

CHAPTER 14

Two Sets of Rules

I had been successful in bidding on many of the SBEP sales in the Quesnel area from 1980 to 85. In 1985, in order to keep our 10 loads a day in summer and 15 to 20 loads per day in winter, working steady, I needed a constant and reliable timber supply. The only place to get timber was through a private land deal or from Crown land made available through the SBEP system. It took some serious juggling to get sufficient SBEP sales to keep my crew rolling. The Ministry, in their wisdom, allowed a bidder to work only two sales at a time. Until each sale was completed, you were not able to bid on another. Their paperwork processing was so slow, it often took a very long time before you got the go ahead to start another sale. Sometimes things got a little dicey; one particular sale, I waited 11 months for clearance. This example is, granted, an extreme case, but it does illustrate the problems that could happen. The process was cumbersome and the delays could be dreadful. Thank heaven, after a while, someone in the Ministry of Forests must have realized that the program had some unnecessary hurdles and started allowing bids to be registered as soon as a forest officer could inspect and "rubber-stamp" each completed job.

In order to allow for bureaucratic delays, I registered myself, my son Blaine, my brother Roy, and my truck boss, Earl, under the SBEP guidelines. In order to qualify you had to own one piece of logging equipment, and pay a registration fee of $100.00 per year. The fee increased to $250.00 a year after the program began. Four registrants allowed us to bid on up to eight sales at one time. It was rare that we came even close to eight sales, but once, the MOF put five small high lead sales up at the same time, all adjoining. In order to move a high-cost cable machine in, and high lead sales require a cable machine, it was imperative for us to have a suitable volume of wood to cut. It was crucial that we get all five sales. They were sold separately but on the same day, which made for some very interesting juggling. We were competing with another high lead logger, a colourful character named Ed Deering. Ed was a plus at a sale because of a habit of his: he talked a running commentary all during the sale. Normally, as the bidders were qualified, everybody in the room was as quiet as mice. Not Ed Deering, and his comments were comical. For example, as the deposit cheques were handed in on the first sale, he said something like, "Oh, oh Eddie is interested (meaning me), and this could be interesting." I always handed in my deposit cheques separately instead of all at the same time because if you didn't get the first one, maybe you didn't want the second, and so on. In this case, I was successful on the first sale, as the bids didn't go too high. The second deposit cheque was called for and handed in. Deering said (he talked to himself, but loud enough for everyone to hear), "I'll probably have to give this one to Eddie too." My bid was high and as Deering didn't try very hard, I was awarded the second sale. He then said, "Well that's two for Eddie and that's his limit so maybe now I'll be able to get a sale." When they called for deposit cheques on the third sale, I got up and handed in another deposit cheque. Deering said, "How can that be?" Then they read out the names as the bidders were qualified and Blaine's name was read. (You could bid for somebody else as long as he qualified and had no sales.) Deering said, "Oh, I see, he's bidding for Blaine." He (Deering) bid more on the next two sales but I was able to end up with the higher bid, and got those two as well. When the fifth sale came up he said, "Well, I certainly will get this one as Eddie is finished." When cheques were called for, I stood up and handed in another one. When they read off Earl Olsen's name, Deering got real excited, and his comments weren't that comical. Anyway, he bid me up pretty high on that last one but I ended up getting it. Ed Deering came to see me that night and asked me how could I make any money bidding so high? "If you have a secret, maybe you can tell me and I'll be able to compete with you." I told him that there was no secret and that I averaged out all my bids for the year and if that average worked, then all was well. He mused, out loud, "Oh, that's how you do it! I see now."

I was successfully bidding on a lot of sales. There were some complaints. One particularly good sale (a definition of a good sale is one that is close to town, with nice timber) drew many bidders. Mine was the winning bid. One person in particular complained to the MOF about it. The sale had been run as a sealed bid and everybody had the same chance, but because it had come to me, I was targetted. Ministry of Forests called me in and explained the system to me. When MOF wanted to talk to you about something important, they would take you to the conference room. There would be at least two ministry personnel and a secretary. It was a bit intimidating and I think that was intentional. In this instance, the representatives said the SBEP was designed to allow small logging operators to get access to some Crown timber. To work best, each small operator would have one sale and when he was finished, he could try for another. That way everyone could have a sale. I said, "Hey guys, let's get real here! The mills would get every sale through their men if they could. Have you noticed who is the top competition on the big sales?" I told them that in order for me to stay in business, I needed enough timber to produce 10 loads per day. I had four trucks and 10 men depending on me to get timber. I said, "In a way, you created me. You designed this program and that's how it works. Have you checked with West Fraser Mills to see how many sales they have at one time? I rest my case!" They, of course, protested that the cases were different.

For many, the Small Business Enterprise Program was a "damned if you do and damned if you don't" program, mostly because the Ministry of Forests didn't put up enough sales, which meant the sales that did go up generated tons of competition. There wasn't enough to go around. It was like throwing a chicken in with a bunch of wolves . . . everyone was fighting for a share. In the meeting I had with them, the one they called me in to, I told them that if I ran the country, the first thing I would do is take the timber back from the big companies and put it up for sale, allowing everyone to compete. That would be fair and then there would be timber enough for everybody. Why should a few big companies be allowed to tie up all our timber? I said, "Have you noticed how big some of these companies have become? Where do you think they get the money to buy out all the little guys? Some not so little, either. They have to do something with their money, they don't want to give any back in taxes so they buy other mills. How do you suppose Slocan, West Fraser, Riverside, and Tolko got so big so fast? Do you really think they earned that money? They got bigger because they control the timber and when you have years of minimum stumpage, this is what happens. This province should be the richest in the world with all its timber, and everybody who wants to, could be working. It's no wonder the U.S. is crying 'foul'. I would be too, if I was in their shoes." I watched their faces as my verbal barrage sank in. They seemed surprised that I knew anything more than cutting down timber on SBEPs. They shuffled their papers and said, "Thank you for coming in, Ed. We'll be getting back to you when we've had a chance to review this." This was so typical of the MOF. Very seldom did anything get resolved.

Not too long after this formal session, our area SBEP supervisor came to me during a sale, one I was participating in, and leaned over to me and said, "I'm cancelling two of the sales that you have in the Webster Lake area." These were two of the better sales I had gotten earlier on, with the requirement that the beetle wood be taken out before flight time. We had done this as soon as we had our logging plan complete. We put in the roads and landings, logged just the beetle wood, hauled it out and left the rest of the sale for later on. We had 12 months to complete it and this left about 8 months. I said to him, looking him straight in the eye, "No, you're not cancelling any of my sales, and furthermore, see me after the sale, not during it." I had taken my wife Vicki and Blaine with me for help during the sale. The moral support this gives you sometimes makes the difference between getting a sale or not, especially during the open auction sales. (I sometimes think they came with me because they didn't trust me by myself.) Both Vicki and Blaine were shocked by this SBEP officer's statement, as was I. After this sale, we went to his office to find out what was going on. He said, again, "I'm cancelling your two Webster Lake sales!" I asked how he could justify this. He stated that I had not completed my obligations on these sales and he had heard that I was logging in Wells, which is on the other side of the area. I asked, "Just what are my obligations, am I missing something?" I was right in his face. He said, "You haven't followed the logging plan, which specifically says 'the beetle wood must be out before flight time' and it is now August. I have no choice in the matter." I said, "Look, don't you keep up? Do you ever go out to the bush? I hate to tell you this, but our roads and landings are in on both sales and our beetle wood has been logged and hauled in." He was flabbergasted. He told us his forest officer had reported no activity on either of the sales after inspecting them two weeks before. I said, "Well, hey, that's your problem. Maybe he got lost out there." He said, "Cut the funny stuff and let me investigate this. I will go to the bush myself. Will you come with me?" No way was I taking time out to do his job and I told him so! But, I suppose he went out to the sales, as I didn't hear anymore about unmet obligations or cancelled sales.

That same summer, 1985, my crew and I were logging a SBEP sale out at Slender Lake, 50 miles east of Quesnel, in the Prince George district. We had set up a camp, as the operation was expected to continue for a year or more. This sale bordered Slender Creek, a nice creek 20 feet wide or so. We had a 30-metre, no machine zone, starting from the creek back (for obvious environmental reasons). I had been down at the Ministry, on purpose, carefully going over the creek rules and other environmental stipulations. We were not allowed to move any machinery within 30 metres of the creek and, if we were going to fall any of the big trees within that 30 metres, we had to drop them away from the creek. I ribboned the 30-metre "off-limits" zone myself and built my skid roads just up to it. I instructed my fallers about steering clear of the creek and about the drop rules. A few days later, I received a call from Blaine, who was in camp at the time, saying that the MOF had just shut our operation down. Something about trees in the creek and I was to come out right away. I said I'd be right out. I phoned Prince George MOF. They informed me that there were trees in the creek and they didn't know how they were going to handle it yet. I said, "I'm going out there now and I'll call you later." I wanted to see for myself. I met Blaine out at camp and we proceeded down to the creek. I asked who had been falling down there and he said he didn't think anybody had been down there yet. As we walked down one of my skid trails to the creek I saw, to my dismay, a huge green patch of trees in the creek on our side. As we got closer something didn't look right. There weren't any stumps! Netherlands Overseas, a big company out of Prince George, had the rights to the timber on the other side of the creek. They had started falling at the creek, falling every tree across the creek on to our side, so they could skid nothing but butts. True story! This was fairly typical of the big companies in Prince George at the time. Apparently, they were bigger than the rules.

Fish creek

In any case, we had a hard time believing what we were seeing, but sure breathed a sigh of relief. Even though it was a terrible thing to do to a creek, we hadn't done it. The original forest officer who had found the creek problems had just walked down our skid trail, and when he saw the mess, had assumed it was made by my crew. Anyway, I called the MOF in Prince George and asked if I could get the forest officer and the supervisor of the SBEP to come out and meet me on the site. They said, "Yes, we'll meet you out there in the morning." The next morning, three people came from Prince George MOF came to see us: the SBEP supervisor, the forest officer in charge and the supervisor in charge of timber. You can imagine the look on their faces when they realized what had happened as we stood by the creek. One comment was, "Boy, they (meaning Netherlands) are sure going to have to get their trees out of the creek." I probably made more comments than I should have as they stood there with egg on their face. Incidentally, Netherlands never got shut down, and they left no buffer between them and the creek. Talk about the same rules for everyone! This was always a frustrating part of the system I had to accept. The big companies could do pretty much as they wanted and the little guy had to follow the so-called "rules" to the letter. The big guys did fall in line later on but at that time, especially in Prince George, they did pretty much as they pleased.

The large Prince George operators were not happy with the SBEP, they never offered to help the smaller operators with anything; their loggers and crews acted like any road in the area was theirs. When their trucks came through loaded, they were not very considerate at all. One time, I was going to town on the main bush road. I came on a company grader parked a bit off to the side. The driver stopped me and said he was out of fuel, and did I have some? I had my diesel tank with me and I emptied my tank into his grader. He said thanks a lot, and that was the last I heard from him or his superiors. He had said that he would have his boss square up. Never happened . . . and I decided they just didn't think we were important enough to even acknowledge, much less repay, a favour. They resented our being in what they called "their territory." Prince George was the only area that acted that way.

One other time, on this same Slender Creek job, we had finished up for the day and had settled down in camp for the night. A Prince George logger was moving into an adjacent area to work and lowbedded nine machines on to one of our working landings during the night. Our camp was about a half a mile from this landing so we were not aware of anything until the next morning. Imagine our shock to discover our landing absolutely full in the morning. You couldn't turn around for machines! Nobody showed up from that outfit until about noon. I went over and asked them who was the boss? This operator said, "Over there," and I found a new pickup, idling away while the boss sat inside talking on his radio. I asked him what was happening? He said they were going to log on the other side of the creek. They hadn't put any roads in there yet, so were going to use our side as their dropoff point. I explained to him that he was on one of our working landings and since we needed it, he would have to move off. He said, "Oh yeah, no problem. I'll have my cat build a spot on the other side of the creek and then we'll move from your landing." They finally did get their equipment moved but I often wondered what would have happened if it had been us that moved on one of their landings.

This same outfit moved a large fuel tank in and parked it on our side of the creek in a little clearing that we were not using. I thought, well okay, it's not in our road . . . but I mentioned it to their foreman saying I didn't like it seeing the fuel tank there and that I felt it was too close to the creek. He looked at me like I'd lost it and replied, "Well, this is Crown land you know and if it's not in your road, we'd like to leave it here for a while." About two weeks later, a MOF forest officer came out to my camp with his ticket book and had written me a note giving me two days to move my fuel tank back from the creek. Imagine his surprise when I explained that it was Netherlands' tank. We had been assigned a brand new forest officer by this time. He was at least sympathetic to us, in dealing with this company and its roughshod ways.

The two-rule system showed up another time, on the Lavington Road, 40 miles west of Quesnel, on a blowdown timber sale. We were logging in the summer and it had been raining steady for a few days. Our forest officer on this sale came out and, since the rules were "very little ground disturbance allowed," he shut us down until it dried up a bit. He explained carefully to us that it was important not to make ruts on the trails or have mud pushed up on the landings. I said I could see that and that we'd clear out and see him in a few days. We talked a bit about the weather and he was on his way. We parked our equipment and left. I came back a bit later to see if it had quit raining and had dried up some. I noticed the sale next to ours was still being worked on. They were skidding in the wet ground and had ruts all over. I thought, oh well, I guess we can go back to work. I went back to town to the MOF office and talked to my forest officer. I told him about our neighbouring logger working and he said, and I quote, "Yes, Ed, that's Quesnel Forest Products' logger, Real Gamache, logging that sale and they do their own site prep after the sale is finished. They are allowed to do as they see fit." I exploded at him, saying, "That's not right! How about all the stuff you were feeding me about damaging the forest? Come on, get real! What kind of logic is that?" To make a long story short, the company logger kept working and we stayed shut down until it dried up.

Not everything the Ministry of Forests did was misguided but I do think there was a higher degree of bungling, at least in the areas that I was logging, than there should have been. Another example of mismanagement happened on a sale near Nyland Lake, east of Quesnel. We were logging alongside a very wet patch of land and the forest officer came out. He and I ribboned this wet spot out, the idea being to keep machines out. Any trees within this wet spot were to be felled out and reached from dry ground. A big stand of cottonwoods was to be left untouched. The forest officer explained the reason for the restriction: the machines would sink through the top layer of soil destroying the integrity of the overall layers of vegetation, and causing no end of problems. It made sense in a way and, heck, we were loggers not soil analysts. Whether we agreed or not, however, we wouldn't have been able to do anything else. The people in the SBEP could and would shut you down for any infraction of the tender package rules. After completing the sale, all the while keeping machines out of the wet area (that had meant lots of long lining to reach some of the trees, a labour-intensive and difficult process), we cleaned up our landings and moved on. I went back a few weeks later to look at another sale and was amazed to see our wet spot with its cottonwood stand all flat and full of ruts. A large cat had been moved in and was pushing these cottonwood trees over and piling them up. What a mess, as the ground was so wet. I couldn't believe what I was seeing. I immediately went to the MOF and asked for an explanation. I was informed that the silviculture branch of the MOF was looking after rehabilitating and reforestation, and they decided these cottonwood trees needed to be removed and replace with conifers. I went to see the silviculture guy and asked him about all those ruts. He said, "Well when our cat just makes one or two passes in one spot, it's okay. It's when you are skidding and carrying a load that it gets packed down and that is when problems occur." Talk about a bunch of "bull."

The Department of Fisheries and Oceans was a bit of a problem at this time as well. This was a federal agency with authority over spawning rivers and water areas that could have an impact on the fish and fishing industries. One of our trees had fallen over a creek in the Wells area. MOF reported it to DFO, can you imagine! A DOF officer came out and explained to me the negative points of a tree falling in a creek. He explained that needles would clog a creek up and fish would have difficulty breathing. I said, "Hey, you have to make sense with this." He went on to say if an accumulation of needles occurred it could hamper the breathing of the creek. I said, "Okay, but this is not even a fish creek." "No" he said, "but as the needles float down stream they could eventually get into a fish creek."

We cleaned out the creek to his satisfaction and said goodbye. I received a call from this DFO officer a few months later, asking me to come and see him in his office, downtown. I called him back from my truck, asking what was this about? He said he would like me to come in and fill out a report about some garbage he had found on one of our landings. Further conversation revealed that two green garbage bags were found on a landing burn pile on my timber sale and would have to be removed. I asked him if he had been out there personally. He had. I then asked him why he hadn't picked up these two green garbage bags and brought them in with him. Dead silence for a while, and then he said in a clipped voice, "I don't pick up garbage!" I said I didn't have time to see him at this time. He said, busy or not, he would like me to come in right now and fill out this report. I wasn't taking this guy very seriously, at this point, and told him I couldn't come in right then but maybe later. He said, "Well, I just happen to have gotten control of your $30,000.00 deposit on that sale and unless you come in today, I am going to have to seize it." I thought, what's happening here, as I said, "I'm on my way." Tampering with my deposit had got my attention in a big way! When I arrived at his office, he had some forms for me to fill out and he went over the problems of garbage in the bush. He said he realized he didn't know who the garbage belonged to but that it was my responsibility as it was on my timber sale. I said, "Look those two bags are mine and I took them out there myself. I always take my burnable garbage out to the bush and put it in the burn pile." He explained that was not allowed and would have to stop. I said, "Okay, as long as I know the rules, I am willing to go along with them." He went on to explain the new rules of keeping the bush in its natural state as best as we could. Over the years I got to know and like this man. His name was Mitch Kindall.

One thing I always had a problem with was that we little guys had to follow these new rules (and, to be fair, I agreed with them to a point) while the big boys didn't. The pulp mills, sitting at the end of the drainage, are allowed to dump their waste into major waterways. A case in point is Quesnel River Pulp. Their four-foot diameter discharge pipe is (still) located one mile from their mill, emptying into the Fraser River. In the fall, as the water goes down and is partially clear, you can see black sludgy, discharge fluid going directly into this main fish river. This is my idea of polluting, not some logger changing oil in the bush miles from nowhere and spilling some, or at least it was until Mitch made us aware of the new rules. With Mitch, I came to realize even a small spill was bad news and set about cleaning up my act. After a while I adopted a different approach: I would imagine this was my land, right next to my living area, and what would I expect of a logger who came in to log it for me. Would I want garbage left, old cans or fallen trees left on my fence, or lawn? No way! With this kind of thinking in place, I modified some of my methods regarding timber sales and I started to have more respect for the forest and its surroundings. I had never been really careless and had always followed the rules, even the two-rule tango. But now, doing something properly without anybody's prompting gave me a sense of well-being, a feeling of rightness. Just knowing and doing it yourself was reward enough. I guess it's called stewardship.

CHAPTER 15

Life Not Logging

For years, most of my life I guess, I had been having trouble with relationships. I was not consciously aware of my problems but anything unresolved shows up somewhere. I had been married three times and, despite business success, was not really very secure within myself. My inability to resolve (or recognize) some personal issues became unhappiness and that discontent leaked out and affected those around me.

My wife, Vicki, had hung in there with me for seven years. It wasn't easy but she is a wonderful lady and was determined to stick things out and struggle to make and keep a marriage. She found a self-help sanctuary on Gabriola Island called Haven by the Sea. She spent some time there herself and realized it was a place people could sort out their problems, and receive help with them. It took some convincing but she persuaded me to go for a session or two.

I was a rough logger. I really didn't think I needed this kind of help. I agreed to go along with Vicki's plan, probably unconsciously knowing I needed help of some kind but, also, to please her. My first visit was quite an eye opener. I realized a very real closeness was expected of each member of the group and I, being me, pulled right back. How did I end up here! I didn't say anything to the session leaders but I wasn't going to do any crying or hugging of other men. No way. My resolve lasted for the whole five sessions. I think the only effect those first five days had on me was to give me a hint, a sneaking inkling that there might be another way to live in the world. A way I didn't know. I went back six months or so later.

After committing myself to go a second time, I arrived prepared to be a bit more open. I let myself talk some. The group leaders were skilled and helpful and able to sense a troubled area and pursue it. With me they found out I had a hard time talking about my childhood, especially when I was around five and six years old. Gently probing, the story came out, with old feelings surfacing. Without realizing it, in a group session, I blurted out my overwhelming boyhood secret, the shameful sexual happenings with my half-sister Edith. As my story came out, I shrank inward. I was sure the group (about 25 people and 4 leaders) would think I was a bad person and would shun me. I wailed away in this tortured inner space. Slowly I came to realize nobody hated me. As I looked around at the faces of those who had gathered around me, I saw compassion and caring. My secret hadn't made the huge impact I had imagined. Just sharing it with others had taken away most of its power. As I realized this, I was overwhelmed with a sense of relief. It was almost laughable. The sense of horror and revulsion I thought would surface in the people around me if they learned my secret didn't! There was no blame, no shunning.

It was time to bring my memories out into the open and expose my fears. I had to work on my problem. I discovered I had blamed myself for these childhood incidents; I assumed only boys could be abusers. Rape, aggression, physical strength . . . male traits . . . this is what I thought of as abuse. It was carefully brought out that it was possible for a girl to be the abuser and maybe I was not so bad after all. The horror of childhood abuse is "the loop": it gets replayed and replayed as you age without you knowing why and, often, without resolution. Victims are driven by a force they don't understand. In my case the undercurrent, the "force" was worthlessness. I believed I would be considered worthless if someone knew my secret. I kept needing secrets in my life; I needed to live with the fear that someone close to me would discover my shame and shun me. If I wasn't being discovered, I would try to help the people close to me to expose my failures. Subconsciously, I wanted them to find out I was not a good person. I would become harder and harder to live with, needling my partner and creating a nightmare. I am still amazed at the effect an early incident can have on a person's life; an early trauma can have an impact on you forever, or at least until it is exposed and dealt with. I came to realize I had been treating women like objects, with all the problems that go along with that. I was very judgemental about people and things. When I look back now, on this portion of my life, I realize that I was not a very nice person.

I can tell you, discovering that about myself and accepting it and trying to fix it hasn't been easy!

I took careful stock of myself and realized I had to do some work and change some of my thinking and beliefs. I kept going back to Haven by the Sea year after year, and each time I discovered something new about myself. I tried to improve. I realized how small the world I lived in was. I discovered that women were human beings with much the same uncertainty and feelings as men (no kidding), and that deep down we are all just little boys and girls, only older. I learned to become more open and sharing of myself, which, in turn, allowed me to gain more confidence and become a better person. I was able to be more comfortable in a group and it became possible to try public speaking. Slowly I became more comfortable with myself. Over the next few years (10 to be exact) I was able to mend my ways and work on my relationship with my wife, fully realizing my part in our troubles, and being able to change it. I am very grateful to my wife, Vicki, for hanging in there through my self-discovery, and to the Haven folk for being there in my time of need. I am now aware of how my actions have an affect on other people. I am trying to be a better person as I practise my new found philosophies.

Some funny things happened to me at Haven over the years. As you may guess, I was uncomfortable around people. I was very reluctant to join strangers at tables in the cafeteria. One of the leaders, Ben Wong, gave me several assignments with this problem in mind. First, he wanted me to get a plate of food and sit at a table for four by myself. Just look at my plate, eat, feel closed, alone and see what happens as the place fills up. Surprise, surprise — no one came and sat with me. The next day I was to get a plate of food, sit at a table for four, face the line and put a smile on my face and make eye contact with my fellow diners, and feel open to anything. I was amazed to find three people joining me as they walked into the room looking for a table, and even though I didn't know them very well, they chose to sit with me. The next day my lesson was to fill my plate a few minutes late and walk into the crowded cafeteria and go up to any table filled with people and stand close by waiting for somebody to make room. I was not to make eye contact and to feel closed. I felt terrible as I stood there imagining all sorts of things. Nobody paid any attention to me. I stood there alone in my misery until I could no longer stand it and I

Haven seminar.
Back Row: leaders, Linda, Jock, and Ben. *Next Row*: author second from right

moved to a corner table for one, sat down and ate my lunch feeling shamed. The next day I was to repeat the process except the table was to have eight people sitting there. I was to have a smile on my face and make eye contact with anybody at this table, and feel open and friendly. Imagine my surprise as I moved close to this table, to see people sliding over to allow some space for me to sit, without their seeming to even notice me. Most of the conversation did not even stop as I slid in. I was accepted, just another human being. Amazing stuff for a logger from the Cariboo to realize.

Vicki and I attended a couples "how to" workshop one year. There are certainly a lot of things to learn about a relationship. Much of the problem solving is common sense but there seems to be much less common sense in a marriage than you'd believe! In the course of the workshop, I found out something quite surprising about myself. We were asked to tell our partner several things while he or she listened. The person who did the listening was then asked to repeat the things that had been said, word for word or as close as possible. Well, I thought I'd have no problem, after all, I figured I was a fairly smart guy. Would you believe, whenever Vicki went beyond three things, I couldn't for the life of me remember what they were. I couldn't believe it. My mind would go blank. It certainly explained why I had trouble with arguments . . . if Vicki went on for any length, I wouldn't hear what she was saying. Phrases like "you don't know what you are talking about" or "what do you mean" were suddenly pointing out my shortcomings. The hard part of all this was that Vicki could repeat pretty much of what I said word for word. That was pretty hard to take! Sometimes it's hard to really listen to someone. Too often we are busy thinking about what we are going to say ourselves when the person who is talking is finished. When you are planning what you are going to say you can't listen to what's being said. Relationships, especially marriages, are better if everyone takes the time to listen carefully.

I have come to realize how little we learn in life when all we do is work and live in a closed, small world. We actually follow the examples our parents set; they are our role models. My parent's early life was filled with just coping, feeding their family, and being busy with a hard pioneer life. Not much time was ever spent on improving things. They lived from day to day and that was not their fault; it was all they knew. They probably did the very best they could at the time. It becomes our own responsibility to expand our lives. I have learned some life lessons: I have become closer to my family, am able to show them love and compassion, can talk to them more effectively than before (I didn't communicate much before. It was difficult for me and that was tough on the people I loved.), and I am happier in my closeness to family and friends. And yes, I can now cry when feelings surface and I am also able to hug men!

Most men, I think, have a hard time showing their feelings. We are brought up, for the most part, thinking we have to be strong, tough and unemotional. I remember when I was raising Blaine, if he got hurt I tell him, "Hey, don't cry. Don't be a wimp. Go to sleep or you'll wish you did! No Blaine, you can't sleep with me. You have to sleep alone. You can do it, be tough. That little scratch doesn't hurt, boys are tough." When I think back at these times now, I cringe. I was not getting a good message across. Without really thinking about it, I was doing the same thing to Blaine that my parents had done to me. I didn't think, I copied. If we don't think, we risk damaging a young mind.

There should be a mandatory course for all new parents, taught by someone who knows what's what. We should have to pass this course before having children. In order to do most things that we value, we have to study for years, taking courses and passing tests . . . i.e., training to be doctors, dentists, veterinarians, foresters, counsellors, bankers, etc. Yet for marriage and raising kids, the most important job of all, we need no licence or training at all. These are the most important lessons that we will ever need. Can you believe this?! I think, slowly, our world is becoming more aware and I hope our attitude to relationships and families is improving. I'm all for more awareness about life in general. It has been a long time coming. One person said to me once, "It took us 700 years to get into this mess and it's going to take a while to straighten it out."

I had met a nice man in the early 1980s, named John Lee Kotnekoff, who was putting on public speaking workshops and generally helping people with their problems. I happened to go to one of his workshops and immediately liked him and his humour. I took some of his workshops on public speaking and enjoyed myself very much. He also taught things along the lines of Haven but, at the time, I was unable to recognize their value and missed an opportunity to grow. One of his sayings often comes to mind, "When the student is ready, the teacher will appear." Well, I had a number of teachers appear in my life, but it was not until I was in my 50s that I realized they were there for me and took advantage of what they had to offer. It's hard not to regret the way I did things in the past but I am now aware of better ways to live and that has become important to me.

In 1980 a grandson came along and two granddaughters followed. I was fortunate enough to live close so I could truly enjoy them. I used to take my grandson, Kyle, for summer holidays as he grew older and went to school. What a pleasure it was to be around a young and impressionable mind. I was amazed at how all I had to do was love him and everything else worked out. I was able to put some of my new understanding to the test and discovered there is no big secret but a big benefit to caring. We just need to be open, loving (unconditionally), and young people will respond accordingly. You love, therefore they love. The hardest part is to know them on their own terms. They are little persons with unique personalities and feelings. They should not be, as I was, just kids to be seen and not heard.

I enjoyed the time I spent with my grandkids, especially our Sunday morning breakfasts. Kyle was the first to start the ritual and then, when her mother said she was old enough, Nikki came along too. Candi joined us when she turned four years old. I would pick the kids up on Sunday morning and we would drive to town for breakfast. We had a game to choose the restaurant: we'd each write our choice on a piece of paper and whichever place got the most votes, that's where we'd go. One particular morning we were having pancakes at Gary's Pancake House and suddenly Candi (at age four) exclaimed, "Grandpa, I have to go to the bathroom and it's number 2." Oh boy! I took her to the bathroom and was faced with an immediate problem, which bathroom do I take a little girl to? The men's? No, she's a little girl! The women's? I can't go in there. We settled on the women's with me standing at the door, waiting. In a few minutes I hear Candi calling, "Grandpa, I'm finished." I said, "Okay, come on out then." She hollered, "No, I can't, you have to wipe me!" I thought, God, what am I going to do? Run and get Nikki, who was two years older, or what? Then common sense took over and I said to myself, "Look you have had kids. You know what it's about," and with that in mind, I marched into the ladies room and into her booth, to find her patiently waiting for me as she leaned over unabashedly offering me her bottom. I quickly took care of things. The innocence was wonderful and made me smile.

Another time, we were having breakfast at the same place when Nikki pipes up and asks, "Grandpa, could we go shopping for toys?" We usually stopped in at the Flea Market on our way home after breakfast. I replied, "No, Nikki, the stores are closed." She persisted, "But Grandpa if they are open, could we?" I felt safe in saying yes, if they were open, we could go toy shopping. "Oh, goodie!" she cried, "Mom says Zellers is open Sundays now!" I said we'd go and see after breakfast was finished. I still didn't believe that the store would be open Sundays. She said, "Oh good, and if they are can we buy anything we want?" I half thought about that and visualized a small, cheap toy section in Zellers, so I said, "Sure, if Zellers is open, you can have any toy in their toy section." Of course they hurried up and finished their breakfasts and off we went to Zellers. Yes they were open! They were all excited at this as we headed for the toy section. Nikki immediately ran up and down the isles looking for something definite. Upon finding it, she proudly grabbed this large box containing a talking boy doll, called Ricky, whom she had seen on TV. Talk about smart at six years old. Now what was I to do? I had imagined a small, inexpensive toy, one that would get their mother's approval and cause no problems. I said, hopefully, "Well Nikki, let's put the doll down and look around some more." She could hardly carry it. She hugged it tighter and stated, "No Grandpa, this is what I want," as she looked at me hopefully, with her big blue eyes. I had said yes, any toy in this store, but this was different. All sorts of arguments went through my head. It's too big, too expensive ($109.00), your Mom won't let you keep it, it probably won't talk, but as I looked at her I realized none of my arguments would work. A promise is a promise. I said okay very reluctantly, silently wondering what on earth I was going to tell her mother? She was so excited on the way home, hardly able to wait to open it. Candi had chosen some building blocks and Kyle couldn't seem to find anything that suited him. Arriving home, Nikki charged into the house, proudly hanging onto her doll, saying to her mother, "Mom, Mom look what I've got. A real Ricky!" Her mother looked at me questioningly, I looked back, lifted my hands up, shrugged, silently saying, "What could I do?" Nikki was so proud of her doll and kept it for many years. Maybe she still has it.

These kids were a joy to take out and they looked forward to each Sunday. Mostly we went to McDonalds, a favourite place for kids. Our deal was that they could have anything they wanted for breakfast. One morning, after seeing an advertisement, Candi ordered chocolate chip cookies and milk. Little do most of us realize the impact advertising has on young minds. I learned very quickly (why had I missed it with Blaine?) how fast children pick up everything from the hard sell on TV to the casual "adult" comments we make in front of them. We need to be vigilant in our talk and actions and what we let them see and hear. At McDonalds I could let my three charges pretty well have free run of things. I soon learned that it was best to decide what the breakfast order would be BEFORE arriving at the restaurant; otherwise the decisions and wait took too long and kids, I found, like to get their food and eat without too much dilly-dallying. I observed mothers with their kids and discovered that most problems seem to show up after the kids had finished eating. They wanted to go and play and the Moms wanted them to stay because, "We're going soon." I learned to allow my brood to play pretty much as they pleased; after all, the place was set up for kids. Would you believe, once the freedom was offered, Kyle, Nikki and Candi would find a comfort zone not too far from me. I think the worst they ever managed was the time Nikki, aged six, put Candi in a high chair with wheels and pushed her around as fast as she could make it go. Candi was screaming, "Stop" and Nikki was laughing. Week after week, they enjoyed their breakfast outings with their Grandpa.

I remember another outing that involved a meal. One time Kyle and I were checking on some land clearing. We'd gone out in an ATV and ended up in between properties around lunchtime. I asked Kyle if he was hungry and he said, yes, he was. I said, "Okay, let's go and get some lunch." I drove to a place I knew had a patch of wild raspberries and they were in season. This patch was a short way from the road and I stopped as close as I could get, shut the machine off, and said to Kyle, "Let's go and eat." He looked at me with a puzzled expression on his face and said, "Where are we going to get lunch out here, Grandpa?" I replied, with a straight face, "Just follow me, Kyle. Today God is providing lunch." What a feast we had. The raspberries were exceptional that year and we enjoyed every mouthful.

Candi and Nikki stayed over some weekends. They were always fun to have around. Nikki was so busy trying to be helpful, she was an accident waiting to happen. One time Blaine and I sat down to have some coffee. Nikki, who was around five then, jumped up on the table exclaiming excitedly that she wanted to pour the cream in our cups. You guessed it, she spilled the cream. She rushed to clean up the cream and as she wiped vigorously, you guessed it, she spilled the coffee.

That same weekend, I had arranged to have some work done on my truck at the local garage. The salesman there, Darrel Collins, had been wanting to sell me a fancy foreign car for some time and took this opportunity to have me try it out. He said, "Hey Ed, take this car for a test drive while we are fixing yours." and tossed me the keys. I said, "Okay. Good deal. Come on kids let's go get some ice cream." Candi and Nikki came running from somewhere. Darrel hadn't noticed that they were with me and I know that all he could see was his beautiful car being messed up by sticky children. I was putting him on, of course. We did go for a ride though and when I opened the moon roof Nikki jumped up on the seat, grabbed the edge of the opening, poked her head out and hollered, "Faster, Grandpa, faster!" Candi just sat quietly, watching the world with a smile, and looking about as if fancy cars and bouncing sisters were an everyday occurrence.

We were cutting hay that same summer and I was raking this large field. Kyle was riding on the tractor with me. He was about 10 years old. There was a nice saskatoon patch beside this field and I said to Kyle, "Why don't you get off and pick us a feed of berries while I make a round." He said okay and took a couple of empty coffee cup containers, and started picking while I raked. It probably took 20 minutes to make a round. As I approached the saskatoon patch I saw a bush come down and I thought, boy that Kyle really means business. I was shocked to see a large black bear busy stripping berries off the bush. I frantically looked around for Kyle. He was on the other side of the bush, unaware of any problems. The bear faded into the bush as I approached and I was soon enjoying a feed of berries. I did not mention the bear to Kyle.

Another time when Kyle was around eight years old, I had to fall a few leaning trees from a powerline after a storm. I settled him in a safe spot, not far from where I was working, so that I could keep him in my line of sight. I worked a bit and then looked over at him only to see him doing a funny little dance. It didn't look right, so I shut off my saw and asked him if he was all right. He screamed at me, "No, there's bees here!" I ran over and sure enough I had put him beside a yellow jacket nest. The insects had crawled up his pants and were stinging him. I hurried to the truck with him, peeled off his clothes and got rid of the bees. He was pretty upset. A short time later, I felt a burning sensation on my leg. Investigating, I found a critter at the top of my work sock, stinging away. Yellow jackets do get serious when they think they are being threatened.

Each summer Kyle stayed with me and Candi and Nikki would visit back and forth. Vicki's boys by then were away at college and rodeoing. Candi and Nikki, for the most part, were too young to go to work with me, but Kyle was old enough and come with me he did. I enjoyed him thoroughly. He was a big help to me as he grew older; helping to pick roots and rocks, cutting hay and baling it, helping to mechanic any broken equipment and driving the truck as we moved machinery. He would mark the trees to be cut on a selective logging sale, help with payroll days, etc. I always missed him when 'back to school' rolled around. I have many fond memories of my summers with Kyle and my many riotous Sunday morning breakfasts with all three grandkids.

Blaine, Candi, Kyle, Nikki, and myself

Shaun and Kyle, aged 3

Daughter Joann with Mandy and Morgan, 1984

CHAPTER 16

Blending Families, Work, and Bears

*V*icki's sons, Steve and Brian, came with her when we got married, and they saw their Dad every two weeks. They were 10 and 8 years old when Vicki and I got together. Blaine was 22 then and was living with his wife, Shaun. My daughter Jo was living in Smithers at this time, though I had yet to spend much time with her.

Steve and Brian didn't have the benefits of an accepting, more compassionate me; my self-improvement efforts were to come when they were close to grown, but they did have a caring mother. Blaine never had the benefits of a caring mother at any time in his life. How was I to be a stepdad? I muddled along, not thinking about it a whole lot, and came to the conclusion that maybe a semi-work arrangement might be a start. As the boys grew older, starting around 13 and 11 years old, I always had some work they could do in exchange for money. I knew they would probably like to have some spending money, maybe for a special bike or an ice cream or just to have. If they worked for it, it would teach them some good habits and tend to keep them out of trouble. One job that kept coming up, that they could do, was slashing timber sales. Slashing was the three-metre knockdown that was required on SBEP sales, a cleanup procedure that was mandatory when the logging was complete. The debris to clean up was small trees and brush, sort of logging leftovers! They (the boys) had been going to the bush with me in the summer holidays from an early age. I had let them take turns and helped them cut limbs from the short log decks. These short logs were the tops of bigger trees and they usually had small branches left on them after bucking. The loader would deck them separately and then the boys would trim them up.

It was a good job for them. They started out with axes and progressed to a small chainsaw. The biggest hurdle to overcome when I started them with the chainsaw was their mother. She was sure they were going to cut themselves, she used all the standard arguments. The saws were too sharp, too noisy, too heavy, too dangerous, would kick back, a log would roll on them, etc. After a few summers cutting limbs with the axe, I knew they could handle a saw. After receiving careful instructions on sharpening the chain, how to keep it on, and general safety tips, they were away. They had driven dirt bikes and skidoos already, so they were familiar with small engines. I taught them chain safety, i.e.; not to file the rakers down too much as the chain wears out. The rakers determine how deep the teeth cut, and a lot of problems come from rakers that are set too low. The chain becomes jerky and will kick back whenever the tip comes in contact with anything. They also needed to know how to keep the chain tight so it wouldn't fly off and cut their leg or handle bars. Low rakers and a loose chain are the most common dangers that amateur wood cutters face . . . the fix is simple but often people learn the hard way because there isn't anybody around to teach them chainsaw safety.

Steve and Brian started slashing a SBEP sale out at Slender Lake where we had a camp. We would all go out for the weekend. Vicki would take over in the camp, the boys would slash and I would do cat work. This way I could keep an eye on them. This first time for Brian was comical. I was showing them how to fall these small trees by leaving a little wood still holding as it fell. That small attachment was a good way to control the tree as it fell. Brian said, "Yeah, I know that," as he confidently approached a 15-foot bushy balsam tree, covered with snow. He reached in through the bottom limbs and with one big roar of his saw, he cut it right off, on a slant. This tree slid off its stump and the jar of the newly cut end hitting the ground caused the snow to fall off in a cloud of white. Brian hunched up and closed his eyes to keep the snow out and the tree slowly toppled on him. I can still see the picture in my mind! Poor Brian, he untangled himself from the branches and crawled out, sputtering, coughing and shaking himself off. This tree was not big enough to hurt him, but it showed him how careful you needed to be, even with small trees.

I had some rules and one was that they were to cut only small trees. If there were any big trees left standing from the logging, they were to leave them and get me to help. I was building skid trails one day, next to the boys, and I saw smoke coming from a large spruce snag, standing alone out in an open spot. I wondered why smoke would be coming from this tree. I turned my cat and headed off to investigate. As I neared the tree I saw Brian with his small saw, standing on his snow shoes, determinedly cutting away on this tree. Before I could get there I saw him pull his saw out of the cut and run down hill as fast as he could go, as the tree started to move. This tree fell slowly, cracking and smashing its way to the ground, making a deafening crash as it hit the frozen ground and broke into pieces. It landed partly on a hard frozen skid trail, luckily away from Brian. This snag had been left by the fallers and was about 30 inches on the stump and over 100 feet tall. When Brian saw this big tree he couldn't resist giving it a try. He had hoped I was far enough away not to see this, but as things usually don't work that way — he got caught. He was pretty scared as he realized how unstoppable these big trees are when they start to go. I was amazed he had been able to cut it down with his small saw. When I looked at the stump, it had been wittled from all sides. We ended up having a good laugh as it dawned on us that everything was safe, and I think Brian learned his own lesson.

Brian always was the rebel, doing things on his own and often finding out the hard way, but sometimes this is the only way. Steve was more conservative, always following instructions to the letter, and as the eldest, he was supposed to keep watch on his little brother. This was a rather difficult job as Brian always thought it should be the other way around. These early jobs in the bush helped both boys to learn about all aspects of the logging industry and they became proficient with most jobs. Falling, bucking, skidding, driving cat, loader, excavator, etc. I think it's a good thing to know more than one job. That way you are never stuck for work, there is always something you can turn your hand to.

The boys liked horses, and all horse-related recreations. They participated in the high school rodeos and became good cowboys. After graduating, they both went to college in Torrington, Wyoming, with scholarships, and became part of the college rodeo team.

I was taking a vet seminar in Las Vegas recently and I ran into a lady from Torrington and I mentioned Steve and Brian attending college there. She was interested and talked about their rodeo skills and what they had excelled in. She asked me then what were their academics. I replied, "Well, Steve took Forestry and Agriculture," and after hesitating a bit I went on to say, "and Brian took Beer and Girls." We had a laugh at this in fun, but there was probably some truth to it. At the time of this writing, both boys have turned professional cowboys, with Steve specializing in calf roping and Brian in steer wrestling. They both are proficient team ropers. In 1998, Brian made the top 10 in steer wrestling and made the Canadian Finals Rodeo. Steve was a hair's breath from the finals himself.

As these two boys grew up and jockeyed for position in life they were torn between rodeo and work. "Should you work or should you rodeo" was a long-standing question. Should I rodeo now while I'm young or should I work now, get ahead and buy some property, and rodeo later when I'm settled and a little older. I encouraged both boys to follow their dream; to rodeo, even though it went against my own example. I had been taught that work comes first in anything and I had a hard time realizing that this could be their work. I do know that people should try and do what seems right for them. To avoid getting into some job or profession that somebody else thinks is right for them. I knew from my own experience that doing something that your heart wasn't in made the days long and the time drag. And that the time flew and spirits were high if you were doing something exciting, that interested you. When I thought about my situation, there was no comparison between fixing a broken machine in 20 below weather and cruising some timber on a warm day. I didn't want to imagine how I would feel if my steady job each day was fixing broken machines on cold days. The other factor that came into play in my deliberations about what Brian and Steve should do was, if they decided to work first and rodeo later, and then realized they were doing the wrong thing just to please Vicki or me, their heart would not be in it, they would be unhappy and the job would suffer. I really think the old saying, "do what you love and the money will follow" holds true with many people.

The enthusiasm that comes with doing something you love shows and makes you successful whether it shows outside or is just within yourself. Think about kids at play, doing something they like, they don't even want to come in for supper. Think how happy you'd be in your job if suppertime went by unnoticed? It is not always possible to do what you love, but just being aware of possibilities changes your thinking and allows for change. Some people are unhappy with their job their whole lives and don't know why they're unhappy with their life. Sometimes just knowing the source of your unhappiness will change your whole attitude and make doing an unpleasant task acceptable.

When I first got to know Steve he was 10 years old and pretty quiet and reserved, at least around me. My marriage to his Mom probably was uncomfortable or put him under some pressure. Back then his first love was hockey until high school rodeo took over. He was good at both but Vicki and I thought he'd be hard pressed to do both sports plus school. In hindsight, he probably could have but we discouraged it. In any case, being good at hockey and at rodeo events was good for Steve. There is a time in young people's lives, in between school and finding your life's work, that is a tough transition. Having an interest or serious hobby can help young people through that difficult period. Rodeo filled this "no place" gap for Steve. As he got older, he became interested in land and timber deals as well. With a bit of help and using some of his rodeo prize money, he bought two five-acre lots for $10,000 each, in a good location, with the market in a downturn. He then held onto them for two years, until the market picked up, and sold them for $30,000 each. That got him hooked, or maybe spoiled, or maybe a little of both.

One time Steve and I went to look at a 160-acre project on Shuswap Lake, near the small town of Seymour Arm. Shuswap Lake is a beautiful piece of water in the north Okanagan. We drove to Kamloops from Quesnel; the plan was to spend the night and contact the real estate people in the morning. As it turned out, the listing realtor couldn't see us that day but he said he'd give us directions. Seeing a property without someone who knows the boundaries, etc., is not ideal but we drove out there anyway, over 60 miles of rough road. When we arrived at the Seymour Arm settlement, we stopped to ask the storekeeper about the 160 acres that was for sale. He said, "Oh yeah, that's over at such and such a place. There's a logger working on the property next to it. You should go see him." He pointed us in the right direction and off we went to find this logger. He turned out to be very informative, showed us the lines and gave us some other pertinent information.

The ad for this land had said, "160 acres, ¼ mile from the lake, with 3 creeks running through the property, with lots of timber." Our imaginations took these words and created a scene of big trees, a view of the lake, and three babbling brooks. The reality was a rain forest that had been logged. The whole area was wet and it was impossible to distinguish where the creeks started and where they stopped. It didn't help that it rained the whole time we were there. It was a good experience, though, for Steve. He learned about acreages and timber and so on, and that even though ads can be misleading, if you are really interested in property and timber you have to go and explore. Somebody once told me I was lucky in my deals. I don't know about that. A good deal does not fall in your lap. I like the saying "luck is where hard work and opportunity meet." Steve and I ended up having a nice two days together, discussing a variety of things, and becoming a little closer.

In the off season, when they are not rodeoing, the boys usually work with me in the bush. One time Brian and I were building roads into a new sale. I was on the cat pushing out trees, slowly working my way through the timber to the landing. In wet country, as this was, the idea is to put your road in with the least amount of disturbance, let it freeze in, then put the finishing touches on it. This has to be done in cold weather, allowing each day's work to freeze in. I would push a trail in, just wide enough for the cat to get through, and Brian would cut the roots off these pushed over trees. I pushed a few trees over and moved them off my trail. I hit an open spot and carried on plowing snow to the first landing, where I had started to rough it in. I started to feel uncomfortable as Brian didn't show up behind me, and I decided I had better go back up the road to check. When I got back to my last pushovers, there was Brian, sitting down with his legs under the end of a large spruce. As he was cutting the root off, it had kicked over, knocked him down and then settled on his legs, pinning him under the tree. His chainsaw had bounced too far away for him to reach and he was helpless although unhurt. The snow underneath his legs was soft and deep enough so that he hadn't broken anything, but hard enough to stop any movement. It wouldn't have taken long to become a big problem if I hadn't been there. Had he been working alone, he would have been in big trouble. I eased the cat blade under the tree and carefully lifted it up and I pushed it off Brian's legs. Other than being a little stiff and sore, he was okay.

When building the landing, we used the same principle. I would push the trees over and Brian would buck the stumps off; then I would push the trees in a pile and push the stumps off the landing into a low spot or pile of its own. One particularly large cedar tree had a den under it. This tree was about eight feet at the stump and this hole was about two-and-a-half feet in diameter, going under the tree. I called Brian over and said, "Go into this hole and see if there is anything in there." He looked at me like I'd lost my mind and, of course, refused. We cut the tree, as it was too big to push over, and underneath was a large bear den, about 10 feet in diameter and about 4 feet high. We both could have comfortably laid down and stretched out in it. Luckily the owner of the den was not at home.

Bears, the bush, and boys, oh my! I remember one time when Brian was young, he and Steve and another friend had been playing in the bush when they discovered a bear den. They excitedly ran home to tell us about it and wondered if there would be a bear in it. All of them were too scared to get too close to see. I told them I knew how to do it in this case, because my method took three boys. "Oh, how?" Brian asked excitedly. "Well," I said, "the two biggest boys take the smallest boy and poke him in the den and he'll be able to find out if the bear is in there." When Brian realized he was the smallest boy, several different expressions flitted over his face. I think he probably remembered this episode when we were discovering this new den.

I have had several encounters with bears in the bush over the years. One time Blaine and I were cruising timber, north of Quesnel, on the Fraser River. Blaine was about 14 at the time and we flushed a mother bear and her two cubs out of a thick patch of willows. There were bear signs all over. They ran snorting and puffing away from us. Blaine said, "Dad, we should go and get a gun or at least our dog." We had a German Shepherd dog then and I don't know why we were without him that day. I said, "No Blaine, they're just black bears and we don't have to be scared of them." He said, "What would we do if we ran into one on the trail?" I said, "I will just holler at it and it will run away." As we broke over a hill on to a flat area, Blaine touched me and whispered, "Dad, there's a bear." I looked where he was pointing and sure enough there was a large brown bear, just standing there looking at us, about 100 feet away. I threw my hands in the air and jumped toward the bear, hollering as loud as I could. Instead of running away, he shook his head and let out a roar, and came toward us in a rush. I turned around, gave Blaine a little push and said, "Let's get the hell out of here," and we started running. A few seconds later I noticed Blaine stopped at a tree and I hollered, "What are you doing?" "I'm climbing a tree," he replied. That's all I had time to hear as I went leaping and running for my life, all thoughts of bravery and saving Blaine gone from my mind. My only thought was to get away from this bear. I ran down the hill and across a steep draw and halfway up the other side before I realized the bear was no longer behind me. I stopped, my heart pounding, and I heard Blaine calling in a broken voice, "Dad, you better come back, he's under my tree." I turned and ran for the pickup parked back on the road, about a quarter of a mile away. I had a chainsaw in the truck. I grabbed it and ran back. The bush was thick and I could not see Blaine or his tree or the bear as I approached. "Is he still there?" I shouted. Blaine said, "Yes," his voice breaking. I took my chainsaw and felled a large fir tree toward the area where Blaine was. As it went crashing down, I shut my saw off and hollered, "Is he still there?" He replied, "Yes, he is." I moved closer and dropped another tree, this one landing not far from where Blaine was. "Is he still there?" I asked as things quieted down. "No," Blaine replied, "I can't see him now." "Well get the hell out of there," I hollered, as I ran toward him carrying my saw. Blaine came out of his tree and we ran to the truck. Blaine was white as a ghost. It was one thing to talk about bears and something else to have one snapping and snarling at the bottom of your tree. I had always told Blaine, and anyone else, that if a bear comes after you, climb a tree, and I guess this had stuck in his head. It was a good thing he had dashed up that tree as, if we had both run, I'm sure the bear could have caught us. I preached climbing trees but that thought never occurred to me as I panicked and ran. I always assumed that I would be good under fire so to speak, but this episode really shook me up as I realized it was survival first. I wasn't in there defending Blaine with my life, I was gone with the wind. I wonder what he really thought of his big protector after that.

Years later, Blaine and I were driving between landings in the bush when a small cinnamon-coloured bear crossed the road in front of us. It stopped at the bottom of a crooked tree and looked back at us. I said, "Blaine, stop the truck, I'm going to kick that bear in the butt!" and I jumped out and ran toward the bear thinking this would redeem me in Blaine's eyes, as I showed him how brave I was. As I ran toward the bear I realized he was bigger than I had first thought. When I was about 30 feet from him (I assumed it was a him), he turned and looked at me. A look of disbelief came on his face, as if to say, "Hey come on, make my day." Well, again fear took over and I came crashing to a halt, about 20 feet away from the bear. He still hadn't moved and I realized that I could have probably kicked him in the butt. What would have happened after that I don't know, but my chance of a lifetime had slipped away. What a thing, to have been able to tell your grandchildren, "Oh yeah, I just kicked him in the butt, and sent him on his way." But it wasn't to happen as I wheeled around and headed back to the truck. After hearing other bear stories I guess I'm lucky I didn't follow through and touch this bear. The saying "where fools rush in" comes to mind.

I was walking in the bush with two of my sisters one time, and we came upon a fresh bear track in the loose dirt. They immediately wanted to go back but I assured them we were safe as I had my bear spray. Coming upon more tracks, my one sister, Joan, said, "Ed you'd better show me your bear spray." I said okay and I pulled a 44-magnum revolver out of my shirt, a tool that I pack when I think I might be in bear country. I have never had to use it but the confidence I have when carrying it means the difference between getting the job done or not. I got this gun after doing some timber layout along the Bowron River during the fall season. I had some thick bottom land to ribbon a road through, and though I couldn't hear any bears, I could see evidence of them all around. I had to abandon my ribboning when I ran into a large grizzly that was not moving out of my way. After getting this powerful handgun, I really didn't pay much attention to bears, and they seemed to realize that and stayed out of my way. Having confidence makes all the difference in the world.

My Mother and Me

Sister Jean and author at our old place at Silver Creek

Steve and Brian as teenagers

They developed into professional rodeo competitors

Vicki, Brian, Kathy and myself at their wedding

CHAPTER 17

Realizing Dreams

*W*ay back in 1952, when Roy and I were newly on our own and trying to survive, my dream was to own a small farm in Silver Creek. By 1965, I was a logger. I was responsible for a family, rent, vehicle payments, grocery bills and all the rest of the costs of day-to-day living. My paycheque was used up on these things each month. I realized, if my dream of owning a farm was to come true, I would have to do something different. I decided to go up north, where I figured the wages were higher and the opportunities greater, and work for five years. I was going to make a "stake," come back and buy a farm.

Well, it was 29 years before I came back. I became established in Quesnel, and before I knew it, all this time had passed. Where did the years go? This is what happens when you get buried in work. You follow a new road and do new things and meet new people and sometimes you forget the life you wanted to start with. Sometimes work becomes too much and you forget how to appreciate things; maybe waking up to realize that life is passing you by. Has the thrill of the deal, the challenge of the next business opportunity taken over your original hopes and dreams and wishes? My dream of owning a farm in the Okanagan had been put on the back burner for a long time while I did other things and lived a different kind of life.

In 1993 Vicki and I drove to the Okanagan to visit Shaun, our daughter-in-law, and our grandkids who had moved to Enderby. After staying a few days, instead of going straight home, we decided to stay overnight in Vernon (I had a touch of the flu). The next day I was still feeling rough and Vicki said, "Let's take a drive through Silver Creek, you always like that." Every time, over the years, that we had come down to this part of the province, I would drive through Silver Creek. Vicki knew I loved the area. It seemed like a good way to feel better so I agreed and off we went. As we were driving through Silver Creek we noticed a "For Sale" sign on a farm. I phoned the real estate agent and talked to him. This farm was not ideal but all of a sudden I realized that we would be able to buy one of these farms if we wanted to. We had been looking at farms in Silver Creek over the years, but never seriously, mostly play-looking. This time realization hit home: I had reached a time in my life both financially and personally that I could buy some land here. Not "could" . . . I knew we *would* be buying some land here.

Vicki and I went home to Quesnel with plans to arrange things so that we could come back in about a week with the idea of buying something. Arriving back in Salmon Arm, I arranged a meeting with a real estate agent. Ron Cameron of Re/Max met us in town and we went with him looking for farms. He asked me if I had any thing specific in mind and I realized I did. I wanted around 80 to 160 acres in Silver Creek, around one mile either way from the Silver Creek Store. I wanted the property to have the Salmon River running through it and I wanted it to border on Crown land. Ron kind of threw his hands in the air and said, "Yeah, don't we all!" Anyway we spent the day looking at farms but nothing seemed right. None were in this two-mile radius I seemed to require. He finally gave up on us and took us back saying, "If something comes up I'll be in touch with you." The next day, we drove out ourselves and I went and visited an old friend from the '50s, Randy Bellows. I thought he might know about property in the area. I asked about one particular nice, older farm, owned for many years by the Wright family. He told me this farm had been sold a few years before to a fellow from England. Randy didn't know if he wanted to sell or not. He went on to tell me that he (Dave Wing from England) was not that nice of a guy. Well, I had nothing to lose so I drove out to the place. I drove onto this lane leading to the house. It was a neat driveway, through thick timber and everything was dark. The trees around the house were thick and didn't let in much light. Two big dogs greeted me as I drove up to the house. Nobody seemed to be around except these dogs, although there seemed to be a dim light on in the house. I thought, well I'm here now and, hoping the dogs wouldn't eat me, I got out and went to the door. The dogs didn't bite but didn't seem too friendly. I knocked on the door and waited, knocked again harder this time. I was just about to give up when I heard something from within and the door opened and this large, unkempt man, of around 55 years said, "Yes, what do you want?" I explained my mission and asked him if this farm was for sale. He seemed interested in finding out more and invited me in. I went in and he asked me in his neat, English accent, "Some tea then?" I said, "Yes," but instantly regretted it as he set a dirty cup in front of me and plugged in his kettle. He made a pot of tea and poured us each a cup. I realized that the cup was just stained and tentatively took a sip. It was good. He told me that he might sell his farm because he wanted to go back to England to retire. He said he wished he knew how long he was going to live and then he would know when to move. I couldn't help him there. He went on to say he would sell but not right now. He said there was a piece of property next to him, over across the river, and he waved in the direction of the mountain. He didn't know if it was for sale but some guy in Calgary owned it, by the name of Ken Evans. I inquired some more, thanked him and said goodbye. He hollered as I was leaving, "Mind you see me next year. I may sell to you."

It was 8:30 in the evening by then, and I had to get back to Quesnel, so I phoned my realtor, Ron Cameron, and told him what I had found out. I asked him to contact Ken Evans in Calgary and ask if the property was indeed for sale, and to contact me in Quesnel the next day. He agreed although he didn't sound too enthusiastic about it. He called me the next evening and said he had reached Ken Evans and that the place was not for sale, but "make him an offer he couldn't refuse" and he might reconsider. We agreed to meet on the upcoming weekend and inspect the property with Ron. We asked Ron to contact Ken and get permission and to make the arrangement to drive over and inspect this property. Ron got the go ahead we met on a Saturday morning and drove out to the Evan's place together.

This was a beautiful property. 155 acres total, 55 acres of valley bottom with the Salmon River running through, and 100 acres of rolling, timbered sidehill, bordering Crown land. The buildings and five acres had been surveyed off and kept by the original owners, Steve and Pat Sima, leaving a vacant farm with no buildings. Perfect in every way for us. After spending most of the day walking around exploring the property, we went to Vernon, where we were staying, to plan a strategy for an offer. Ron Cameron appraised it as best he could, i.e., $3,000 per acre for the bottom land and $1,000 per acre for the sidehill, or a total of $265,000.00. Ken had owned this property for two years and had paid $150,000.00 for it. We agonized over this for the weekend, knowing if we offered too little he would say no. Although we wanted it we also wanted to get it for a reasonable price. In my own calculations I had come up with a value of $365,000.00 and Vicki came up with $250,000.00. We sort of met in the middle and decided to offer him $275,000.00, thinking this would be enough to pique his interest, also knowing he would probably counter with $325,000.00. We could then counter with $300,000.00, which would be fine. We would have a deal. This sounded okay the night before, but who knew. Monday morning bright and early we were off to the real estate office. At 9:30 (we had been up since 5:00) we met Ron and discussed our offer. He agreed $275,000.00 was a good start. He called Ken and said he had an offer ready and would fax it over for review, and Ken could get back to us. I butted in and said to just give him the details over the phone. Ron did and Ken said that it was a good offer but he wouldn't sell for less than $300,000.00. Ron said he would talk it over with his clients and get back to him. As soon as Ron was off the phone I told Ron to offer to meet him in the middle, $287,000.00. Ron complied but Ken was firm, $300,000.00 or nothing. We agreed and I left Ron to take care of details.

Vicki went outside for a smoke while I went to the coffee room for a coffee. I met a man in the coffee room and we talked a bit. I was wound up. About 10 minutes later Ron stormed into the coffee room and stated angrily, "Boy, I sure told him. This deal is off!" I thought, "oh no," and asked what happened? Ron said he had called Ken and said he was faxing over the agreement for sale along with a listing agreement. Ken had asked him what the listing agreement was for and Ron had said, "I have to do this as that is how I get paid." Ken said, "I'm not signing a listing agreement. I have just agreed to sell for $300,000.00 and I'm not paying anything out of that to no real estate." Ron said, "Yes you are!" and of course the fight was on with Ken finally saying "no deal" and hanging up. Oh boy, what a mess. I said, "Ron, let's go back to your office." Ron was still bristling about this. I said, "Ron, cool down and here's what I want you to do. You get Ken back on the phone and you apologize to him, saying you made a mistake about the listing agreement and your client is taking care of any fees incurred from this deal, real estate fees and any legal fees." He did this and Ken said he would have to think about it and get back to us. After a long hour, Ken phoned back and said, "Okay, Ron." Ron faxed him the agreement for sale and asked him to sign and return it. As soon as the agreement was returned, signed by Ken and his wife, we had a deal. Vicki and I went back out and spent the rest of the day exploring and planning for our new property. We planned, in a year or two, we would move down and build a house on the property.

Meanwhile back in Quesnel, I took stock of my situation, realizing I would have to plan a bit for the move to Salmon Arm. I made a file of my property and timber and with the help of a real estate friend, we put a value on the property. The timber had its own value. It just needed someone to cruise it. As I had the most experience in this field, this job fell on my shoulders. I ended up with 24 properties, totaling 4,000 acres and approximately 40,000 M³ of timber, for a total value of $4.7 million. The equipment and miscellaneous would round it out to $5 million. I put the land and timber together and tried to sell it as a package. It didn't sell, as there was too much land and too little timber. I could have sold the timber separately, but I didn't want it stripped off. I ended up selling four parcels with the best timber value to Dunkley Lumber for $2 million. The rest of the timber and property I kept. This sale would enable me to develop my Salmon Arm property. I sold my logging outfit to my brother-in-law, Wayne Roch, with five timber sales to finish and look after. Wayne bought some of my equipment and I kept some myself. I decided to buy a quota job in Clearwater for Blaine, Steve and Brian to run, giving them a project to work on. Steve chose rodeo at this time and Brian and Blaine went to Clearwater to run this show. Within a year Brian returned to rodeo, leaving Blaine to run the show himself. (At the time of this writing, Brian and Steve are both enjoying success at the professional level of rodeo and Blaine is doing well with the logging show.)

After selling to Dunkley, I planned a home for Salmon Arm. I was building a log house in Quesnel at the time: it was at lock-up and I was getting cedar logs from a log yard I had in Wells. We were hauling logs from timber sales in the area to this log yard, bucking and sorting them there. It made an ideal way of getting building logs. I had my trucks haul four more loads to Quesnel for the new home. We started it right away, with the intention of building it in Quesnel and moving it to Salmon Arm when the log work was finished. This technique is possible with a log home. You can build it — walls, roof, and everything — and then take it apart and move it. This is what we did.

I needed to go to Salmon Arm to choose good spot on the farm for the house and build a basement. We finally picked a site, with much difficulty as there were so many good choices. Do you build in the trees, by the river, on the hill with a view, off to one side . . . ? We settled on a setting in the trees, on the bank of the river, in the centre of the property. We would have privacy and also have the sound of the river coming in our bedroom at night. That spring I hauled down my D8 cat (a bit of overkill), cleared and levelled a building site, hauled in some 147 dump truck loads of good rocky fill to lift the foundation up a bit as I felt it needed to be higher than it was. We raised the building site five feet to give us some protection from the river in case of flooding. With this accomplished, I put in the foundation. I had to forego a basement because the water table was too high. I excavated through the fill down to old ground, built forms, poured the footings and the frost wall. It was quite a job as the walls were as high as a regular basement taking into account this five feet of fill. After backfilling, the walls were just two feet above the ground level and perfect for a no-basement house. Just a two-foot crawl space. (Although after the fact I would now put in a four-foot crawl space as there is lots to do under there. Two feet is not much room to manoeuver in.) Now I was ready for the floor joists and floor.

I had bought 25 thousand feet of lumber from Dunkley and had it hauled down on a B-train truck so we had lots of material to work with. Dunkley had the best lumber of all. They were proud of their quality and I had bought their best grade. You could use every board; nothing had to be picked over. I had moved a 30-foot 5th wheel travel trailer down to the property to stay in while we were building the house. I parked it on the riverbank beside the house. The first four months I was there I had no power or water, but it was summer so it was okay. I could wash in the river and go to bed when it got dark. My grandson, Kyle, came and stayed with me during the summer holidays and helped on the house. He was 14 years old and learned to drive the Bobcat that summer. After finishing the floor, I went back to Quesnel to finish off the house we would bring down. I had a good helper working for me at the time, Terry Hook, whose Dad and brother build log houses. Terry had rodeoed with Steve and Brian for a while when they were in high school together.

To get on with it, I decided to build the roof structure in Salmon Arm. Terry and I sorted out extra logs to haul down. We had built six "king" trusses for the roof already. We brought in three highboy trucks, dismantled the house with a crane, carefully numbering every log, 176 logs in total. As we were taking down the walls, I compared the size to the cement work in Salmon Arm. It sure didn't look like it would fit. I hoped I had measured properly. We loaded up all three trucks, (it took them all), and we headed to Salmon Arm, making arrangements for a crane down there. We had a crane hired in Quesnel but of course he couldn't come down all that way. We had fun getting the first truck in to get started with the bottom logs. It didn't seem right that the last truck was the first truck loaded. The trucker was hardest to convince, as the first one to be loaded was parked by the basement waiting to be unloaded. We had six people altogether, counting the crane operator, to put the logs up. We had to insulate as we went up. Luckily the house fit on the cement. I had a deck on three sides covered by a roof making the total floor space 7,000 square feet, a huge floor. The finished floor space inside the house was 5,500 square feet. I had lots of comments on the size, like, "Boy, Ed, this is going to be a large house." I'd say yes it is but there are going to be two of us living here. . . . I had stayed at a house my brother-in-law had built in Calgary. He had built an extra wing on his house with four bedrooms and bathrooms. As he had a large family on both sides, he wanted room for guests. It sure worked good to have your own bedroom and bathroom when you visited. It was nice for him too as he could get up when he wanted and go to bed went he wanted. Then and there, I decided if I ever built my dream house, I would have some extra bedrooms with baths just for guests.

So this house in Salmon Arm had a total of 16 rooms. four bedrooms, four bathrooms, a kitchen, front room, foyer, laundry room, utility room two recreation rooms, and a library/office. We had a nice ensuite in the master bedroom with a Jacuzzi tub and a walk-in shower, a vanity with two sinks. At first Vicki said, "Okay Ed, you can have half the counter space." I agreed not realizing that when she said half she meant six feet for her and two feet for me.

I used to tell a story I had heard about an interview a newscaster had with Johnny Cash. Johnny was asked 'To what did he attribute his long marriage to June Carter?' He thought for a while and then said, "Two bathrooms." It's funny that when we are first starting out, raising a family, we often have only one bathroom; then, after we become empty-nesters, we have two. Should be the other way around. I know with kids going to school, the bathroom gets to be a pretty popular place in the morning.

I spent over two years, full time, building and finishing this house, and I had lots of help. I contracted the drywall, plumbing and heating (I put in radiant heat), and the wiring. I helped the electrician by doing all the drilling and cutting into the logs. I had made a rule, no one was to cut into the logs except me. I had a carpenter, Greg Robinson, come in to help me with the cupboards. Greg was a good carpenter and he worked on a few jobs with me. We became good friends. Finally the house was done. We had hardwood and tile floors on the main floor and carpet in the rest. In one rec room, upstairs, I put down tongue-and-groove fir. I had always wanted to do a fir floor. This house was completed at a cost of over $650,000.00, not counting the cost of the land. I had to bring in hydro, natural gas, telephone and cable, all 2,000 feet from the main road to the house. We also had to build a 2,000-foot driveway. I drilled a well and put in a pump septic system. This house also had three fireplaces, all done with local rock. The windows and doors were made locally from cedar. The doors were something else, there were nine outside doors, seven of them double glass, two single doors, and ten inside doors. This house had lots of glass. For me, lots of outside light makes log houses really homey.

About half way through building the house, the neighbouring property came up for sale again. This was Dave Wing's property that I mentioned before. He had contacted me twice before, to buy his place and both times he had changed his mind. This particular time I was driving to Quesnel when I received a call from Vicki saying that Frank Popane (a Re/Max realtor), who had Dave's listing earlier, had been out saying that Dave wanted to sell his place and that we would buy it. I called Frank and asked him if he had a signed listing agreement? He said, "No," and then I said that I would not deal until he had a signed agreement because I had been through this before. Frank went back to Dave and got the listing agreement signed, at great length, with a full price of $450,000.00 for the bare place. Dave had tried to sell it to me months before for $450,000.00 including the stock and machinery. His price, one way or the other, kept going up. I instructed Frank to go to Vicki and get a $10,000.00 deposit and offer the full price. I knew that any offer less than full price would be met with "no way, she's not for sale." Frank got the deposit and took the agreement for sale with a full price cash offer back to Dave to sign. This was about 10:00 a.m. By 2:00 p.m., Frank phoned me in Quesnel and said, "Ed, I don't know what to do. Dave keeps stalling and will not sign. I'm at my wits' end as to know what to do." I told him to just stay with it, "If Dave really wants to sell he will eventually sign." At 4:30 p.m. Frank called me to say that Dave had finally signed but that he wanted the deal closed in three days because he was going on a trip to England. This would be nearly impossible normally. Normally you have 30 days to close. I told Frank I'd get my lawyer, Gary Quinn, and the banker, Rod Wallace, working on it and we'd see what could be done.

Frank faxed up the paper work and I took it over to Gary. Gary Quinn had become a good friend over the years. Any deals I had I would get him to handle them. Gary was a "no nonsense" guy and made sure my (sometimes) somewhat unorthodox deals were letter perfect. Gary would insist that every "T" was crossed and every "I" was dotted. I sometimes got impatient with this and would try to shortcut but I never got away with anything ever, Gary made sure of this. This particular time I took this deal to Gary and he said, "No problem," until I mentioned the three-day closing. He burst out with, "You son of a bitch, Reierson, what do you mean three days?!" I said, "Yeah, well we are dealing with an eccentric here. This Dave Wing wants to deal but he wants to make it miserable for everybody. I think this is how he has his fun." Gary said, "Well, here's what you have to do and let's try to get it done." I went to the bank got a draft for $450,000.00 and, on the morning of the third day, I picked up the paperwork from Gary and headed to Salmon Arm. At around 4:30 that afternoon, I arrived at Dave's lawyers' office and handed over the draft and the paperwork. Everything was in order and this deal closed. That part of it anyway. Dave made it complicated by stating his cattle would stay until the following spring, the machinery until December 30th, and he would occupy the premises until December 30th. I agreed to all of these conditions, as I had no immediate plans for the place. Owning it was enough for now. Frank and I went to see Dave the next morning to tidy up our deal.

I had mentioned earlier to Frank that the cattle could stay but would have to be contained in the feedlot which was a 10-acre piece that was fenced and had feeders. Frank had said he would look after that. I didn't want the cattle running around as the outside fences were in bad shape and as soon as they got hungry they would break out into the neighbours. Dave had 40 head of cattle and these cows had spent as much time at the neighbours as in his place. I had had no end of trouble with these cattle as I had hay fields next to him. He would put the cows in the river and they would go downstream, and end up at my place. I eventually had to fence the river off and fix the rest of my fence. When his cattle did get over, Dave would do nothing about it. You had to get them out and fix the fence yourself. I was pretty frustrated with these cattle. Fisheries had helped him (Dave) fence the river off from the rest of his property to keep the cattle from the river and he used this as another pasture. With him the cattle came first and to heck with the environment and the neighbours. Anyway, when I said feed yard to Dave he said, "No, they won't have water. They need to go to the river for water." I said, "Yes, that's right and I will supply fence panels and we will make a lane to the river with a drinking station at the river." A drinking station is a place where animals can drink but cannot get into the water to walk around. Dave said, "You better show me," and the three of us headed for the river. I explained what I was prepared to do and Dave said, "Okay, but I reserve the right to open this gate if I run short of feed." I said, "No way! That's exactly what I don't want." Dave hollered, "Okay you guys, I've tried to accommodate you but I was on the phone to my lawyer at eight this morning and he says I can have full run of this place until spring." This was November 15th. I said, "Sorry Dave," and I turned to Frank and said, "Tell him, Frank," meaning our feed yard restriction. The look on Frank's face told me, Frank had not mentioned this to Dave. Dave was furious, red-faced and he hollered at me, "What do you mean 'tell him Frank'? Frank bloody works for me!" I replied, "Well, these cows are staying in the feed yard." To this Dave screamed, "No, these cattle are going to have free run of the place and what are you going to do about it!?" He had approached me and was standing close, his face red, his eyes bulging and his fists clenched. It was hard to believe how fast he had changed. I glanced at Frank and realized "no help there." Frank was trying to make himself invisible. I realized that this was time for a poker face and a bluff. I stood up as big as I could, looked Dave right in the eye and said, with as much authority as I could muster, "I will impound them, that's what I'll do!" "You'll what?" screeched Dave. "I'll impound them," I said calmly. I was shaking in my boots but I stood there. Dave looked like he would burst. He looked at Frank then back at me and like all bullies, he backed down saying, "Okay, but if they run out of feed will you sell me some hay?" I said, "Yes, I will," allowing him to save face, however little. Until this point, Dave had bullied the whole neighbourhood.

This new property had everything. Eighty acres in four titles, two houses, outbuildings, 50 acres in bottom land hay field and the rest in pasture and timber, and it joined our 155 acres on the south side making it one property. There was thick timber all around the buildings. It was nice but didn't let much light in and the trees were in bad shape. The pine beetle had gotten into the pine and the fir was riddled with root rot. This forest had not been cared for in years. A forest like that needs care. The beetle trees needed to be taken out and the root rot needed to be addressed. I had to take out most of these trees as it was too late to save them.

As soon as our possession date came, I immediately renovated the newest house. I stripped it down, put in new floors, cupboards, appliances, a new water system with outside hydrants, a new bathroom, added a dishwasher and a washer and dryer. Then we promptly moved in as we had been living in our 5th wheel travel trailer. We were happy to get out of that I'll tell you. While this trailer was comfortable it was very cramped, especially in the winter. When I first came down to Salmon Arm to begin the serious work on the log home, the contractor I hired to put the septic system in looked over this situation and asked what our plans were. I had said, "We're planning on staying in the trailer all winter until we get the house finished." He said, "Is your wife going to stay the winter too?" I said, "Yes." He thought about that a while and then he said, at lunch time one day, "Well Ed, I think I'll save half your property for you." I looked at him questioningly, not knowing what he meant. "What do you mean?" I asked. He said, "Well, if your wife is going to spend the winter in there with you, I am going to hook it up to the septic system so you'll at least have a bathroom that'll work. If she had to stay with you over the winter with no bath facilities she would divorce you and take half the property." We laughed but he was partly right. A proper bathroom would be a life-saver. We did hook up to the main septic line and also to our water system. Although it was cramped we were quite comfortable.

I lived in this trailer for about a year starting in April. Kyle was with me in July and August. Vicki moved in October and we stayed until the fol-lowing spring when we moved into our newly renovated "new house next door." We were in the neighbouring house until the following October when our log house was completed. These moves were short as these houses were only one km apart. We had great fun picking out furniture, beds, etc., for the new place.

That fall I went back to Quesnel to log the five-year cut on my woodlot. I arrived in Quesnel and needed to talk to the head scaler about woodlot scaling stuff. He was not in, I was told, he was up at West Fraser's scale shack that morning. I drove up there to see him. I parked in the front lot at the scales and got out. There were about six trucks lined up waiting to get weighed. There was a loader unloading trucks. Another loader was spreading logs. There was lumber piled high in the distance. This was coming home for me. The smell of newly cut logs, sawdust and lumber was like a drug to me. It was euphoric. I stood there transfixed as I breathed in deeply and listened to these familiar sounds. I then realized how I missed this life. I liked building houses as well, but the difference is hard to explain. I was looking forward to this winter of logging.

I had hired Bob Huard to log my woodlot as he was working his own right next door. Bob was good at selective logging, which is what you have to do on a woodlot. Woodlot logging is slower paced than regular logging is, and it takes a caring sort of guy to do it properly. My cut control ended in December and Bob needed help to finish in time. I borrowed a skidder from my brother-in-law, Wayne Roch, and with Brian as my operator, we joined in. I did the falling, Brian skidded and we both bucked. We had a self-loader haul our wood. Arnie Larson worked well for us. It took a while to get my logging muscles back in shape, I'll tell you. It seems the older you get the longer it takes you to get in shape, and the quicker you get out of shape. Falling is a tough job but I loved it. Trees falling, the skidder roaring and brush cracking, it was music to my ears and I thoroughly enjoyed it.

Back in Salmon Arm the next year, Vicki wanted a barn for our horses. We had around 20 head. Brian and his wife, Kathy, were living in the white farmhouse and Brian wanted to learn to build, so Brian, Vicki and I planned and built this barn. We had high ceilings and open air stalls. This was the first barn that we didn't follow convention. Most barns are not built with horses in mind. This one was. We had a 12-foot alleyway with stalls on both sides, an office with a washroom, a wash stall, a couple of storage stalls, a tack room and five tie stalls with a four foot feed alley in the front of them. When the horses came in and saw all the light, high ceiling and open air stalls, they seemed happy and content. And why not when you think of it . . . they need to see their neighbours. They were calm and happy as they were brought in.

We had five mares coming up to foal, and when their time came, we would bring them in. When these foals made their appearance, it was quite exciting. We were raising paints and you would never know what colour you would get. We had a paint stallion, quarterhorse mares and of course we expected all paints. These little foals are neat, they all have their own personalities, being so friendly and receptive at first. It depends on how you handle them whether they stay that way on not. We had a large foaling stall with a manger with two oat bins and two ties. It was cute to see mother and foal tied together, eating away, within a few short days of being born. When the little guy is trained right along with his mother, he never gets too excited. If he can look over at his mom and she is just standing calmly, he will soon calm down himself. Working with these little guys is so rewarding and resulted in happy times. Over the years we have learned some new training methods that work wonders. More working with them (horses) than against. Starting young and getting their trust is a big thing. A horse is happy to work with you if they trust you. It's amazing how they respond when handled this way. I am happy to see the old force-ful training methods being slowly phased out. Books like Monte Roberts' *The Man Who Listens to Horses* could help a lot of people to understand horses better. About time too. Horses are wonderful animals and should not just be the "beast of burden" that they have been for many years. They should be treated as partners when we ride or drive them.

About this time I saw an ad in the local newspaper, an ad asking for applications for a woodlot in our area. A woodlot is a 1,500-acre parcel of Crown land that is to be logged selectively, only as much as it grows. Theoretically it will always be the same. Fifteen hundred acres will grow approximately 1,000 cubic metres of wood per year, so if the woodlot farmer takes only 1,000 cubic feet per year the growth and yield will balance out. You could compare it to a tree farm licence. Actually, a mini TFL is what it is. The MOF always charged the going rate for stumpage fees. I said to Vicki, "Let's apply for this woodlot and we will each have one, mine in Quesnel and yours here. She said, "Okay, good idea." I was familiar with woodlot applications and knew the system. These woodlots are awarded on the basis of proximity, forestry experience, private land contribution and development plan, awarding roughly 35 points for each qualification. The more private land you contribute toward this woodlot, the better your chances. We put up our 155 acres. We formed a new company, putting the property in the new company name, and made Vicki the sole director or owner. Then we prepared the application, stating her forestry experience. Her credentials were fairly extensive when put on paper: two years forestry secretary for West Fraser Mills, two years tree planting, 10 years assisting with SBEP applications, slashing, rehabilitation of landings, paperwork and forestry business relating to crew payrolls, trucking and logging payrolls. Proximity was good as we lived four kilometres from the woodlot. I had done management plans before so that was not much trouble. We put the package together and sent it in.

It takes a few months for the MOF to evaluate these applications. For this particular woodlot there were approximately 15 applications. I could not figure out why it took so long to evaluate these applications at this time. The first woodlots that were given out, back in the earlier days of the program, were figured out the same day, with the applicants attending. Talk about making things complicated. After three or four months, we received a letter that advised we were tied for this woodlot and would have to now send in a one-time-only, bonus bid, which would be returned if we lost or kept if we were awarded the woodlot. We had a few weeks to do this so had time to plan it out. How much was a woodlot worth? How was it possible to tie with somebody else with such a complicated point system in the first place? We phoned a friend and business associate, Marv Kempston, a forester in Kamloops who handled this type of work. He managed woodlots, logging projects and log brokering. I asked Marv what he thought and had this ever happened before? He said he would get back to us. In a few days, Marv called and said, yes this had happened numerous times with a bonus bid being the tiebreaker. The bonus bids to date were studied; the highest had been $50,000.00. With that knowledge, we prepared a bid of $51,500.00, and sent it in. In a few days, we received a letter stating we had been successful and now had a woodlot, depending on final approval from the district manager.

Then, within days, Vicki received a disturbing phone call from the MOF. She was asked who else was a shareholder in her company and how could she possibly buy this woodlot? To answer these questions the district manager requested a meeting the following day, alone! Vicki was worried. She was easily intimidated especially by people in authority and they had indicated that they "assumed somebody else was behind this." She said this man, Gary Nielsen, who was in charge of woodlots, seemed angry as he asked her these questions. I was pretty upset at this turn of events. Who did this guy think he was talking to Vicki this way. I said to Vicki, "Look, this is a proper application and you won fair and square. There is obviously some favouritism going on or these guys are an 'old boys club' hangover who thinks a woman belongs in the kitchen!" She said, "Well I'm worried about this meeting. What will I say?" I told her not to worry about the meeting, that I would prepare a list of questions for her to ask these guys! I wanted her to put them on the spot and in their place. Strong-arm tactics are ridiculous. I said, "Here is what you will say to these guys at the meeting. Be calm but firm and let them talk first if they wish and then hit them with this statement." My list was as follows:

1. My bonus bid amount is none of you business.
2. How I log this is explained in my development plan.
3. And now I would like to know who I tied with on this woodlot and how a tie is possible seeing as I am located right next to the property and I put up all this private land?

I went on to explain to her how to interact with them, to look them in the eye and take her time. I instructed her to ignore any questions she didn't like and ask her own instead.

Vicki went in by herself and after the first few uncomfortable minutes, it soon took a turn for the better as she laid it on them. They soon realized they were dealing with a legitimate person and changed their tune. I was very proud of her for her brave front. Of course they wouldn't tell her who her competition was but we found out via the grapevine that the person she tied with, had put up 15 acres of private land and was 17 miles from the woodlot and had bid a $15,000.00 bonus. This person must have had a lot of experience as a forester or something was "fishy." I was pretty sure "fishy" was the way of it.

Anyway we went on the hire Marv Kempston of Westwood Fibre to manage this woodlot. There are a lot of details in woodlot management and it is best to have a professional handle this type of work. Marv is a very competent guy in this field, an R.P.F., and he knows how to handle this type of planning. He is familiar with the do's and don'ts of the MOF in woodlot situations. The paperwork that goes with a woodlot these days, the new rules and regulations, would swamp an individual. This is something Marv and his company just take in stride. He prepared the five-year development plan, cruised the woodlot, the private land and did everything necessary to get the cutting permit part of it. We had to build a road into the lot as the original access was through private land. All this preparation cost approximately another $50,000.00, so we were behind for a long time, probably still are, but these woodlots are a long-term project. As Marv finished all the preliminary work, we phased him out and phased ourselves in. It seemed sensible with us right there as opposed to Marv in Kamloops, 75 miles away.

Vicki and I learned a lot from Marv about woodlots, and about long-range forestry for that matter. This is definitely Marv's field. We have continued to work together on other projects and exchange information on miscellaneous forestry-related stuff. After all is said and done, we have a good relationship with the MOF regarding the woodlot. Gary Nielsen has been especially friendly and helpful. A few bumps in the road to start with and then it smoothed out. Vicki has gained a lot of confidence over the course of this project and now can quite comfortably handle any aspect of the woodlot.

◆ ◆ ◆

All in all, I am proof that dreams can come true. When you dream about something long enough it seems to happen. I don't mean sleep dreaming but a kind of day dreaming: a wishing-dreaming-seeing that you imagine before you go to sleep. As you lie down and prepare for sleep, you start to think of something you really want, or would really like, and you imagine it each day for as long as it takes. You need to be aware of what you are doing though or, if the dream comes about, you won't recognize it.

I was always day dreaming about something or other and the things I thought about consistently happened. When I was young I used to dream about owning a chainsaw and a pickup truck. Later, I used to see myself driving a big cat, levelling off big humps of dirt. I would put myself to sleep with these images in my head. As I got older, I would visualize having 1,000 acres of land with timber on it. I would see myself walking through this forest. These dreams of mine went on for years, and the funny part of it is, they all came true. It seems that when you close your eyes and visualize yourself doing something or having something, something happens . . . your mind begins to devise ways to bring this about. My dreams did come true. I did get a pickup and a chainsaw. I did get a large cat and did a lot of pushing and levelling with it. I did get 1,000 acres of land with timber. I didn't recognize the realization of these dreams at the time, however. It was not until years later in life, when I was attending a self-help seminar by John Lee Kotnekoff and he was explaining the power of visualization, that it dawned on me that I had been practising his technique without knowing it. I had almost missed the significance of the 1,200 acres at Abbott Heights. I had dreamed for years of owning flat ground with timber on it. I owned the property for three years before it suddenly came to me, "Hey, this is my 1,000 acres!" I had a hard time believing it. All the other strange happenings, wishes that became horses, came to me at the same time. I thought, "Yes, dreams do come true." You just have to think hard enough and long enough and let opportunity direct you.

Roy and I, so many many times, made or tried to make deals with car salesmen. We always needed a working vehicle and we never had enough money. Because of that, for years I dreamed of walking into a car dealership and saying, "I'll take that car," paying cash for it and shocking the salesman. It was a favourite dream of mine, perhaps because it involved another person. Anyway, it happened in spades. In 1969 I went into F & W Equipment in Quesnel, ordered a new pickup from the salesman,

Roy Trombley, and paid cash for it. I felt really important and proud as I did it, though I didn't associate it with my before-sleep day dreaming. In 1989, I walked into Cariboo Ford in Quesnel and said to the salesman, Hartley Quest, "I'd like to buy four new trucks." Hartley smiled real big and said, "Come with me," and I paid cash for them.

I believe that anyone can do this. It seems to come from the visual part of the dreaming. For example, if you wanted a boat, you'd close your eyes and see yourself skiing behind this fast sleek boat. You would imagine warm air, blue water, the colour of the boat and maybe even its name. Give it enough time to come true . . . I don't think you can control the time factor on these happenings. If you think, dream and visualize hard enough, things start to happen. The mind is a powerful tool and I don't think we use it to the fullest. Dreams allow our minds to shape and make happen what we want. This is one of those cases where it would be safe to say, "Try this at home." But, be very careful what you wish for because it will likely come true. Wish for good things, or things you would like to happen to you.

Kyle, myself and Blaine at Kyle's 13th birthday

Vicki and Kyle with Rainbow trout from Salmon River

My neighbour and friend
Mackie Ramsey "on stage"
in Hawaii.

My friend Art Smith with
daughter Lillian, 1994

Telling stories to my nephews Ashley and Spencer in Calgary

269

Myself, Joann and Vicki in Smithers

Blaine fishing at Stuart, 1990

Nikki modeling a new hat

House going up in Salmon Arm

Dunkley's finest lumber for building in Salmon Arm

Salmon river as it runs through our property at Silver Creek

Kyle ready for supper at Silver Creek
as our house was being built

Two loads of house logs ready for Salmon Arm home

Our house at Silver Creek

Rock fireplace at Salmon Arm house

Vicki on the deck at Silver Creek

CHAPTER 18

The End and the Beginning

I guess you get through life one way or another. I've muddled my way so far. There seem to be easy ways and hard ways and fewer in-betweens than I'd like. Unfortunately, we don't usually find out the easy ways until later on. If you could find the secrets to life early, it would be okay. But no, it seems most things have to be learned the hard way (Vicki's favourite saying — Pain is the teacher).

I know for myself when I was 20, I didn't think anybody who was 60 could teach me anything in the way of smarts. I was much too busy for that, I didn't have time. . . . I didn't take time. . . . and that's all too often the way when we are young. You are too busy running into things. I remember a time with Vicki that illustrates this point. I liked to take her along with me when I looked at a new property or cruised timber; it gave us time together and kept her up-to-date on stuff that affected us both. This one time, I was looking over some timber sales in the high country, east of Wells, and Vicki was along. On one particular sidehill the buck brush grew about four feet tall and was very thick and brambled. Buck brush is a dense branchy, willow type of bush that hugs the ground. It grows in thick clumps, sometimes covering acres of ground and sometimes just small patches. I was busy looking at trees and terrain and not paying particular attention to Vicki when I heard her exclaim, "These damn bushes are driving me crazy! They stick to my legs and I get my boots tangled up in them." I watched her fighting this brush and realized I had not taught her the way of buck brush. "Vicki," I said, "stop for a minute. Look I'll show you. You have to ease your way through this stuff. Find any little opening, put your foot in it and go slow." After a few minutes she said, "Hey, this works!" In any kind of brush this is how you have to go, easing your way through trees and limbs, over or under windfalls, not getting caught on limbs or not bumping into things. Vicki learned this method and started enjoying our trips to the bush. Life is much like that. You have to ease your way through, much like going through a forest — slow and careful.

Some sayings come to mind:

If you greet a man with a clenched fist he will likely clench his — if you meet a man with a smile he will likely smile back.

What you sow, so shall you reap. (For myself, I know that what I give comes back, at the very least in the good feeling that comes to me just from the act of doing something nice. Giving is important, even if it is just time.)

The faster you go, the behinder you get.

Too soon old and too late shmart.

And then there is my favourite saying for raising kids — "Give a man a fish and you will feed him for a day. Teach him how to fish and you will feed him for the rest of his life." Too often we take the easy way out and just give to our kids. Teaching kids is a big responsibility, and far too many times we think we are too busy, or it is easier and faster just to do something ourselves. My Dad was a carpenter (among other things) and when he had me help him, it was to either blow sawdust as he was sawing, or bring him boards. "Hand me that tool," he'd say. He never included me in his work. Did he think I could learn by just watching him? Of course you have to start somewhere, by carrying boards and pulling nails but you also, along the way, have to be shown how to do it yourself. I vowed I would teach my own kids by letting them do rather than watch. It is hard to remember to do this especially when they are young. Too young, you think! Then, before you know it they are grown up and haven't learned some basic stuff.

I remember a time with Blaine, when he was around 17 or 18, I was building a house and he was helping me. I decided that on this job I would teach him what jobs I knew and get him to do them rather than just be a helper. As a helper you don't have enough interest in a job to learn it. When building the cupboards, I said, "Okay, we'll set up the table saw and start cutting doors." I gave him the measurements and said, "Here, cut them out." I showed him how to change the blade and put the dado blade on to cut out the edge. While he was doing the "important stuff," I was building the frames and showing him as we went along. It's amazing how interested he became when he was actually doing something. Then we came to the fireplace and I said, "Okay, now we are going to lay rock." I showed him how to make mortar and said to him, "Look how easy it is. You used to do this when you were three years old, making mud pies." I showed him how to place mortar down and then place a rock on it, picking out one that you figured fit in that place, patting it down, then doing it all over again. We broke our own rock, made our own mortar and placed our own rock. I let Blaine do it himself and he was both excited and interested to do it. Sometime after we finished this house, Blaine's cousin, Bernie Marchewka ,was going to build a brick well on his lawn and was talking to Blaine about it. Blaine said, "No problem, I'll come and help you. I'll see you in the morning." The next day, Blaine was a bit late getting there and Bernie had already started, but some of his work was not quite right as he had no experience with this type of project. "No Bernie," Blaine said, "this is what you have to do. This mortar is too thick and these bricks have to be placed like this," and he proceeded to show him how to do it properly with confidence.

I've learned a lot of things in my life. I didn't head into life with much confidence or self-esteem but I have learned along the way. Sometimes I was bull headed and stubborn, or defensive, and took longer to learn something than I should have; other times I picked things up real quick and, over time, I've learned to learn from others. With each thing I came to know, I gained a notch in confidence. Amazing how this works. When you learn to do something yourself there is a transformation that happens that is hard to explain. You start to realize how simple most jobs are. You don't have to be a rocket scientist to figure things out. You just need confidence and confidence comes from doing it yourself. It's surprising what you can do if you are by yourself and a task confronts you. You imagine that you can't do it and you have to figure out a way to do it. You explore different avenues; some may seem ridiculous but some may work. The thing is that you are thinking, and when you think, things happen. I now look at older people differently. I think, "I wonder what all that person knows?" Or, "boy, that person must know a lot from his long years." Maybe it's because now I'm older myself and I see things differently.

I guess you never see yourself as old though. I remember at a seminar one time, we were to split into groups and had to find one older person as a leader. I was busy looking around for an older person to team up with and what a shock it was to find three young men had chosen me for their older person. It makes you wonder . . . !

There is one more saying I like — Life is what you make it. I have had more good fortune than misfortune, more luck than adversity, lots of adventures and lots of love. And I'm still taking life as it comes and making the best I can of it. Whatever is around the corner, it seems pretty sure that it will be interesting. And so, the story continues. . . .

My sister Shirley

My five sisters Joan, June, Shirley, Ines, and Jean

Mother and her magnificent seven.
Back row: June, Joan, and Ed. *Front row*: Roy, Shirley, Jean, Mom and Ines

Clearing a landing on a timber sale with the trusty D8. Silver Creek, 1998

Right: the author off his cat D8 →